Accounting Technician

**INTERMEDIATE STAGE
NVQ/SVQ 3**

Unit 5

Maintaining Financial Records and Preparing Accounts

TEXTBOOK

FOULKS LYNCH
PUBLICATIONS

British Library Cataloguing-in-Publication Data

A catalogue record for this book is available from the British Library.

Published by Foulks Lynch Ltd
4, The Griffin Centre
Staines Road
Feltham
Middlesex
TW14 0HS

ISBN 0 7483 5946 X

© Foulks Lynch Ltd, 2003

Printed and bound in Great Britain by Ashford Colour Press Ltd, Gosport.

Acknowledgements

We are grateful to the Association of Accounting Technicians for permission to reproduce extracts from the Standards of Competence for Accounting.

All rights reserved. No part of this publication may be reproduced, stored in a retrieval system, or transmitted, in any form or by any means, electronic, mechanical, photocopying, recording or otherwise, without the prior written permission of Foulks Lynch Ltd.

CONTENTS

		Page
Introduction		v
Standards of competence		vi
Assessment		x

Chapter

RECORDING TRANSACTIONS

1	Double Entry and the General Ledger	1
2	Credit transactions and VAT	13
3	Books of prime entry and the general ledger	23

RECORDING CAPITAL EXPENDITURE

4	Capital and revenue expenditure	55
5	The acquisition of assets: recording	61
6	The acquisition of assets: authorising and funding	73
7	Depreciation	81
8	Disposal of fixed assets	93

PREPARING FINANCIAL STATEMENTS

9	The trial balance	103
10	Stock	119
11	Accruals and prepayments	133
12	Bad and doubtful debts	147
13	The extended trial balance	159
14	Producing the accounts	175
15	Partnership accounts	197

INCOMPLETE RECORDS

16	Incomplete records: techniques	221
17	Incomplete records: example	239

LEGAL AND PROFESSIONAL ISSUES

18	The accounting and business framework	251
Answers to activities		259
Index		285

INTRODUCTION

This is the new edition of the AAT NVQ/SVQ Textbook for Unit 5 – *Maintaining Financial Records and Preparing Accounts*.

Tailored to the new Standards of Competence, this Textbook has been written specifically for AAT students in a clear and comprehensive style.

This book takes a very practical approach, with the inclusion of numerous examples and activities to help you practise what you have learnt. Self test questions and key terms at the end of each chapter reinforce your knowledge.

STANDARDS OF COMPETENCE

A unit of competence (for example, Unit 1 *Recording Income and Receipts*) is made up of **elements** which contain all the essential information to define the standard and how it can be achieved. These elements consist of **performance criteria**, **range statements** and **knowledge and understanding**.

Performance criteria: These are the tasks you need to do to complete each element.

Range statements: These are the methods to use to complete the performance criteria.

Knowledge and understanding: These statements are the underpinning requirements to be able to complete the tasks.

Listed below are the elements, performance criteria, knowledge and understanding and range statements. These have been referenced to the chapters in the book where they are covered.

Unit 5 Maintaining Financial Records And Preparing Accounts

Unit commentary

This unit relates to the maintenance of accounts from the drafting of the initial trial balance through to the preparation of information required to produce a set of final accounts.

The first element is concerned with the records for capital items, how to deal with acquisitions, on-going depreciation and the rules for disposal. The second element requires you to collect relevant information for preparing the final accounts and to present the information to your supervisor in the form of a trial balance or an extended trial balance.

The third element requires you to prepare final accounts for sole traders and partnerships. You must also be responsible for communication in relation to the handling of queries, for making suggestions for improvements and maintaining confidentiality.

Element: 5.1 Maintain records relating to capital acquisition and disposal

Element: 5.2 Collecting and collating information for the preparation of final accounts

Element: 5.3 Preparing the final accounts of sole traders and partnerships

Knowledge and understanding

To perform this unit effectively you will need to know and understand:

The business environment *Chapter*

1	The types and characteristics of different assets and key issues relating to the acquisition and disposal of capital assets (Element 5.1)	4
2	The relevant legislation and regulations (Elements 5.1, 5.2 and 5.3)	18
3	The main requirements of relevant Statements of Standard Accounting Practice and Financial Reporting Standards (Elements 5.1, 5.2 and 5.3)	18
4	Legal requirements relating to the division of profits between partners (Element 5.3)	15

		Chapter
5	The methods of recording information for the organisational accounts of sole traders and partnerships (Elements 5.2 & 5.3)	1, 2, 3
6	The structure of the organisational accounts of sole traders and partnerships (Elements 5.2 & 5.3)	14, 15
7	The need to present accounts in the correct form (Elements 5.2 & 5.3)	14
8	The form of final accounts of sole traders and partnerships (Element 5.3)	14, 15
9	The importance of maintaining the confidentiality of business transactions (Elements 5.1, 5.2 and 5.3)	18

Accounting techniques

10	Methods of depreciation and when to use each of them: straight line; reducing balance (Element 5.1)	7
11	The accounting treatment of capital items sold, scrapped or otherwise retired from service (Element5.1)	8
12	How to use plant registers and similar subsidiary records (Element 5.1)	5
13	How to use the transfer journal (Elements 5.1 and 5.2)	3
14	The methods of funding: part exchange deals (Element 5.1)	6
15	The accounting treatment of accruals and prepayments (Elements 5.2 & 5.3)	11
16	The methods of analysing income and expenditure (Element 5.2)	3
17	The method of closing off revenue accounts (Element 5.2)	9
18	The methods of restructuring accounts from incomplete evidence (Element 55.2 & 5.3)	16, 17
19	How to identify and correct different types of error (Elements 5.2)	9
20	How to make and adjust provisions (Elements 5.2 and 5.3)	12
21	How to draft year final accounts of sole traders and partnerships (Element 5.2)	14, 15

Accounting principles and theory

22	Basic accounting concepts that play a role in the selection of accounting policies– accruals and going concern	4, 18
23	The objectives and constraints in selecting accounting policies – relevance, reliability, comparability and ease of understanding, materiality (5.1, 5.2, & 5.3)	18
24	The principles of double entry accounting (Elements 5.1, 5.2 & 5.3)	2
25	The distinction between capital and revenue expenditure and what constitutes capital expenditure (Element 5.1)	4
26	The function and form of accounts for income and expenditure (Element 5.1, 5.2 & 5.3)	14
27	The function and form of a trial balance and an extended trial balance (Element 5.2)	9, 12
28	The function and form of a profit and loss account and balance sheet for sole traders and partnerships (Elements 5.3)	14, 15
29	The basic principles of stock valuation including those relating to cost or net realisable value and to what is included in cost (Elements 5.2 & 5.3)	10
30	The objectives of making provisions for depreciation and other purposes (Elements 5.1, 5.2 & 5.3)	7

The organisation

31	The ways the accounting systems of an organisation are affected by its organisational structure, its administrative systems and procedures and the nature of its business transactions (Elements 5.1, 5.2 & 5.3)	18

Element 5.1 Maintaining records relating to capital acquisition and disposal

Performance criteria *Chapter*

In order to perform this element successfully you need to:

A	Record relevant details relating to capital expenditure in the appropriate records	5
B	Ensure that the organisation's records agree with the physical presence of capital items	5
C	Correctly identify and record all acquisition and disposal costs and revenues in the appropriate records	5, 8
D	Correctly calculate and record depreciation charges and other necessary entries and adjustments in the appropriate records	7
E	Ensure that the records clearly show the prior authority for capital expenditure and disposal and the approved method of funding and disposal	6
F	Correctly calculate and record the profit and loss on disposal in the appropriate records	8
G	Ensure that the organisation's policies and procedures relating to the maintenance of capital records are adhered to	5
H	Identify and resolve or refer to the appropriate person any lack of agreement between physical items and records	5
I	Make suggestions for improvements in the way the organisation maintains its capital records where possible to the appropriate person	5

Range statement

Performance in this element relates to the following contexts:

Records:

- Asset register 3
- Books of original entry 3
- Ledgers 3

Depreciation:

- Straight line 7
- Reducing balance 7

Element 5.2 Collecting and collating information for the preparation of final accounts

Performance criteria

In order to perform this element successfully you need to:

A	Correctly prepare reconciliations for the preparation of final accounts	9
B	Identify any discrepancies in the reconciliation process and either take steps to rectify them or refer them to the appropriate person	9
C	Accurately prepare a trial balance and open a suspense account to record any imbalance	9
D	Establish the reasons for any imbalance and clear the suspense account by correcting the errors, or reduce them and resolve outstanding items to the appropriate person	9
E	Correctly identify, calculate and record appropriate adjustments	9, 12
F	Make the relevant journal entries to close off the revenue accounts in preparation for the transfer of balances to the final accounts	9
G	Conduct investigations into business transactions with tact and courtesy	18

		Chapter
H	Ensure that the organisation's policies, regulations, procedures and timescales relating to preparing final accounts are observed	18

Range statement
Performance in this element relates to the following contexts:

Reconciliations:

- Purchase ledger reconciliation — 9
- Sales ledger reconciliation — 9
- Closing stock reconciliation — 9

Reasons for imbalance:

- Incorrect double entries — 9
- Missing entries — 9
- Numerical inconsistencies and wrong calculations — 9
- Insufficient data and incomplete records have been provided — 9
- Inconsistencies within the data — 9

Adjustments:

- Prepayments and accruals — 9
- Provisions for doubtful debts — 9
- Provisions for depreciation — 9
- Closing stock — 9

Element 5.3 Preparing the final accounts of sole traders and partnerships

Performance criteria
In order to perform this element successfully you need to:

A	Prepare final accounts of sole traders in proper form, from the trial balance	14
B	Prepare final accounts of partnerships in proper form and in compliance with partnership agreement, from the trial balance	15
C	Observe the organisation's policies, regulations, procedures and timescales in relation to preparing final accounts of sole traders and partnerships	15
D	Identify and resolve or refer to the appropriate person discrepancies, unusual features or queries	9

Range statement
Performance in this element relates to the following contexts:

Final accounts of sole traders:

- Profit and loss account — 14
- Balance sheet — 14

Final accounts of partnerships:

- Profit and loss account — 15
- Balance sheet — 15
- Partnership appropriation account — 15
- Partners' capital and current accounts — 15

ASSESSMENT

Unit 5 is assessed by both **Skills Testing** and **Examination**. If you take the examination, you may also need to provide further evidence of your competence in this unit in your portfolio.

Examination

- The examination will be **three hours** long (plus 15 minutes reading time) and will include practical tests linked to the performance criteria and questions focusing on knowledge and understanding.

- **Double entry book-keeping**: you will be asked to complete a number of accounts. For example, the cash book, disposal account or purchases ledger control account might be requested. This could be in section 1 or section 2 or both. Double entry book-keeping will also be tested by use of the journal.

- You must know the difference between **writing up an account** and **preparing a journal entry**. Dates and narratives will not be required.

- Either or both sections will contain a **memo** or **letter-style** task. This will often be linked to a previous task where the student will be expected to justify an accounting entry or explain an adjustment.

- If a scenario using a **computerised system** is used, it will be based on an integrated system of ledgers, which could include an integrated stock ledger. Where records are kept, these will consist of a main ledger, where double entry takes place, a sales ledger and a purchases ledger. You can assume (but will also be told) that the sales ledger control account and purchases ledger control account will be contained in the main ledger, forming part of the double entry. The individual accounts of debtors and creditors will be in the sales ledger and purchases ledger and will therefore be regarded as memoranda accounts.

Section 1: This will assess your competence in elements 5.2 and may also cover some aspects of 5.1. Tasks may include:

- Produce information from data given and/or incomplete records for either a sole trader or a partnership.

- Provide brief explanations, calculations, accounting entries, or select from a number of given answers.

- Process, restructure and produce information including, for example:
    - Calculation of opening and/or closing capital.
    - Restructuring the cash and/or bank account.
    - Preparation of sales ledger control account and purchases ledger control account to calculate, for example, sales and purchases.

- Use mark-up and margin to calculate or check sales or purchases figures.

- Restructure ledger accounts, for example to calculate expenses paid, accruals and prepayments, profit or loss on the sale of an asset.

- Draft journal entries.

- Produce a trial balance or extended trial balance from reconstructed accounts or information.

- Produce a memo, letter or notes in response to a client or supervisor.

Section 2: This will assess your competence in element 5.3, but some aspects of 5.1 and 5.2 may also be covered. Tasks may include:

- Preparation of journal entries to clear the suspense account or make adjustments.
- Preparing capital accounts or journal entries for changes to partnerships (see guidance below)
- Completion of the extended trial balance.
- Preparation of profit and loss account for sole trader or partnership, in good form.
- Preparation of appropriation account for partnerships.
- Preparation of current accounts for partnerships.
- Preparation of balance sheet for sole trader or partnership, in good form.
- Short questions, explanations, letters or memos concerning the underpinning knowledge relating to the tasks undertaken.

Skills testing

Skills testing when your approved assessment centre (AAC) is a workplace

You may be observed carrying out your accounting activities as part of your normal work routine. You need to collect documentary evidence of the work you have done in an accounting portfolio.

Skills testing when your AAC is a college

This will use a combination of:

- documentary evidence of activities carried out at work, collected in a portfolio
- realistic simulations of workplace activities
- projects and assignments.

Skills testing when you don't work in accountancy

Don't worry – you can prove your competence using one of AAT's simulations, or from case studies, projects and assignments. The AAT simulation will always be based on a partnership,

Portfolio building

Your portfolio is where you will keep all of your **evidence** to show your competence. It should contain different types of evidence from a range of sources.

Rules of evidence

Evidence must be:

- Valid – clearly related to the standards being assessed
- Authentic – must be your own work
- Current – make sure it is as recent as possible
- Sufficient – all performance criteria need to be met

Sources of evidence

- Prior achievement
- Performance in the workplace

- Performance in specially set activities
- Questioning: oral, written or by computer

Portfolio contents

For Unit 5, ensure your portfolio contains the following:

- Title page (your name, contact details and what you are studying)
- Your CV
- Information about your organisation (name and address, type of business, staff numbers, organisation chart if you have one)
- Job description
- Summary of your previous and current work experience (if appropriate)
- Witness statements from supervisors at work listing performance criteria and details of the job undertaken (these need to be on headed paper, be signed by your supervisor and have their job title on it)
- Evidence that you have performed all of the necessary performance criteria.
- Evidence that you possess the underpinning knowledge and understanding (this could be written answers to questions set in class or a statement from your tutor outlining the oral questioning you received)
- Evidence grid (from the AAT's student record)
- Index to evidence

Chapter 1

ELEMENTS OF BOOK-KEEPING AND ACCOUNTING

This is an introductory chapter to remind you about how accounting systems are structured, with accounts and ledgers, and how transactions are recorded in the accounting system. It describes the accounting equation, on which the principle of double-entry book-keeping is based. It then explains in broad outline the nature of double entry book-keeping and balances on accounts. Finally, it explains how the balances on accounts in the main ledger can be presented in an initial trial balance and that the initial trial balance is a starting point for producing two financial statements, the profit and loss account for a period and the balance sheet as at the end of the period.

The content of this chapter should be largely familiar to you. However, elements of book-keeping will be described in the chapters that follow.

CONTENTS

1 Book-keeping and financial accounting
2 The accounting equation
3 The basics of double-entry book-keeping
4 Initial trial balance
5 Introducing the profit and loss account and balance sheet
6 Definitions

KNOWLEDGE AND UNDERSTANDING

		Reference
1	The methods of recording information for the organisational accounts of sole traders and partnerships	Item 5
2	The principles of double entry accounting	Item 24

LEARNING OUTCOMES

At the end of this chapter, you should be able to:

- describe the basic structure of a book-keeping and accounting system
- describe the basic structure of a profit and loss account
- describe the basic structure of a balance sheet

- understand that an initial trial balance provides the starting point for preparing a profit and loss account and a balance sheet.

1 BOOK-KEEPING AND FINANCIAL ACCOUNTING

Businesses are required to record details of their monetary transactions, such as sales to customers, purchases from suppliers, paying wages and salaries to employees and receiving and paying cash to settle transactions. Transactions involving the sale of goods or services, and transactions involving expenditures are recorded as income and expenses.

Businesses also keep a record of the assets they own (including money owed to them by debtors), the amounts of money they owe to creditors ('liabilities') and the amount of money invested in the business by its owners ('capital').

The process of recording transactions in the 'books of account' is called book-keeping, which is a basic element of accounting.

When transaction data has been entered in the accounting system, it can be used to extract information for the managers and owners of the business. Extracting and presenting information from the accounting system, for example to prepare a profit and loss account and a balance sheet, is called financial accounting.

1.1 BOOKS OF PRIME ENTRY

Details of business transactions are recorded in the accounting system initially in a book of prime entry or 'day book'. This is used simply to list the transactions and the data that will be recorded in the accounts.

There are several books of prime entry, for recording different types of transaction.

- A sales day book is used for listing credit sales transactions.
- A purchases day book is used for listing purchase transactions on credit terms.
- The cash book is used to record details of payments received and paid into the business bank account, and payments made out of the bank account.
- The petty cash book records details of cash withdrawn from the bank and transactions paid for in notes and coins.

There are other day books: the sales returns day book, the purchases returns day book and a transfer journal for recording any transactions not recorded in any other book of prime entry.

After transactions have been recorded in a book of prime entry, they are then transferred to (or 'posted to') relevant accounts in one or more ledgers.

1.2 LEDGERS

A ledger is a term for a set of similar accounts. A business usually has three ledgers:

- a main ledger, also known as the general ledger or nominal ledger
- a sales ledger
- a purchase ledger.

The sales ledger and purchase ledgers are sometimes called 'subsidiary ledgers'.

The **main ledger** contains many different accounts for sales, expenses, assets, liabilities and capital. There is an asset account for trade debtors, which records the total value of transactions with credit customers. This is called the sales ledger control account or debtors control account. There is also a liability account for trade creditors, called the purchase ledger control account or creditors control account. This is used to record the total value of transactions with suppliers.

The **sales ledger** contains accounts for individual credit customers. These are used to record transactions with each customer (whereas the main ledger is used to record the total value of transactions with all credit customers).

The **purchase ledger** contains accounts for individual suppliers/trade creditors. These are used to record transactions with each supplier/trade creditor (whereas the main ledger is used to record the total value of transactions with all trade creditors).

The focus of interest in this text is with the main ledger, because the information in the main ledger is used to prepare a profit and loss account and a balance sheet.

1.3 ACCOUNTS IN THE MAIN LEDGER

The following types of account are held in the main ledger. Some examples of each type of account are shown, but the actual accounts set up in the main ledger can vary widely between different businesses.

Asset accounts

Land and buildings
Plant and machinery
Equipment
Fixtures and fittings
Motor vehicles
Stock (inventory)
Debtors
Cash in bank (unless there is an overdraft balance)

Liability accounts or creditor accounts

Trade creditors
Bank (if there is an overdraft)
Tax payable
Bank loans

Capital accounts

Owner's capital
Drawings (i.e. withdrawals of capital)

Income accounts

Sales
Interest receivable

Expense accounts

Purchases
Wages and salaries
Rent
Insurance
Motor vehicle expenses
Telephone charges
Electricity charges
Charges for contracted-out services
Interest charges
Audit fees

When transactions are posted from the day books to the nominal ledger, they are recorded in the appropriate accounts.

The process of recording transactions in the main ledger is based on the double entry principle of book-keeping. To understand the concept of double entry, it helps to begin by looking at the accounting equation.

2 THE ACCOUNTING EQUATION

The double entry concept starts with the assumption that a business and its owner (or owners) are separate entities. An owner puts capital into the business, and the business is assumed to owe this capital to its owner.

If a business owes all its capital to its owner, we can state that the assets of a business must always be equal to the sum of what it owes to its creditors and what it owes to the owners. In other words, at any time:

> **Assets = Liabilities + Capital**

Transactions by a business alter the values of its assets and liabilities, but the accounting equation will always apply.

We can show this with a series of transactions for a newly-established business.

Situation

Jo Green invests £5,000 of her own money setting up a garden design business. The business will be called *Lynx Landscaping*.

2.1 SETTING UP IN BUSINESS

Jo Green (the owner) pays £5,000 of her own money into a business bank account to set up the business. This £5,000 is business capital, which the business now owes to Jo. So we have an asset of £5,000 in the bank, and capital of £5,000.

Assets		=	*Liabilities*	+	*Capital*	
	£		£			£
Cash in bank	5,000	=	0		Initial capital	5,000

2.2 BUYING ASSETS FOR CASH

The business pays cash for gardening equipment costing £1,000 and for stock (inventory) costing £2,000. The capital remains the same, but there are now three types of asset.

Assets		=	*Liabilities*	+	*Capital*	
	£		£			£
Equipment	1,000					
Stock	2,000					
Cash in bank	2,000		0		Initial capital	5,000
Total	5,000	=	0	+		5,000

2.3 BORROWING MONEY

The business needs to buy a second-hand van costing £7,000. A bank agrees to provide this money as a loan. When the loan has been obtained and the van purchased with the money, the accounting equation will be as follows:

Assets		=	*Liabilities*		+	*Capital*	
	£			£			£
Van	7,000						
Equipment	1,000						
Stock	2,000						
Cash in bank	2,000		Bank loan	7,000		Capital	5,000
Total	12,000	=		7,000	+		5,000

CHAPTER 1 : ELEMENT OF BOOK-KEEPING AND ACCOUNTING

2.4 TRADING AT A PROFIT

So far the business has not done any trading. It has purchased some stock (and purchases are normally recorded initially as an expense rather than as an addition to stock). However, it has not made any sales.

Now let's suppose that the business does some work for a client. This uses up all the stock. In addition, the business pays £800 cash in wages to an employee to do the work. The customer is charged £4,000 for the job, for which he is invoiced, but he has not yet paid.

The job earns a profit of £1,200.

	£	£
Sales		4,000
Cost of stock	2,000	
Wages	800	
		2,800
Profit		1,200

Profit adds to the owner's capital, and at the end of the transaction, total capital will be higher by the profit of £1,200. This can be shown as an accounting equation, as follows. Notice how the transactions creating income or expenses affect assets, liabilities and capital in the accounting equation.

Assets		=	Liabilities		+	Capital	
	£			£			£
Van	7,000						
Equipment	1,000						
Stock (stock now at cost of sale)	0					Initial capital	5,000
Debtors	4,000						
Cash in bank (2,000 less wages 800)	1,200		Bank loan	7,000		Profit	1,200
Total	13,200	=		7,000	+		6,200
			Sales		Adds to assets (debtors)		4,000
			Expenses				
			Purchased stock		Reduces stock		(2,000)
			Wages		Reduces cash at bank		(800)
			Profit		Adds to capital		1,200

2.5 DRAWINGS

Jo Green is pleased with the profit earned and decides to withdraw £500 in cash as a payment to herself. Drawings are a reduction in capital, so the accounting equation after this transaction is:

Assets		=	Liabilities		+	Capital	
	£			£			£
Van	7,000						
Equipment	1,000						
Stock	0					Initial capital	5,000
Debtors	4,000					Profit	1,200
Cash	700		Bank loan	7,000		Drawings	(500)
Total	12,700	=		7,000	+		5,700

3 THE RUDIMENTS OF DOUBLE-ENTRY BOOK-KEEPING

These examples of the accounting equation show that whenever a transaction occurs, there is a change in the value of assets, liabilities and/or capital, which might also affect the amount of income (sales) or expenses. The end result, however, is that the accounting equation still holds true and Assets = Liabilities + Capital.

It follows that if a transaction increases or reduces the amount of an asset, a liability or capital, or if a transaction increases sales income or expenses, there must be a counterbalancing change in the value of something else. Without a counterbalancing change, the accounting equation could not be true. In accounting terms, we can say that there are two matching sides to every transaction.

Double entry book-keeping is a process of recording transactions in the main ledger accounts in a way that shows the two sides to the transaction. The two sides of each transaction are recorded as:

- a debit entry in one account and
- a matching credit entry in another account.

In practice, more than two accounts might be used to record the details of a transaction, but the rule that the total of debit entries equals the total of credit entries must apply.)

Every account in the main ledger can be portrayed as a 'T account', with a debit side and a credit side, as follows.

Account name

Details	£	Details	£
DEBIT SIDE		CREDIT SIDE	

3.1 DEBIT OR CREDIT?

A transaction is recorded on the debit side or the credit side of an account as follows:

Assets

Asset account

DEBIT SIDE	£	CREDIT SIDE	£
Record any increase in the asset value		Record any decrease in the asset value	

CHAPTER 1 : ELEMENT OF BOOK-KEEPING AND ACCOUNTING

Liabilities

Liability/creditor account

DEBIT SIDE	£	CREDIT SIDE	£
Record any decrease in the liability		Record any increase in the liability	

Capital

Capital account

DEBIT SIDE	£	CREDIT SIDE	£
Record any decrease in capital		Record any increase in capital	

Income

Income/sales account

DEBIT SIDE	£	CREDIT SIDE	£
		Record any increase in sales	

Expenses

Expense account

DEBIT SIDE	£	CREDIT SIDE	£
Record any increase in the expense			

3.2 MATCHING DEBITS AND CREDITS

The basic rule for recording transactions in the main ledger accounts is that every transaction should be recorded in two (or more) accounts, such that the total of debit entries equals the total of credit entries. Examples of matching debits and credit are as follows.

		Possible matching effect	
Increase in the value of an asset	1	**Decrease in the value of another asset**	
		Example	
		A debtor pays an invoice for £1,000.	
		Debit Bank (increase)	£1,000
		Credit Debtors (decrease)	£1,000
	2	**Increase in a liability**	
		Example	
		Buy equipment on credit for £2,000	
		Debit Equipment (increase)	£2,000
		Credit Creditors (increase)	£2,000

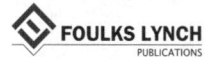

	3	**Increase in income** *Example* Sell goods on credit for £750 Debit Debtors (increase) Credit Sales (increase)	£750 £750
	4	**Increase in capital** *Example* The owner of a business puts another £3,000 cash into the business. Debit Bank (increase) Credit Capital (increase)	£3,000 £3,000

		Possible matching effect	
Increase in the value of a liability	1	**Increase in the value of an asset.** *Example* Buying equipment on credit, as above	
	2	**Increase in an expense** *Example* Receive a telephone bill for £350 Debit Telephone expenses (increase) Credit Creditors (increase)	£350 £350
Increase in an expense	1	**Increase in a liability** *Example* As above	
	2	**Reduction in an asset** *Example* Pay wages of £500 in cash Debit Wages (increase) Credit Bank (decrease)	£500 £500

Recording transactions by double entry is described in more detail in the next chapter.

3.3 DEBIT BALANCES AND CREDIT BALANCES

Transactions are recorded in the accounts in the main ledger, on either the debit side or the credit side of the account. In many cases, particularly with asset and liability accounts, transactions are recorded on both sides of the account. For example, in the Cash at Bank account, cash paid into the bank account is recorded as a debit entry and payments from the bank account are recorded as credit entries.

- If the total of debit entries in the account exceeds the total of credit entries, there is a **debit balance** on the account.
- If the total of credit entries in the account exceeds the total of debit entries, there is a **credit balance** on the account.

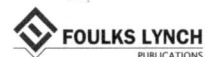

CHAPTER 1 : ELEMENT OF BOOK-KEEPING AND ACCOUNTING

Due to the double-entry system, whereby all debit entries are matched by equal credit entries, it must follow that at any time (unless there has been an error in recording transactions in the accounts) the total of all debit balances in the main ledger accounts must equal the total of all credit entries.

4 INITIAL TRIAL BALANCE

A list of all the accounts on the main ledger, showing the balance on each account and the total of debit balances and the total of credit balances, is called a trial balance. A simple example, with hypothetical figures, is shown below. (In practice, there are usually many more accounts in the main ledger).

	Debit £	Credit £
Sales		76,000
Creditors		2,900
Debtors	15,000	
Equipment	14,000	
Motor vehicles	17,000	
Motor vehicle expenses	2,000	
Cash at bank	3,100	
Capital		20,000
Stock at start of year	800	
Purchases	25,000	
Telephone expenses	5,000	
Electricity charges	6,000	
Rent	14,000	
Insurance	5,000	
Bank loan		8,000
	106,900	106,900

When the accountant wishes to prepare a profit and loss account and a balance sheet, the starting point is to prepare a trial balance. This trial balance is called an initial trial balance.

- The account balances for income and expenses, with some adjustments, go into calculating the profit or loss for the period.
- The account balances for assets, liabilities and capital, with some adjustments, go into preparing a balance sheet as at the end of the period.

This text will explain how a profit and loss account and balance sheet are prepared.

5 INTRODUCING THE PROFIT AND LOSS ACCOUNT AND BALANCE SHEET

5.1 PROFIT AND LOSS ACCOUNT

In broad terms, a **profit and loss account** is a statement for an accounting period, usually one year, setting out the income and expenses for the period, and the resulting profit or loss. If income exceeds expenses there is a profit, and if expenses are higher than income there is a loss.

Some businesses present the results for a period as a trading profit and loss account. The trading account is used to calculate a gross profit for the period, with is the sales for the period less the 'cost of goods sold'. The profit and loss account is then used to deduct other expenses such as administration and marketing expenses from gross profit, to establish the net profit or loss for the period.

A trading, profit and loss account is typically presented as a financial statement as follows.

MAINTAINING FINANCIAL RECORDS AND PREPARING ACCOUNTS : UNIT 5

	£	£
Sales		221,000
Opening stock	7,000	
Purchases	107,000	
	114,000	
Closing stock	12,000	
Cost of sales		102,000
Gross profit		119,000
Administration expenses	40,000	
Selling and distribution expenses	50,000	
Other expenses	6,000	
		96,000
Net profit for the period		23,000

5.2 BALANCE SHEET

In broad terms, a balance sheet is a statement of the accounting equation as at the end of the accounting period: Assets = Liabilities + Capital.

However, it is usual to present it as Assets − Liabilities = Capital, and in a vertical format, as follows.

	£	£
Fixed assets		120,000
Current assets	80,000	
Short-term (current) liabilities	(30,000)	
Current assets less current liabilities		50,000
Total assets less current liabilities		170,000
Long-term liabilities		(45,000)
Assets less liabilities		125,000
Capital		
At the start of the period		105,000
Profit for the period	60,000	
Less drawings	(40,000)	
Retained profit		20,000
At the end of the period		125,000

6 DEFINITIONS

Check that you understand the meaning of the following terms used in this chapter.

Asset An asset is something that is owned by the business,
- for use within the business, or
- cash, or
- investments, or
- something that will be converted to cash as part of day-to-day trading activities. These assets include purchases for resale (stock or inventory), and debtors.

Owner's capital - The amount owed by the business to the owner. Initially, this is the total amount of money put into the business (invested) by the owner, but it is increased by retained profits and reduced by losses.

Liability/creditor - A liability is an amount of money owed by the business to people other than the owner.

CHAPTER 1 : ELEMENT OF BOOK-KEEPING AND ACCOUNTING

Stock (inventory) - Items purchased or produced for resale at a later date.

Debtors (receivables) - Amounts owed to the business, for example by customers purchasing on credit terms.

Trade creditors (payables) - Amounts owed by the business to its suppliers.

Profit - The excess of sales over the cost of sales and other expenses. Profit adds to the business capital.

Drawings - Any amounts taken out of the business by the owner for his or her personal use. Drawings can include money taken out of the business, stock taken for personal use or personal expenses paid by the business. In companies, drawings are called dividends.

CONCLUSION

The starting point for preparing a profit and loss account and a balance sheet is an initial trial balance. The balances for income and expenses go into preparing the profit and loss account. The balances for assets, liabilities and capital go into preparing the balance sheet.

The process of preparing financial statements isn't quite so simple, however, and various adjustments have to be made (and other entries have to be made in accounts in the main ledger).

The following chapters provide an explanation of double-entry book-keeping in more detail, and in addition explains how to account for fixed asset items. It will then go on to explain the adjustments that have to be made in order to draw up an extended trial balance, and then a profit and loss account and balance sheet.

SELF-TEST QUESTIONS

		Paragraph
1	What are the books of prime entry?	1.1
2	What is a ledger?	1.2
3	What are the three ledgers in an accounting system?	1.2
4	What types of account are held in the main ledger (general ledger)?	1.3
5	What is the accounting equation?	2
6	Is an increase in a liability recorded as a debit entry or a credit entry in the liability account?	3.1
7	Is an increase in an expense recorded as a debit entry or a credit entry in the expense account?	3.1
8	What is a trial balance?	4

KEY TERMS

Book of prime entry – the point at which a transaction first enters the accounting system.

Ledger – a set of related accounts.

Main ledger (nominal ledger) – a set of accounts for assets, liabilities, capital, income and expenses.

Accounting equation – Assets = Liabilities + Capital

Profit and loss account – a statement for an accounting period, usually one year, setting out the income and expenses for the period, and the resulting profit or loss.

Balance sheet – a statement of the accounting equation as at the end of the accounting period: Assets = Liabilities + Capital.

Chapter 2

CREDIT TRANSACTIONS AND VAT

This chapter continues the revision of double entry bookkeeping. In particular it looks at credit transactions, VAT and loan interest.

CONTENTS

1. Credit transactions in the general ledger
2. Elements of VAT
3. Accounting for VAT
4. Repayment of loan

KNOWLEDGE AND UNDERSTANDING

		Reference
1	The methods of recording information for the organisational accounts of sole traders and partnerships	Item 5
2	The principles of double entry accounting	Item 24

LEARNING OUTCOMES

At the end of this chapter, you should be able to understand and account for:

- credit purchases
- credit sales
- credit expenses
- accounting for the VAT on sales and purchases
- day books, control accounts and memorandum accounts
- receiving and repaying a loan to a business.

MAINTAINING FINANCIAL RECORDS AND PREPARING ACCOUNTS : UNIT 5

1 CREDIT TRANSACTIONS IN THE GENERAL LEDGER

1.1 INTRODUCTION TO CREDIT TRANSACTIONS

Most business-to-business transactions are done on credit. This means that the goods are exchanged before they are invoiced or paid for. Under the accruals concept, these transactions should be recorded when they occur, rather than when they are paid for. Generally speaking it means that both sales and the purchases will be recorded when the related goods or services are physically delivered.

Normally, for the sake of convenience, transactions are recorded when the invoice is raised or received. At the year end an adjustment is then made for goods or services that have been received but not yet invoiced.

1.2 CREDIT PURCHASES

When a business buys goods on credit they will owe money to a supplier. Until paid, the supplier will be a trade creditor. Trade creditors are classified as current liabilities in the balance sheet.

The double entry on purchase will be:

| Debit | Purchases |
| Credit | Trade Creditors |

When the goods are paid for the double entry will be:

| Debit | Trade Creditors |
| Credit | Bank and Cash |

Expenses incurred on credit will be dealt with in the same way, except that the appropriate expense heading, say electricity, in the P&L will be debited instead of the purchases account.

Example – credit purchases

Swing Dancewear purchases some leotards on credit for £10,000

Purchases		Trade creditor	
10,000			10,000

After a short period of time the supplier will be paid. Following the double entry rules, the asset account, cash at bank, is being reduced therefore there will be a credit entry to that account. The liability account creditor is also being reduced thus requiring a debit entry to that account.

Purchases		Trade creditor		Cash at bank	
£	£	£	£	£	£
10,000		10,000	10,000		10,000
(1)		(2)	(1)		(2)

CHAPTER 2 : CREDIT TRANSACTIONS AND VAT

1.3 CREDIT SALES

With a credit sale, the sale is made, the goods go out of the business and somebody owes the business some money. That person is known as a trade debtor. Trade debtors are normally classified as current assets in the balance sheet.

The double entry on sale will be:

    Debit   Trade debtors

    Credit   Sales

When the customer pays up the double entry will be:

    Debit   Bank and cash

    Credit   Trade debtors

Example – credit sales

Swing Dancewear sells all the leotards for £14,000 on credit; they had previously been purchased for £10,000.

(a) Sale on credit

Sales	Trade debtors
14,000	14,000

(b) Receipt of cash

Two months later the cash is received from the trade debtor.

Sales	Trade creditor	Cash at bank
14,000	14,000 14,000	14,000
(1)	(1) (2)	(2)

2 ELEMENTS OF VAT

2.1 THE VAT SYSTEM

The purpose of this section is to look at the double entry in respect of accounting for VAT. It is not intended as a definitive guide on VAT. The procedures set out below only apply to businesses that are **registered** for VAT.

- VAT is levied (charged) on sales at 17.5% of the net amount (e.g. list price). The VAT is added on to the list price. This VAT is collected by the selling company and then paid over to Her Majesty's Customs and Excise (HMCE). VAT on sales is often called output VAT.

- VAT at 17.5% is also levied on most purchases. The VAT on purchases can be recovered from HMCE. This is often called input VAT or recoverable VAT.

- The output VAT is owed **to** HMCE, and the input VAT is owed **by** HMCE. The net amount is normally settled on a quarterly basis. Most businesses will end up paying VAT to HMCE.

MAINTAINING FINANCIAL RECORDS AND PREPARING ACCOUNTS : UNIT 5

- The business merely collects VAT on behalf of HMCE. At no time does the VAT belong to the business.

2.2 WORKING OUT VAT

At work and in exams, there is often a need to work out VAT from either the VAT inclusive figure (gross), or the VAT exclusive figure (net).

Net to gross

The net (VAT exclusive) figure is given and VAT is added to this. The VAT is calculated at 17.5% of the net amount. Therefore the gross amount is built up as follows:

Assume that the net selling price is £200.

	%	£
Net amount	100.0	200
Add VAT @ 17.5%	17.5	35
Gross amount	117.5	235

Gross to net

The gross (VAT inclusive) figure is given, and the VAT element has to be calculated. Using the structure above we can see that the VAT will be $\frac{17}{117.5}$ of the gross amount. This will be deducted to find the net amount, as shown below.

Assume that the gross selling price is £705. The VAT will be $\frac{17}{117.5}$ of this, which is £105.

	%	£
Gross amount	117.5	705
Less VAT @ $\frac{17.5}{117.5}$	(17.5)	(105)
Gross amount	100.0	600

ACTIVITY 1

Calculate the VAT element on the following supplies:

(a) £117.50 gross
(b) £470.00 gross
(c) £200.00 net
(d) £1,245.50 gross
(e) £17,117.40 gross

For a suggested answer, see the 'Answers' section at the end of the book.

2.3 STANDARD RATED, ZERO RATED AND EXEMPT SUPPLIES

In an AAT assessment, VAT will either be ignored or levied at the standard rate. At work, you may have noticed that there are three different rates of VAT. These are explained below.

(a) **Standard rated supplies**

Traders in standard-rated items are charged VAT on their purchases and charge VAT on their sales. Consequently VAT should have no effect on their profit and loss account.

(b) **Zero rated supplies**

Traders in these items charge VAT at 0% on their sales. As they are making taxable supplies they can recover VAT suffered on their purchases. Once again VAT should have no effect on their profit and loss account.

(c) **Exempt suppliers**

Traders in such items do not charge VAT on their sales but are not allowed to recover VAT on their purchases (unlike the zero rated situation). In such cases the irrecoverable VAT will be added to the trader's costs, and there will be no VAT account.

3 ACCOUNTING FOR VAT

3.1 OVERVIEW

The business must record:

- The gross amount payable to suppliers and receivable from customers. 'Trade creditors' and 'Trade debtors' are shown gross in the balance sheet.
- The net amount of purchases, expenses and sales.
- The VAT owed to HMCE and the VAT recoverable from HMCE. The net amount is normally a liability in the balance sheet.

3.2 CREDIT SALES AND VAT

This section looks at the accounting for VAT on a credit sale. The example is based on the sale of goods with a net price of £6,000. The total invoice price will be made up as follows:

	£	Double entry	
Net	6,000	Credit P&L Sales	This is the net sales value to the business. The profit and loss account will record a sale of £6,000.
VAT @ 17.5%	1,050	Credit B/S VAT Liability	This VAT will be collected from the customer by the business, and then paid over to HMCE.
Gross	7,050	Debit B/S Trade debtors	This is the trade debtor, the total amount receivable from the customer.

MAINTAINING FINANCIAL RECORDS AND PREPARING ACCOUNTS : UNIT 5

The steps to accounting for VAT on this transaction are:

1 The net sale is credited to the sales account, the VAT is credited to a VAT account and finally the total is debited to trade debtors.

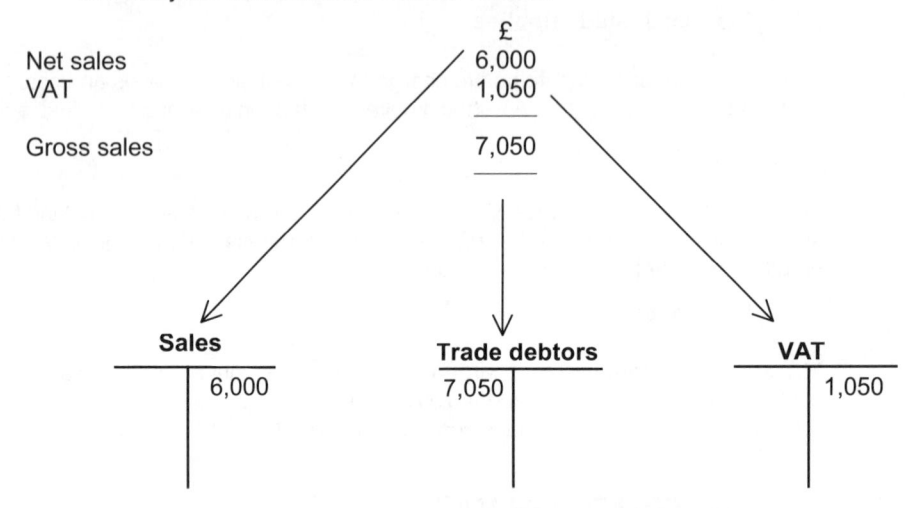

	£
Net sales	6,000
VAT	1,050
Gross sales	7,050

Sales	Trade debtors	VAT
6,000	7,050	1,050

2 The customer pays the gross amount, clearing the debt.

Note that VAT is not accounted for when the money is received from the customer. The VAT has already been accounted for when the sale was made.

Sales	Trade creditor		VAT	Cash at bank
6,000	7,050	7,050	1,050	7,050
(1)	(1)	(2)	(2)	(2)

3.3 CREDIT PURCHASES AND VAT

This section looks at the accounting for VAT on a credit purchase. The example is based upon the purchase of goods with a net cost of £4,000. The total invoice cost will be as follows:

	£	*Double entry*	
Net	4,000	Debit P&L Purchases	This is the net cost to the business. The P&L will record a purchase of £4,000.
VAT @ 17.5%	700	Debit B/S VAT Recoverable	This VAT will be paid over to the supplier, but then recovered from HMCE.
Gross	4,700	Credit B/S Trade creditor	This is the trade creditor, the total amount payable to the supplier.

The steps to accounting for VAT on this transaction are:

1 The net purchase is debited to the purchases of stock account as normal. VAT is debited to the VAT account. Finally the total is credited to the trade creditors account.

CHAPTER 2 : CREDIT TRANSACTIONS AND VAT

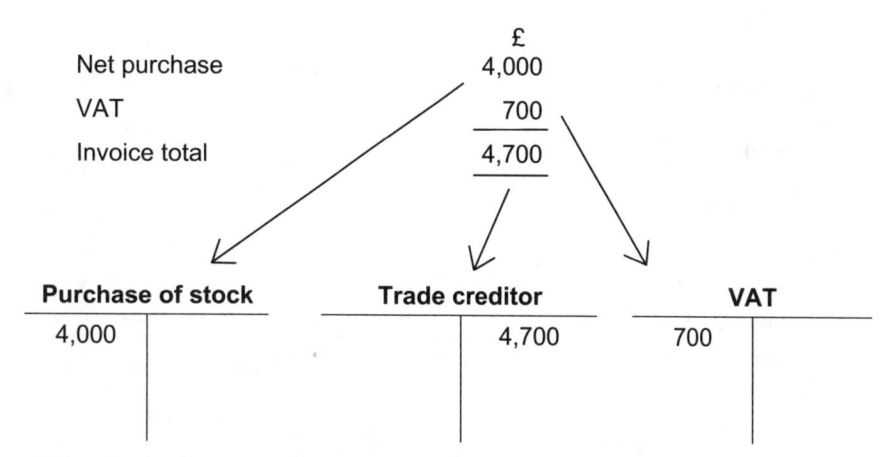

	£
Net purchase	4,000
VAT	700
Invoice total	4,700

Purchase of stock	Trade creditor	VAT
4,000	4,700	700

2 When the business pays the debt to the supplier the total invoice amount is paid from the bank account and the amount showing as owing in creditors is eliminated.

Purchases of stock		VAT		Trade creditors		Cash at bank	
4,000		700		4,700	4,700		4,700
(1)		(1)		(2)	(1)		(2)

As before, VAT is accounted for when the invoices are processed, not when they are paid.

3.4 COMBINING CREDIT SALES, PURCHASES AND VAT

In reality the business will be buying and selling goods all the time. The VAT account therefore will have amounts of VAT from sales transactions recorded on the credit side (VAT payable to HMCE), and also amounts of VAT from purchase transactions recorded on the debit side (VAT recoverable from HMCE).

When a payment date to HMCE falls due, the business will find the net balance on the VAT account and this will be the amount paid to, or reclaimed from, HMCE. So if the above two transactions were combined the VAT account would look like this:

VAT account

	£		£
Input VAT on purchases	700	Output VAT on Sales	1,050
Net payment to HMCE	350		
	1,050		1,050

Example

Credit purchases are made for £9,400. This figure includes VAT.

Half those goods are sold on credit for £6,400 exclusive of VAT.

Record the above transactions in the following T accounts: purchases of stock, trade creditors, VAT, sales and trade debtors.

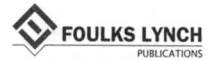

MAINTAINING FINANCIAL RECORDS AND PREPARING ACCOUNTS : **UNIT 5**

Solution

Step 1   Work out the VAT elements

On purchases:

	%	£
Gross amount	117.5	9,400
Less VAT @ $^{17.5}/_{117.5}$	(17.5)	(1,400)
Gross amount	100.0	8,000

On sales

	%	£
Net amount	100.0	6,400
Add VAT @ 17.5%	17.5	1,120
Gross amount	117.5	7,520

Step 2   Record the transactions in the T accounts

Purchases

			£				£
1	Creditors		8,000				

Sales

			£				£
				2	Debtors		6,400

VAT recoverable & payable

			£				£
1	Creditors		1,400	2	Debtors		1,120

Trade creditors

			£				£
				1	Gross amount		9,400

Trade debtors

			£				£
2	Gross amount		7,520				

ACTIVITY 2

During the March 20X8 Flagon made the following sales and purchases:

Sales: 258,500 gross
Purchases: £158,625 gross at the standard rate
               £23,456 exempt purchases

At the start of March the balance on the VAT account was £24,837 Credit.

CHAPTER 2 : CREDIT TRANSACTIONS AND VAT

Task

Write up the VAT Account for March, and identify what should be paid over to HM Customs and Excise in respect of the First Quarter (January – March) of 20X8.

For a suggested answer, see the 'Answers' section at the end of the book.

4 REPAYMENT OF A LOAN

4.1 COMPONENTS OF A LOAN REPAYMENT

When a bank lends a business some money that money (the capital or principal) has to be repaid along with interest on the loan. This section looks at the double entry for loan repayments, not at how the interest is calculated.

A loan is usually repaid in instalments, with each instalment consisting partly of a capital repayment and partly of an interest payment. The capital element reduces the balance of the loan in the balance sheet, while the interest element is charged to the P&L.

Example

Swing Dancewear borrows £30,000 from a bank. It repays the loan in monthly instalments of £350, of which £50 is interest. Show the first two months' monthly payments.

Loan (Principal only)

		£			£
			1	Initial loan	30,000
2	Capital element of repayment	300			
3	Capital element of repayment	300			
	Closing balance	29,400			
		30,000			30,000

Bank and cash

		£			£
1	Initial loan	30,000	2	First instalment	350
			3	Second instalment	350

Interest expense

		£		£
2	Interest element of repayment	50		
3	Interest element of repayment	50		

ACTIVITY 3

On 1 January 20X6 Barrel took out a £15,000 loan. The loan was repayable in eight instalments of £2,100 commencing on 1 April 20X6 and finishing on 1 January 20X8.

£225 of each instalment relates to interest.

MAINTAINING FINANCIAL RECORDS AND PREPARING ACCOUNTS : **UNIT 5**

Task

Write up the Loan Principal Account, Loan Interest Account and Bank Account for 20X6. Balance off the Loan Account at the end of the year.

For a suggested answer, see the 'Answers' section at the end of the book.

CONCLUSION

This chapter has looked at how credit transactions are recorded in the general ledger. The transaction is recorded when it occurs, not when it is paid.

This chapter has also shown how input and output VAT is calculated, recorded and paid over to Her Majesty's Customs and Excise. VAT is collected by a business on behalf of HMCE.

Finally, the split between the capital and interest elements of a loan repayment was illustrated.

SELF TEST QUESTIONS

		Paragraph
1	What are credit transactions?	1.1
2	What is a trade debtor?	1.3
3	What is the standard rate of VAT?	2.1
4	What must a business do with the VAT collected in from it sales?	2.1, 3.2
5	What happens to the VAT on business's purchases?	2.1, 3.3

KEY TERMS

Credit transaction – the buyer doesn't have to pay for the item on receipt, but is allowed some time before having to make the payment.

Value added tax (VAT) – a sales tax that is collected by businesses on behalf of the government.

Chapter 3

BOOKS OF PRIME ENTRY AND THE MAIN LEDGER

This chapter explains how and why day books, cash books and control accounts are used. It also explains the need for reconciliations between personal accounts and control account.

CONTENTS

1   Purpose of books of prime entry day books
2   Creating and using the purchase day book
3   Day books, journals and the nominal ledger
4   Creating and using the sales day book
5   Settlement discounts
6   Bookeeping entries for settlement discounts
7   Creating and using the analysed cash payments book
8   Creating and using the analysed cash receipts book
9   Bank reconciliations
10 Personal ledger accounting
11 Debtors and creditors ledger control accounts
12 Petty cash

KNOWLEDGE AND UNDERSTANDING

		Reference
1	The methods of recording information for the organisational accounts of sole traders and partnerships	Item 5
2	How to use the transfer journal	Item 13
3	The methods of analysing income and expenditure	Item 16

MAINTAINING FINANCIAL RECORDS AND PREPARING ACCOUNTS : UNIT 5

LEARNING OUTCOMES

At the end of this chapter you should be able to:

- explain the purpose of books of prime entry
- create and fill in a purchase day book
- create and fill in a sales day book
- create and fill in a cash book
- record settlement discounts correctly
- set up a personal ledger accounting system and post transactions from the day books and cash book to the personal ledger
- post transactions from the day books and cash book to the general ledger
- explain the use of control accounts
- perform a control account reconciliation
- perform a bank reconciliation.

1 THE PURPOSE OF BOOKS OF PRIME ENTRY

1.1 BOOKS OF PRIME ENTRY

Books of prime entry are the books in which all transactions are initially recorded.

In a business there will be a large number of transactions each day, making it very difficult to record individual transactions directly in the general ledger accounts. The solution is to group similar transactions together and record them in one of the *books of prime entry*. Periodically, the totals of each group of transactions are transferred to the general ledger. The transferring or posting to the general ledger was traditionally performed daily but may be performed weekly or monthly, depending upon the needs of the business.

The main books of prime entry are:

- sales day book
- purchase day book
- cash book (payments and receipts)
- petty cash book
- transfer journal.

1.2 DAY BOOKS

A **day book** is where the credit transactions of a business are initially recorded. The sales day book and purchase day book record sales invoices issued and purchase invoices received, respectively.

Day books are the starting point for recording credit transactions with individual suppliers and customers. In addition to the posting of those transactions to the general ledger, credit transaction details are taken from the day book and grouped

CHAPTER 3 : BOOKS OF PRIME ENTRY AND THE MAIN LEDGER

together by supplier or customer so that a business can see how much is owing from individual customers or owed to individual suppliers.

1.3 THE PURCHASES AND SALES CYCLES

The following sections describe how the day books and general ledger accounts are used to record credit transactions. We study how invoices are originally entered in the day books and from there are posted to the ledger accounts. We then look at how the payment of these invoices are recorded.

2 CREATING AND USING THE PURCHASE DAY BOOK

2.1 USE

The purchase day book is used to:

- record all credit purchase invoices for goods and services received (or returned)
- record all credit notes relating to credit purchase invoices.

An **invoice** is a document produced by the seller and sent to the purchaser, recording all the details of the sale.

A **credit note** is a document produced by the seller and sent to the purchaser cancelling all or part of an invoice. The credit note may be issued because of:

- an error on the invoice e.g. incorrect price charged
- an error in the goods delivered e.g. wrong quantity or wrong type
- the customer has returned the goods.

Note that the day book is a list of invoices. It is not itself part of the double entry, but it is used to originate the double entry procedures.

What a purchase day book looks like

1	2	3	4	5	6	7	7	7	7	7	7
Date	Invoice number	Supplier	Creditors ledger ref	Total £	VAT £	Stock purchases £	Repairs £	Fixed Assets £	Electricity £	Rent and Rates £	Motor expenses £

Notes on completing the purchase day book

The numbers refer to the column references above.

(1) The date on the invoice should be entered here.

(2) Each supplier invoice should be given a sequential number when it is received by the business. The invoice will be filed in this number order, making it easier to find in the future.

(3) The supplier's name is entered here.

(4) Each supplier is given a code (creditors ledger reference). This helps to ensure that invoices get posted to the correct supplier's account.

(5) The total amount includes VAT.

(6) The VAT shown on the invoice is entered in this column. This input VAT will be reclaimed from HMCE.

(7) The final entry is for the net amount shown on the invoice (excluding VAT). The amount will be entered into one of the analysis columns depending on what the invoice was for. For example, an invoice for stock purchases would be entered in the column headed 'Stock purchases'.

The procedure for credit notes is identical except that the figures are entered in brackets to denote that they will be deducted from the total. An alternative treatment, relevant for larger businesses, is to have a separate day book recording all credit notes received. This day book is known as the **purchase returns** or **returns outwards** day book and it operates in the same way as the purchase day book.

Example

The Flying Fortress Partnership purchases the following items on credit.

Invoice (8) from N Hudson (whose creditors ledger reference is H3) dated 6/6/X3 for purchases of stock - total £4,830, VAT £700. A discount of £130 is available for early settlement of this invoice.

Invoice (9) from Doors Ltd (creditors ledger reference D10) dated 10/6/X3 for a repair - total £940, VAT £140.

Credit note (CN6) from N Hudson (H3) dated 20X3 in respect of stock purchases - total £470, VAT £70.

Invoice (10) from G Farr (F8) dated 30/6/X3 for a building work which will be capitalised as a fixed asset - total £2,350, VAT £350.

Set up a purchase day book and fill in the relevant columns.

Solution

Purchase day book

Date	Invoice number	Supplier	Creditors ledger ref	Total	VAT	Stock purchases	Repairs	Fixed assets	Electricity	Rent and Rates	Motor expenses
				£	£	£	£	£	£	£	£
6/6/X3	8	N Hudson	H3	4,830	700	4,130					
10/6/X3	9	Doors Ltd	D10	940	140		800				
20/6/X3	CN6	N Hudson	H3	(470)	(70)	(400)					
30/6/X3	10	G Farr	F8	2,350	350			2,000			
				7,650	1,120	3,730	800	2,000			

Note how the Total of £7,650 'cross-casts' with the sum of the VAT and analysis columns. This is an essential part of the double entry bookkeeping system, and this check is performed before any postings are made to the main ledger. If it does not cross cast, then either the columns have been added up incorrectly or an invoice has been entered incorrectly. The error must be identified and corrected before any postings are made.

ACTIVITY 1

Vincent Corsair trades as a crop-duster. The following invoices were received in April 20X6.

6 April	Invoice 67 from Lightning Avgas (Reference L23) for purchase of aviation fuel. £8,225 gross.
9 April	Invoice 291 from Wildcat Services (W36) for repairs and maintenance. £2,115 gross.
15 April	Invoice 618 from Avenger Agrochemicals (A17) for weed killer. £5,000 net. There is a 3% settlement discount available for early payment.
19 April	Credit note (CN99) from Wildcat Services in respect of the repairs and maintenance. £400 net.

Tasks

Set up a purchase day book and fill in the relevant columns. Ensure that the PDB cross-casts.

All items are subject to VAT at the standard rate.

For a suggested answer, see the 'Answers' section at the end of the book.

3 DAY BOOKS, JOURNALS AND THE MAIN LEDGER

3.1 THE LINK BETWEEN DAY BOOKS AND THE MAIN LEDGER

The column totals from the day books are posted to the main ledger, rather than the individual invoices. The totals are normally summarised on a *Journal*, which will be checked and signed by a manager before the postings are made.

3.2 JOURNALS

Journals are used for routine postings from the day books, for routine adjustments such as deprecation, and to correct mistakes. Firstly we will look at the journal for posting the Day Book totals.

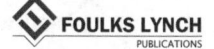

Number	Date	Account Number	Account name	Dr £	Cr £
1	June 20X3	GL 202	Purchase ledger Control account		7,650
		GL 300	VAT	1,120	
		GL 002	Stock purchases	3,730	
		GL 003	Repairs	800	
		GL 101	Fixed assets	2,000	
				7,650	7,650

Narrative
Being the posting from the analysed Purchase Day Book for June 20X3.

Authorised *A Manager*

Before authorising the journal, the manager will have checked to ensure that the amounts and codings are correct and that it balances.

3.3 THE LEDGER ACCOUNTS

The entries in the individual ledger accounts will look as follows.

Purchase ledger control account

	£
	Purchase day book (PDB) June 7,650

VAT account

	£	
PDB June	1,120	

Stock purchases account

	£	
PDB June	3,730	

Repairs account

	£	
PDB June	800	

Fixed assets account

	£	
PDB June	2,000	

3.4 THE PURCHASE LEDGER CONTROL ACCOUNT

The Trade Creditors Account is also called the **Purchase Ledger Control Account**. This account only shows the total amount owed to trade creditors. How much is owed to each individual supplier will be recorded in the **Personal Accounts**. The purpose for having a Purchase Ledger Control Account plus individual Personal Accounts will be discussed in detail later.

CHAPTER 3 : BOOKS OF PRIME ENTRY AND THE MAIN LEDGER

3.5 THE TRANSFER JOURNAL

Journals are sometimes known as Transfer Journals. For example, a transaction may have been recorded in the wrong account. Whenever an amount is moved from one account to another a record of the movement must be made and kept. This Journal acts as an instruction to the clerks carrying out the double entry, as authorisation of the changes being made, and as a record of what has been done. This means that all entries in the nominal ledger can be traced back to a transaction (via the day books and cash books) or to an adjustment authorised by a manager.

The example below follows on from 3.2 and 3.3 above. Assume that the £2,000 (net) paid to G Farr which was capitalised should have been charged to repairs. The net amount must therefore be transferred (the VAT will be unaffected).

Number	Date	Account Number	Account name	Dr £	Cr £
2	July 20X3	GL 003	Repairs	2,000	
		GL 101	Fixed assets		2,000
				2,000	2,000

Narrative
Being the reclassification of capitalised building work as repairs.

Authorised *A Senior - Manager*

The two ledger accounts will now look as follows:

Repairs account

	£		
PDB June	800		
Journal 2 July	2,000		

Fixed assets account

	£		£
PDB	2,000	Journal 2 July	2,000

Example

In reviewing his accounting records on 25 September 20X3, Adrian Plant decides that a £400 expense recorded in the sundry expenses account would be better described as vehicle maintenance. Prepare a journal to record the transfer of the amount from the sundry expenses account to a motor repairs account.

Solution

Number	Date	Account Number	Account Name	Dr £	Cr £
	25 – 9 – X3		Vehicle Maintenance	400	
			Sundry Expenses		400

Narrative
Being the reclassification of sundry expenses as vehicle maintenance.

The ledger accounts will look as follows:

Vehicle Maintenance account

Journal September	400		

Sundry Expenses account

PDB	400	Journal September	400

4 CREATING AND USING THE SALES DAY BOOK

Use

The purpose of the sales day book is to:

- record all credit sales invoices
- record all credit notes issued in respect of credit sales invoices.

What a sales day book looks like

1	2	3	4	5	6	7	7	7
Date	Invoice number	Customer	Debtors ledger ref	Total £	VAT £	Region 1 sales £	Region 2 sales £	Region 3 sales £

Notes on completing the sales day book

The numbers refer to the column references above.

(1) The date of the sales invoice is entered here.

(2) Each invoice is given a sequential number.

(3) The customer's name is entered here.

(4) Each customer is given a code (debtors ledger reference). This helps to ensure that invoices are posted to the correct personal account.

(5) The total amount includes VAT.

(6) The VAT shown on the invoice is entered here. The output VAT on sales will be collected from the customer and paid over to the HMCE.

(7) The final entry is for the net amount shown on the invoice (excluding VAT). This may be analysed depending on the needs of the business. For example it might be by geographic area (as here) or by product type, salesman, etc.

The procedure for credit notes is identical except that the figures are entered in brackets to denote that they will be deducted from the total. Alternatively, a separate **Sales Returns** (or **Returns Inwards**) Day Book may be used for credit notes.

4.1 SALES DAY BOOK

Example

GDP Ltd has two sales regions, North and South. The following invoices were raised in September 20X3.

Invoice number 68, dated 15/9, sent to Forks Ltd (whose debtors ledger reference is F3), total £23,500, VAT £3,500. This was a sale to the North region.

Invoice number 69, dated 18/9, sent to BL Lorries (debtors ledger reference L1), total £4,700, VAT £700. This was a Southern region sale.

Invoice number 70, dated 30/9, sent to MA Meters (debtors ledger reference M2), total £2,860, VAT £420 with a settlement discount of £40 if paid within 30 days. This was a sale to the North region.

Set up a proforma sales day book to record the above entries. (You may use the example in 4.2.)

Solution

Date	Invoice Number	Customer	Debtors ledger ref	Total £	VAT £	North sales £	South sales £
15/9/X3	68	Forks Ltd	F3	23,500	3,500	20,000	
18/9/X3	69	BL Lorries	L1	4,700	700		4,000
30/9/X3	70	MA Meters	M2	2,860	420	2,440	
				31,060	4,620	22,440	4,000

4.2 POSTING FROM THE SALES DAY BOOK

Using the sales day book from the example above we shall post the column totals to the nominal ledger.

Debtors ledger control account

	£		
Sales day book (SDB) Sept	31,060		

VAT account

			£
		SDB (Sept)	4,620

North sales account

			£
		SDB (Sept)	22,400

South sales account

			£
		SDB (Sept)	4,000

5 SETTLEMENT DISCOUNTS

5.1 SETTLEMENT AND TRADE DISCOUNTS

A **settlement discount** is a discount given for early payment of a debt i.e. within a stated period of time.

A credit transaction involves buying or selling goods or services some time before money changes hands. For example, suppose a business sells on credit. It is in the best interests of the customer to delay paying for the goods for as long as possible. In contrast, the business will want payment as soon as possible. Typically an invoice will state that payment is due 30 days from the invoice date. However, to persuade the customer to pay early, a percentage discount will be offered if payment is made before the due date. This discount is known as *settlement discount.*

A **trade discount** is a discount given for ordering in large quantities or as an incentive for regular customers.

A trade discount has nothing to do with payment. They are merely a reduction in the selling price of goods. Once they have been calculated, the transaction will be recorded in the normal way.

5.2 SETTLEMENT DISCOUNTS AND VAT

Settlement discounts raise the question of whether VAT should be charged on the original price or on the settlement price. Customs and Excise have agreed that **VAT should be charged on the settlement price**. (On business to business sales, this merely delays the receipt of VAT by HMCE. The reduced output VAT by the seller will turn into reduced input VAT for the purchaser.)

Example

An invoice with a net price of £400 offers a 2.5% discount for settlement within twenty days. The total invoice amount would be as follows:

	Invoice	
		£
Net		400.00
VAT	*Working 1*	68.25
Total		468.25

A 2.5% discount is offered for settlement within twenty days.

Working 1   VAT

	£
Net amount	400
Less: Settlement discount @ 2.5%	(10)
	390
VAT @ 17.5% on £390	£68.25

CHAPTER 3 : BOOKS OF PRIME ENTRY AND THE MAIN LEDGER

6 BOOKKEEPING ENTRIES FOR SETTLEMENT DISCOUNTS

6.1 DISCOUNTS RECEIVED

Discounts received are where a settlement discount is taken by a business when it pays a debt to a supplier, that is to say, it has 'received' a discount.

As a result, less money is paid by the business to clear the debt than was originally recorded in the books.

The remainder of the debt is then transferred to the profit and loss account as a credit entry, thus increasing profit. This makes sense as the business is paying less for the goods than it originally thought it would.

The double entry for claiming the discount is:

Debit   B/S   Trade creditors

Credit   P&L   Discount received

Example

Speedy bought goods with a net cost of £500. A 2% discount was available for early settlement. Speedy paid the invoice early and claimed the discount. Ignore VAT.

Step 1   Record the original debt

Creditors account

			£
		Purchases (1)	500

Purchases account

	£		
Creditors (1)	500		

Step 2   Record the reduced payment

Creditors account

	£		£
Cash at bank (2)	490	Purchases (1)	500

Bank & Cash

			£
		Creditors (2)	490

Step 3   Record the discount received

Creditors account

	£		£
Cash at bank (2)	490	Purchases (1)	500
Discounts received (3)	10		

Discounts received account

		£
	Creditors (3)	10

Speedy has made a £10 profit by paying early.

6.2 DISCOUNTS ALLOWED

Discounts allowed are where a business 'allows' its customers to take a discount in return for early settlement of the amount owing to the business.

In this case there will be less money received than the amount at which the debtor is shown in the books. The remaining amount is transferred to the profit and loss account as a debit entry (an expense). This makes sense as the business is receiving less than it thought it would be.

The double entry for allowing the discount is:

Debit   P&L   Discounts allowed
Credit   B/S   Trade debtors

Example

Generous sells goods with a net invoice value of £1,000. A 2.5% discount is offered for early settlement. The customer pays early and claims the discount. Ignore VAT.

Step 1   Record the original sale

Sales

		£
	Trade debtors (1)	1,000

Trade debtors

	£	
Sales (1)	1,000	

Step 2   Record the reduced receipt

Trade debtors

	£		£
Sales (1)	1,000	Bank & cash (2)	975

Bank & Cash

	£	
Trade debtors (2)	975	

Step 3   Record the discount allowed

Trade debtors

	£		£
Sales (1)	1,000	Bank & cash (2)	975
		Discount allowed (3)	25

CHAPTER 3 : BOOKS OF PRIME ENTRY AND THE MAIN LEDGER

Discounts allowed account

	£	
Trade debtors	25	

Generous has made a £25 cash loss by allowing the discount. However, there should be savings from reduced overdraft interest and reduced administration costs (now that there is no need to chase this debt.)

7 CREATING AND USING THE ANALYSED CASH PAYMENTS BOOK

Many organisations have a combined cash receipts and payments book. In this chapter we will look at the receipts and payments separately. This section looks at payments, the next one looks at receipts.

7.1 USE AND FORMAT OF THE CASH PAYMENTS BOOK

The purpose of a cash payments book is to:

- record payments of credit purchase invoices
- record all other payments out of the business's bank account.

The format of an analysed cash payments book is as follows:

1	2	3	4	5	6	7	8	8	8	8	8	9
Date	Payee	Cheque number	Total £	Creditors ledger £	Creditors ledger ref	VAT £	Insurance £	Wages £	Drawings £	Petty cash £	Other £	Discount received £

The notes on completing the cash payments day book are explained below:

The numbers refer to the column references above.

(1) The date of the payment is entered in this column.

(2) The person to whom the cheque was made out is entered here.

(3) The cheque number is entered next.

(4) The total value of the cheque is entered in this column.

(5) If the cheque is to pay a credit invoice or a series of credit invoices, the **whole** amount is entered in this column headed 'Creditors ledger'. **No other entry is made for the VAT or the net of VAT amounts. The reason for this is that the details of what the invoice was for and the reclaimable VAT have already been recorded in the purchase day book.** If the detailed amounts are entered again in the cash payments day book then they would be double counted.

(6) If there is an entry in column five, it must have a reference to the supplier. This reference will be the same code that was used when recording an invoice or a credit note from the supplier. The code is not needed if there is no entry in column five.

(7) If the payment is for non-credit purchase invoices then the VAT must be recorded in this column. Details of amounts paid for non-credit invoice payments have not been previously recorded, so VAT is recorded at this point.

MAINTAINING FINANCIAL RECORDS AND PREPARING ACCOUNTS : UNIT 5

(8) The net amount of non-credit invoice payments and other payments will be entered in the appropriate analysis column depending on what the payment is for.

The total column (**4**) should agree to the sum of the other columns above (columns **5, 7 & 8**).

These totals form the basis of the double entry.

They must balance, otherwise the double entry will be incorrect.

(9) The final column, for settlement discounts received, is a memorandum column. It is used to note any amounts of settlement discounts taken by a business because it has paid an invoice earlier than it had to. Discounts will be discussed in detail later in this chapter. The settlement discount taken is recorded in this column, but will not be included in the totals added across.

Example

Following on from our previously described example, the Flying Fortress Partnership, now makes the following payments:

Payment of £4,230 on 23/7/X3 to N Hudson in payment of the stock invoice net of the credit note. The settlement discount of £130 was taken. This was paid by cheque, (cheque number 1003).

On 24/7/X3, £2,350 to G Farr in respect of invoice number 10, by cheque, (cheque number 1004).

On 28/7/X3, purchase of stock, **not on credit** of £940 including VAT of £140, (cheque number 1005).

On 30/7/X3, payment of wages, £2,500 using cheque number 1006.

The cash payments book for these transactions is shown below.

Analysed cash payments book

Date	Payee	Cheque number	Total	Creditors ledger*	Creditors ledger ref	VAT	Insurance	Wages	Drawings	Petty cash	Other	Discount received
			£	£	£	£	£	£	£	£	£	£
23/7/X3	N Hudson	1003	4,230	4,230*	H3							130**
24/7/X3	G Farr	1004	2,350	2,350*	F8							
28/7/X3	Purchases	1005	940			140					800	
30/7/X3	Wages	1006	2,500					2,500				
			10,020	6,580		140		2,500			800	130**

* Note that there is no entry for VAT as the VAT on the invoices has already been accounted for in the purchase day book.
** Note that this entry is outside the 'balancing' of the total of the columns of the cash payments book.

7.2 POSTING THE ANALYSED CASH PAYMENTS BOOK

Using the cash payments book studied above we shall post the column totals to the nominal ledger.

Where applicable, figures already posted to the accounts are shown in *italics*.

CHAPTER 3 : BOOKS OF PRIME ENTRY AND THE MAIN LEDGER

Creditors ledger control account

	£		£
Cash payments book (CPB)	6,580	*PDB*	7,650
CPB (settlement discount)	130		

VAT account

	£		
PDB	1,120		
CPB	140		

Cash at bank account

			£
		CPB	10,020

Purchases account

	£		
PDB	3,730		
CPB	800		

Wages account

	£		
CPB	2,500		

Settlement discounts received account

			£
		CPB (double entry with creditors control account)	130

8 CREATING AND USING THE ANALYSED CASH RECEIPTS BOOK

8.1 USE OF THE ANALYSED CASH RECEIPTS BOOK

The purpose of the analysed cash receipts book is to:

- record the receipts of monies from credit sales invoices
- record all other receipts of monies into the business's bank account.

What an analysed cash receipts book looks like?

1	2	3	4	5	6	7	7	7	8
Date	Receipt from who	Total	Debtors ledger	Debtors ledger ref	VAT	Capital introduced	Cash sales	Deposit a/c interest	Discount allowed
		£	£		£	£	£	£	£

Notes on completing the cash receipts day book are explained below:

The numbers refer to the column references above.

(1) The date of the receipt is entered in this column.

(2) The person from whom the cheque was received is entered here.

(3) The total value of the cheque is entered in this column.

(4) If the cheque is received to settle a credit sales invoice or a series of credit sales invoices, the **whole** amount is entered in this column headed 'Debtors ledger'. **No other entry is made for the VAT or the net of VAT amounts. The reason for this is that the details of what the invoice was for and the VAT have already been recorded in the sales day book**. If the detailed amounts are entered again in the cash receipts day book then they would be double-counted.

(5) If there is an entry in column four, it must have a reference to the customer. This reference will be the same code that was used when recording an invoice or a credit note to a credit customer in the sales day book. The code is not needed if there is no entry in column four.

(6) If the receipt is for income other than credit invoices then any VAT must be recorded in this column as details of amounts paid for a non credit invoice receipt have not been previously recorded. The VAT is recorded at this point.

(7) The net amount of a non credit invoice receipt will be entered in the appropriate analysis column depending on what the receipt is for.

The total column (**3**) must agree to the sum of the other columns above (Columns **4**, **6** & **7**).

These totals form the basis of the double entry.

They must balance; otherwise the double entry will be incorrect.

(8) The final column, for settlement discounts allowed, is a memorandum column. It is used to note any amounts of settlement discounts allowed to the customer in return for the early payment of their debt to the business. The settlement discount allowed is recorded in this column, but will not be included in the totals added across.

Example

This follows on from our Sales Day Book example in 4.4. In October 20X3 GDP Ltd received the following:

Payment of invoice number 69, on 18/10, from BL Lorries (debtors ledger reference L1), total £4,700.

Payment of invoice number 70 on 28/10, from MA Meters (debtors ledger reference M2), total £2,820. The settlement discount of £40 was taken.

A cash sale of £1,175 including £175 VAT on 31/10.

Set up a proforma cash receipts book and post the above entries.

Analysed cash receipts book

Date	Receipt from who	Total	Debtors ledger	Debtors ledger ref	VAT	Capital introduced	Cash sales	Deposit interest	Discount allowed
		£	£		£	£	£	£	£
18/10/X3	BL Lorries	4,700	4,700	L1					
28/10/X3	MA Meters	2,820	2,820	M2					40
31/10/X3	Cash sale	1,175			175		1,000		
		8,695	7,520		175		1,000		40

Posting the analysed cash receipts book

The column totals in the cash receipts book above will be posted to the nominal ledger.

Note, that where applicable, figures already posted to the accounts from the day books are shown in *italics*.

Debtors ledger control account

	£		£
Sales day book (SDB)	*31,060*	Cash receipts book (CRB)	7,520
		CRB (settlement discount)	40

VAT account

	£		£
PDB	*1,120*	*SDB*	*4,620*
		CRB	175

Cash at bank account

	£		
CRB	8,695		

Cash sales account

			£
		CRB	1,000

Settlement discounts allowed account

	£		
CRB (double entry with debtors ledger control account)	40		

9 BANK RECONCILIATIONS

9.1 INTRODUCTION

The two Cash Books record the receipts and payments for the business's Bank Current Account. Between them they provide the detail for the Cash at Bank Ledger Account. The Cash Payments Book represents the Credit side of the account, and the Cash Receipts Book is the debit side.

The balance on the Cash at Bank Account can be found from the Cash Books as follows:

	£
Opening balance	246
Add: Receipts for the period from the Cash Receipts Book	357
Less: Payments for the period from the Cash Payments Book	(468)
Closing balance	135

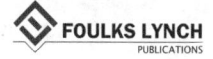

MAINTAINING FINANCIAL RECORDS AND PREPARING ACCOUNTS : UNIT 5

Some organisations have a combined receipts and payments cash book. The receipts (debits) will be on the left-hand page and the payments (credits) will be on the right-hand page. They will still need to do the above calculation in order to calculate the balance on the account.

9.2 BANK STATEMENT

At regular intervals the bank will send the organisation a statement detailing the amount that the bank thinks that the organisation has in its bank account.

The balance on the cash book at a particular date should agree with the balance shown on the bank statement for the same date with two important provisions:

(a) The bank statement is produced from the bank's point of view. Therefore the entries are the opposite way around compared with the business's own cash book. So, the business will classify a receipt as a debit, whereas the bank will record it as a credit. Also, a positive balance from the business's point of view will be a debit, but the bank will record it as a credit. This is because the Bank owes the money to the business. (In the same way, a debtor in one business's records will be a creditor in another.)

(b) There are timing differences between the cash book and the bank statement. A cheque payment is recorded in the cash book as it is written but will only be recorded by the bank when the cheque clears through the banking system.

9.3 BANK RECONCILIATION

The purpose of a bank reconciliation is to ensure that the cash book balance and the bank statement balance agree (subject to timing differences). There will be two types of reconciling items:

- Items which appear on the bank statement but have not yet been entered into the cash book
- Items that have been entered into the cash book but have not yet appeared on the bank statement.

Items on the bank statement but not in the cash book

These will normally be items that the organisation does not know about until the bank statement arrives such as:

- bank charges
- bank interest (charged or credited)
- standing order and direct debit payments
- credit transfers (where a receipt has been paid directly into the organisation's bank account).

These items will be identified on the bank statement and must eventually be entered into the cash book.

Items not yet on the bank statement

These items are due to timing differences between entries being made in the cash book and the same transaction appearing on the bank statement. There are two types of timing difference:

CHAPTER 3 : BOOKS OF PRIME ENTRY AND THE MAIN LEDGER

- outstanding or unpresented cheques.
- outstanding deposits or lodgements.

Unpresented cheques

These are cheques that have been written by the organisation and entered into the cash book. However they do not appear on the bank statement until they are received by the payee, paid into the payee's bank account and finally gone through the banking clearing system.

Unpresented cheques must be deducted from the bank statement total in order to reconcile with the cash book total.

Outstanding deposits

Outstanding deposits or lodgements are receipts that have been paid into the bank account by the organisation and therefore entered into the cash book but they have not yet gone through the banking clearing system and therefore have not appeared on the bank statement.

Outstanding deposits must be added to the bank statement total in order to reconcile with the cash book total.

Errors in the cash book

There is one further reason why the cash book total may not agree with the bank statement total. This might be due to the fact that there have been errors made in the writing up of the cash book. These must be identified and corrected in order for the cash book to agree to the bank statement total.

9.4 PREPARATION OF A BANK RECONCILIATION STATEMENT

1. Update the cashbook with items that have been included in the bank statement but are not in the cashbook (i.e. standing orders and direct debits).
2. Balance the cashbook and correct any errors.
3. Ensure that the opening balance on the cashbook agrees with that on the previous bank reconciliation statement.
4. Lay out the bank reconciliation format.
5. Tick the cashbook to the bank statement to identify uncleared cheques and deposits.
6. Complete the bank reconciliation.
7. Agree the cashbook balance to the bank reconciliation balance.

Example

On 31 March 20X3 the balance on an organisation's cash book was a debit of £1,042. On the same date the bank statement showed that the organisation was in credit with a total of £838. The following was then discovered:

(a) Bank charges of £24 were shown on the bank statement but had not been entered into the cash book.

(b) The payments side of the cash book had been undercast by £100.

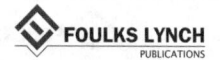

MAINTAINING FINANCIAL RECORDS AND PREPARING ACCOUNTS : UNIT 5

(c) A standing order payment of £70 appeared on the bank statement but had been omitted from the cash book.

(d) Cheques drawn by the organisation for £120, £60 and £35 had not yet been presented at the bank by 31 March and therefore did not appear on the bank statement.

(e) A cheque receipt from a customer of £225 had been paid into the bank account on 30 March but did not appear on the bank statement until 3 April.

(f) Prepare the bank reconciliation statement as at 31 March 20X3.

Solution

Step 1 Identify any items that have not yet been entered into the cash book and put through the entries. For assessment purposes this will generally be done in a ledger account that represents the balance of the cash receipts book and cash payments book.

Cash account

	£		£
Balance per cash book	1,042	Bank charges	24
		Standing order	70

Step 2 Identify errors that have been made in writing up the cash book and correct these in the cash ledger account. Balance the cash book.

Cash account

	£		£
Balance per cash book	1,042	*Bank charges*	24
		Standing order	70
		Undecast of cash payments	100
			194
		Revised balance	848
	1,042		1,042

Steps 3, 4 & 5 Identify any errors that have been made in writing up the cash book and correct these in the cash ledger account. Balance the cash book.

	£	£
Balance on the bank statement		838
Less: Unpresented cheques	120	
	60	
	35	
		(215)
		623
Add: Outstanding lodgements		225
Revised bank balance		848

Step 6 Ensure that the adjusted bank statement total aggress with the amended cash book total.

Both the amended cash book balance and the adjusted bank statement balance are £848. Therefore the bank statement has been reconciled.

The correct balance from the business's point of view is £848. This takes into account specific errors and omissions identified by the bank reconciliation. The timing differences (unpresented cheques and outstanding lodgements) are not errors. These should work through the system over the next few days.

10 PERSONAL LEDGER ACCOUNTING

10.1 WHAT ARE PERSONAL LEDGERS?

Earlier in this text it was stated that the purpose of the accounting system is to show the financial position of the business at a point in time and to show its financial performance over a period of time. This information is taken from the ledger accounts in the **nominal ledger.** The balance sheet and the profit and loss account are based on these nominal ledger accounts.

Two components of the balance sheet are trade debtors and trade creditors. We have seen that the total of the Total column in the Purchases Day Book was posted to the Purchase Ledger Control Account. The balance on the Purchase Ledger Control Account shows the total amount owed to suppliers. The amounts owing to individual suppliers is not recorded in the nominal ledger.

Likewise, total sales were posted from the Sales Day Book to the Sales Ledger Control Account.

However, a business needs to know how much it owes to each individual supplier, and how much it is owed by each individual customer. The solution to this problem is to keep a separate (personal) record for each credit customer and credit supplier that the business deals with. These records take the form of ledger accounts and follow the accounting conventions of double entry. However, they are totally outside of the double entry system of the general ledger. Entries recorded in these records are simply an analysis of the entries in the control accounts. The personal accounts duplicate the real double entry, which is with the control accounts. These personal accounts are also known as **memorandum accounts.**

10.2 THE LINK BETWEEN THE DAY BOOKS AND THE PERSONAL LEDGERS

Day books are the starting point for recording credit transactions with individual suppliers and customers. The credit transaction details are taken from the day books and recorded in the personal ledgers. In a manual system this requires a lot of copying out of invoice details. In a computerised system the control account and the personal accounts are normally updated automatically when an invoice is first processed. (In a computerised system the day book is often referred to as the 'audit trail'.)

10.3 POSTING FROM THE SALES DAY BOOK AND CASH RECEIVED DAY BOOK TO THE DEBTORS LEDGER

From the earlier examples of day books we reproduce the sales day book:

Date	Invoice number	Customer	Debtors ledger ref	Total	VAT	North sales	South sales
				£	£	£	£
15/9/X3	68	Forks Ltd	F3	**23,500**	3,500	20,000	
18/9/X3	69	BL Lorries	L1	**4,700**	700		4,000
30/9/X3	70	MA Meters	M2	**2,860**	420	2,440	
				31,060	4,620	22,440	4,000

MAINTAINING FINANCIAL RECORDS AND PREPARING ACCOUNTS : UNIT 5

These transactions will be posted individually to the debtors ledger.

Forks Ltd F3

		£		£
15 - 9 – X3	Invoice 68	23,500		

BL Lorries L1

		£		£
18 - 9 – X3	Invoice 69	4,700		

MA Meters M2

		£		£
30 - 9 – X3	Invoice 70	2,860		

The Cash Received Book for October was as follows:

Date	Receipt from who	Total	Debtors ledger	Debtors ledger ref	VAT	Capital introduced	Cash sales	Deposit interest	Discount allowed
		£	£		£	£	£	£	£
19/10/X3	BL Lorries	4,700	**4,700**	SLBLL1					
28/10/X3	MA Meters	2,820	**2,820**	SLMam2					40
31/10/X3	Cash sale	1,175			175		1,000		
		8,695	7,520		175		1,000		40

These amounts will also be recorded in the debtors ledger accounts individually. If a settlement discount is taken or is allowed, then this fact needs to be recorded in the personal ledger as well.

Forks Ltd F3

		£			£
15 - 9 – X3	Invoice 68	23,500			

BL Lorries L1

		£			£
18 - 9 – X3	Invoice 69	4,700	19 – 10 – X3	Cash received	4,700

MA Meters M2

		£			£
30 - 9 – X3	Invoice 70	2,860	28 – 10 – X3	Cash received	2,820
			28 – 10 – X3	Discount allowed	40
		2,860			2,860

10.4 POSTING FROM THE PURCHASE DAY BOOK AND CASH PAYMENTS DAY BOOK TO THE CREDITORS LEDGER

Post the following transactions from the Purchase Day Books to the Personal Accounts in the Creditors Ledger.

CHAPTER 3 : BOOKS OF PRIME ENTRY AND THE MAIN LEDGER

Purchase day book

Date	Invoice number	Supplier name	Ledger reference	Total
				£
03 – 03 – X3	6	P Jones	J1	2,415
05 – 03 – X3	10	Windows Ltd	W5	470
10 – 03 – X3	Credit Note 3	P Jones	J1	-235
25 – 03 – X3	15	A Smith	S4	4,700

Cash payments book

Date	Payee	Total	Creditors ledger	Ledger reference	Discounts allowed
		£	£		£
21 – 04 – X3	P Jones	2,115	2,115	J1	65
25 – 04 – X3	A Smith	4,700	4,700	S4	

P Jones J1

		£			£
10 – 03 – X3	Credit Note 3	235	03 – 03 – X3	Invoice 6	2,415
21 – 04 – X3	Cash paid	2,115			
21 – 04 – X3	Discount allowed	65			

Windows Ltd W5

	£			£
		05 – 03 – X3	Invoice 10	470

A Smith S4

		£			£
25 – 04 – X3		4,700	25 – 03 – X3	Invoice 15	4,700

11 DEBTORS AND CREDITORS LEDGER CONTROL ACCOUNTS

11.1 CONTROL ACCOUNTS AND PERSONAL ACCOUNTS

The debtors and creditors ledger control accounts in the main ledger record the total amount owed by debtors and owed to creditors and form part of the double entry system. The totals of the day books are posted to the control accounts whilst the individual entries are posted to the personal accounts. If the accounting has been done accurately, the balance on the control accounts should equal the sum of the balances on the individual accounts in the personal ledgers. If the balances do not agree, then there has been an error in the accounting.

This principle is illustrated in the diagram below. It shows postings from the Sales Day Book.

Sales day book

	£
A Smith	100
B Jones	3,100
C Francis	2,500
D Collins	900
E Jefferies	500
F Hamilton	2,600
	9,700

Individual entries → Recorded in personal accounts

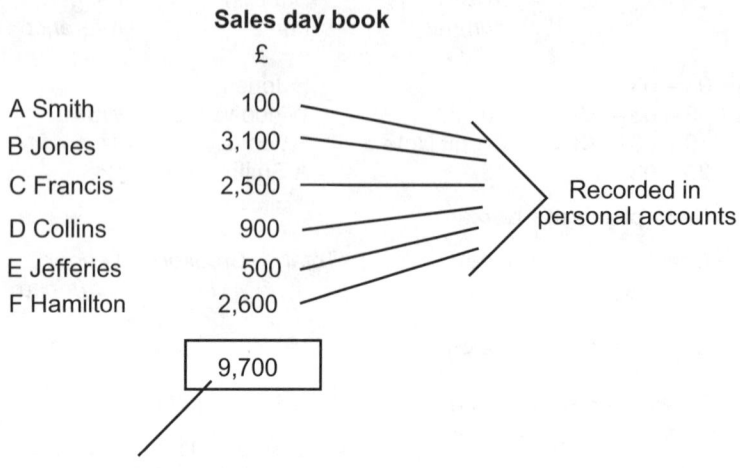

Total (9,700) → Recorded in control account

Occasionally businesses will not keep debtors and creditors control accounts. In these situations the double entry will be with the Personal Ledgers. The total amount owing to trade creditors will then be calculated by adding up the individual account balances. This is fine for a small business, but is obviously inconvenient for a larger business.

11.2 CONTROL ACCOUNT RECONCILIATIONS

The control accounts and the personal ledgers need to be checked at regular intervals, usually monthly, to make sure they do still agree. This check or control over the accuracy of recording debtors and creditors gives the 'control' accounts their name. Any discrepancies between the two indicates that an error has been made which needs to be identified and corrected.

11.3 ERRORS REVEALED BY THE CONTROL ACCOUNT RECONCILIATION AND THEIR CORRECTION

Although it is impossible to consider every possible error that may occur, it is possible to identify common errors with which you may have to deal both in practice and in the exam. These are detailed below, along with the course of action required to correct them.

(a) The sales day book is undercast by £300. Undercast means that numbers have been added up incorrectly giving a total that is too low. (Overcast means that an adding mistake has caused the total to be too high). This casting error will affect the total in the sales day book and therefore the posting to the main ledger will be wrong: the ledger control account and sales account will be £300 short. However, the individual entries recording each sales invoice are, we must assume, correct and therefore the debtors ledger will be correct.

The corrective action is therefore a double entry in the general ledger:

    Dr   Debtors ledger control account   £300
    Cr   Sales account   £300

(b) A transposition error occurred in the recording of a purchase invoice of £890 from J Longshaw in the creditors ledger. The actual amount recorded was £980.

In this case, the only error that occurred was when the creditor's personal account was credited with £90 too much. The creditors ledger control account is unaffected.

The corrective action required is to reduce the amount owing to J Longshaw in the creditors ledger, thus reducing the total amount of creditors shown by the creditors ledger. This is a single entry as the creditors ledger is not usually part of the double entry system:

    Dr   J Longshaw account in the creditors ledger   £90

(c) Cash received of £250 from K Flint had been correctly recorded in the cash receipts book, but had been debited to K Flint's account in the debtors ledger.

The error here is in the posting of the debtors ledger: a debit of £250 was recorded instead of a credit of £250. Therefore, the debit of £250 will need to be cancelled by a credit, and the credit of £250 put through, all in K Flint's personal account. This will decrease the total debtors in the debtors ledger by £500. The correcting entry is therefore:

    Cr   K Flint account in the debtors ledger   £500

(d) The discount received column in the cash payments book had not been totalled and posted to the main ledger. Total discounts received were £64.

It is safe to assume that the individual discounts received were recorded in the cashbook and the creditors ledger. However, the total has not been recorded in the nominal ledger and therefore the creditors ledger control account is incorrect. The correcting entry is to record the discounts received:

    Dr   Creditors ledger control account   £64
    Cr   Discounts received   £64

(e) A balance of £700 owing to J Hudson was omitted from a list of balances from the creditors ledger.

In this case the accounting entries are correct, but an error was made when the total of all creditors' balances in the creditors ledger was listed.

The corrective action is merely to add the omitted balance to the list of balances, increasing creditors per the creditors ledger by £700.

(f) A credit balance of £120 on the account of P Hobbs in the debtors ledger arose from the overpayment of an invoice by the customer. This balance was included on the list of balances as a debit balance.

Again, there are no errors in the accounting entries. This time, a credit balance which would reduce the debtors total by £120 has been included as a debit, increasing debtors by £120. The corrective action is therefore to reduce debtors by £240.

11.4 THE MECHANICS OF A CONTROL ACCOUNT RECONCILIATION

As already mentioned, a list of individual balances is prepared from the personal ledger. The total of the list of balances is compared with the balance on the control account. Any discrepancies are followed up and appropriate adjustments made. The adjustments to the control account are put through in the general ledger to obtain an amended control account balance. The adjustments to the list of balances, whether due to incorrect extraction of balances from the personal ledger or accounting entries

MAINTAINING FINANCIAL RECORDS AND PREPARING ACCOUNTS : UNIT 5

incorrectly performed (and therefore adjusted in the personal ledger), are shown on the control account reconciliation. A proforma reconciliation is given below.

Reconciliation of debtors control account and list of debtors ledger balances at 31 March 20X5

	£
Total list of balances originally extracted	X
Less: Credit balance extracted as a debit	(X)
Add: Debit balance omitted	X
Adjusted list of balances and control account balance	XX

Example

Colin Robbins extracts a list of balances from his creditors ledger on 30 June 20X3 and arrives at a total creditors figure of £1,730. The balance on the creditors ledger control account in the general ledger is £1,885. Further examination of his accounting records reveals the following errors.

(a) The purchase day book total for the month was overcast by £80.

(b) The cash payments book total in the analysis column headed 'creditors' was recorded as £936 instead of £963.

(c) A balance of £48 owing to G Radcliffe had been omitted from the list of balances.

Show how the creditors control account is adjusted for these errors and produce a reconciliation of the creditors control account and the list of creditors ledger balances.

Step 1 Read through the errors and decide how each one affects the control account and/or the list of balances.

(a) Total posted to the ledger is £80 too high. Corrective action:

Dr Creditors control account £80
Cr Purchases of stock £80

(b) Such an error in the cash book totals would mean that the overall totals posted to the general ledger do not form a complete double entry. To complete this double entry an extra £27 should be added to the 'creditors' total in the cash book and posted to the creditors control account:

Dr Creditors control account £27

(c) Add the omitted creditors balance of £48 to the list of creditors ledger balances.

Step 2 Open up a control account and bring down the balance given, before adjustment. Put through any adjustments noted in Step 1 which affect the control account, and find the amended balance.

Creditors ledger control account

	£		£
		Original balance brought forward	1,885
(a) Overcast PDB	80		
(b) Cash book error	27		
Revised balance carried down	1,778		
	1,885		1,885

48

Colin Robbins
Reconciliation of creditors ledger control account and list of creditors ledger balancesat 30 June 20X3

	£
Total list of balances originally extracted	1,730
Add: Balance omitted	48
Adjusted list of balances and control account balance	1,778

12 PETTY CASH

12.1 INTRODUCTION

A business will spend money on small expenses that do not warrant an account being set up in the creditors ledger. For example, some coffee is needed for the office. It is not practical to buy a jar of coffee on credit from the local shop or even for a business cheque to be written out to pay for it. A better system would be if the business had an amount of cash which could be used in such circumstances.

However, there is a danger. Cash is probably the most easily stolen asset of the company, both directly by the actual money being stolen and indirectly by expenses being claimed that have not been incurred.

Both situations and the required control are taken care of by using a method of dealing with cash expenses called the imprest system.

12.2 THE IMPREST SYSTEM

The petty cash float is set at a level that is thought sufficient to cover everyday expenses over a period of time such as one week. When an item is purchased, money is taken out of petty cash and is replaced by an authorised petty cash voucher detailing the transaction and supported by a valid receipt. When a check is made on petty cash there must always be cash and vouchers with receipts which, together, add up to the imprest amount.

At regular intervals the vouchers will be removed from the petty cash and the imprest value will be replenished from the bank account. The cheque drawn to restore the imprest will be an amount equal to the total vouchers removed. The transactions (expenses and cash replenishment) will be recorded in the petty cash book, which will then be posted to the general ledger along with the other day books.

12.3 THE PETTY CASH BOOK

The petty cash book is very similar in appearance to the cash payments book. It uses the columnar format to record the total amount of the expense, a VAT column to record any VAT on an expense and then the expense will be analysed into general ledger categories depending on its nature.

When the petty cash book is closed off, usually at the month end, the columns are totalled up. Because there is usually only one entry on the receipts side of petty cash, the cash replenishment, a separate book or page would not normally be kept for receipts. Instead a small reconciliation would be performed below the expenses totalled. This reconciliation would show the balance brought down on petty cash, less the expenses out of petty cash plus the cash replenishment. The final total will be the amount carried down to the next month.

MAINTAINING FINANCIAL RECORDS AND PREPARING ACCOUNTS : **UNIT 5**

Notice that under the imprest system the brought down total and carried down total are always the same unless the imprest is changed.

A full petty cash book can be seen in the example below.

The double entry to record the expense items in the general ledger would be:

Dr   profit and loss expense accounts
Dr   VAT account
Cr   petty cash account.

In T account form:

P&L expense a/c	VAT a/c	Petty cash a/c
X	X	X

These postings are made from the petty cash book.

To record the cash replenishment:

Dr   petty cash account
Cr   bank account

Bank a/c	Petty cash a/c
X	X

These postings are made from the cash payments book. As the cash must come out of the bank account, it is already recorded in the cash payments book and therefore it is not necessary to post the receipt of the cash from the petty cash book as well.

Petty cash book

Date	Details	Voucher reference	Total	VAT	Cleaning	Repairs	Tea	Travel	Sundry
			£	£	£	£	£	£	£
			X	X			X		
			X	X		X			X
Totals			XX	X	X	X	X	X	X

Imprest voucher

	£
Balance brought down	Required float
Less total expenses	(X)
Add cash replenishment	X
Balance carried down	Required float

The balance brought forward and carried down would normally be the same. It would only change if management decided that more (or less) Petty Cash was needed.

The total expenses normally equals the total replenishment.

Example

Record the following transactions in the petty cash book and post the month-end totals to the main ledger T accounts.

The balance brought down on the petty cash account on 1 September 20X1 is the imprest amount of £50.

CHAPTER 3 : BOOKS OF PRIME ENTRY AND THE MAIN LEDGER

Day

2   Coffee purchased for £1.89 (no VAT)

4   Repair to light switch £11.75 (£1.75 VAT)

10   Taxi fare £5 (no VAT)

15   Pay cleaner £15 (no VAT)

25   Repairs £5.88 (£0.88 VAT)

The imprest float was restored on 30 September.

Solution

Step 1   Draw up petty cash book.

Step 2   Record the transactions for the month.

Step 3   Total the columns.

Step 4   Perform the cash replenishment reconciliation.

Step 5   Post the petty cash book totals to the main ledger.

Petty cash book - September

Date	Details	Voucher Ref	Total	VAT	Cleaning	Repairs	Sundry
			£	£	£	£	£
02 Sep	Coffee	9-1	1.89				1.89
04 Sep	Light switch	9-2	11.75	1.75		10.00	
10 Sep	Taxi	9-3	5.00				5.00
15 Sep	Cleaner	9-4	15.00		15.00		
25 Sep	Repairs	9-5	5.88	0.88		5.00	
			39.52	2.63	15.00	15.00	6.89

Imprest voucher

	£
Balance brought down	50.00
Less total expenses	(39.52)
Add cash replenishment	39.52
Balance carried down	50.00

Petty cash account

	£		£
Balance b/d	50.00	Petty cash book (expenses paid)	39.52
Cash at bank account	39.52	Balance c/d	50.00
	89.52		89.52

Cash at bank account

	£		£
Balance b/d	x	Petty cash account	39.52

VAT account

	£		£
Petty cash book	2.63	Balance b/d	x

Cleaning account

	£		£
Balance b/d	x		
Petty cash book	15.00		

Repairs account

	£		£
Balance b/d	x		
Petty cash book	15.00		

Staff catering account

	£		£
Balance b/d	x		
Petty cash book	1.89		

Travel account

	£		£
Balance b/d	x		
Petty cash book	5.00		

ACTIVITY 2

A business requires a petty cash float of £70 which is the brought down balance on the petty cash account.

During the month of July the following transactions took place.

1	J Smith was reimbursed for a receipt for parking of £10
4	Cleaning materials £15
16	Tea and milk for refreshments £3
20	New keys cut for the office door £2
25	Flowers for a leaving present £25

At the end of the month it was decided to raise the imprest float to £80 which will be the new balance carried down on the petty cash account. (The way to deal with this last point is to ensure the cash replenishment takes the balance on the petty cash account to £80.)

Record the transactions in the petty cash book and post the totals to the general ledger.

Ignore VAT.

For a suggested answer, see the 'Answers' section at the end of the book.

CHAPTER 3 : BOOKS OF PRIME ENTRY AND THE MAIN LEDGER

CONCLUSION

The **Day Books** and **Analysed Cash Book**s are used for the initial recording of the cash and credit transactions of the business. They are called **Books of Prime Entry**.

The totals of the analysis columns in the day books and cash book are posted to the **Control Accounts** in the **General Ledger** in double entry form.

Individual credit transactions are posted to the **Personal Ledgers**, which keep a running total of amounts owed to and owing by the business. They provide the detail behind the totals shown in the control accounts. They are not part of the double entry system.

The memorandum settlement discounts column in the cash book has its own double entry.

The balance on the debtors ledger and creditors ledger control accounts should agree to the sum of the balances on the individual accounts in the respective personal ledgers. A **reconciliation** should be performed periodically to ensure that this is so.

Bank Reconciliation Statements should also be performed at regular intervals as a check on the accuracy of the recording of cash entries in the accounting records.

Petty Cash is controlled by using the **Imprest System**.

SELF TEST QUESTIONS

		Paragraph
1	What are the books of prime entry?	1.1
2	Set out the layout of a purchase day book.	1.2
3	What is posted from the day books to the nominal ledger accounts?	3.1
4	What is a settlement discount?	5.1
5	Is VAT on a credit purchase invoice ever recorded in the cash payment book?	7
6	What are personal ledgers?	10.1
7	What is the imprest system?	12.2

KEY TERMS

Book of prime entry – the point at which a transaction first enters the accounting system.

Day book – a name for a book of prime entry.

Credit note – a document issued to a customer or received from a supplier, indicating that the amount owed is being reduced for sales returns/purchase returns.

MAINTAINING FINANCIAL RECORDS AND PREPARING ACCOUNTS : UNIT 5

Purchase day book – is used to record all credit purchase invoices for goods and services received and to record all credit notes relating to credit purchase invoices.

Invoice – document produced by the seller and sent to the purchaser, recording all the details.

Journal – a book of prime entry that is used as for recording any transactions that are not recorded in any other book of prime entry.

Sales day book – is used to record all credit sales invoices and all credit notes issued in respect of credit sales invoices.

Sales discount – discount given for early payment of a debt, i.e. within a stated period of time.

Bank reconciliation – a process of checking the difference in the balance in the cashbook and on the bank statement, and making sure that the differences can be properly explained.

Unpresented cheques – payments by cheque entered in the cash book but not yet appearing on the bank statement because the bank has not yet processed them.

Outstanding lodgements – payments received and entered in the cash book, but not yet appearing on the bank statement because the bank has not yet processed them.

Control account – a 'totals' account and can be used to check the accuracy of the accounting records and prevent errors from remaining unidentified.

CREDITORS

Sales ledger control account – records the total value of transactions with credit customers.

Debtors ledger control account – records the total value of transactions with debit customers. *SUPPLIERS.*

Debtors control account reconciliation – the comparison of the balance on the total debtors account in the main ledger with the sum of the balances on the individual debtor accounts in the sales ledger, in order to ensure that the figures for total debtors are correct.

Creditors control account reconciliation – the comparison of the balance on the total trade creditors account in the main ledger with the sum of the balances on the individual creditor accounts in the purchase ledger, in order to ensure that the figures for total creditors are correct.

Petty cash book – book of prime entry for recording transactions involving petty cash (notes and coins). Often used as a main ledger account for petty cash.

Chapter 4

CAPITAL AND REVENUE EXPENDITURE

In previous chapters expenditure has been classified as an expense, an asset or as drawings. This chapter explains the actual rules for classifying expenditure. The accounting treatment of capital expenditure is then covered in Chapters 5 to 8.

CONTENTS

1. The need to classify expenditure
2. Determining whether an item is an expense or not
3. Different types of assets
4. Tangible and intangible fixed assets

KNOWLEDGE AND UNDERSTANDING

		Reference
1	The types and characteristics of different assets and key issues relating to the acquisition and disposal of capital assets	Item 1
2	Basic accounting concepts that play a role in the selection of accounting policies – accruals	Item 22
3	The distinction between capital and revenue expenditure and what constitutes capital expenditure	Item 25

LEARNING OUTCOMES

At the end of this chapter you should be able to:

- explain why a distinction is made between certain types of expenditure
- distinguish a purchase as being either capital in nature or an expense
- distinguish between current and fixed assets
- distinguish between tangible and intangible fixed assets.

MAINTAINING FINANCIAL RECORDS AND PREPARING ACCOUNTS : **UNIT 5**

1 THE NEED TO CLASSIFY EXPENDITURE

The main reason for recording commercial transactions in an accounting system is to enable a business:

- to determine its financial performance over a period of time
- to determine its financial position at the end of that period.

Performance is measured in terms of profit. If revenues (sales) are greater than expenses, then the business has made a profit.

The financial position is assessed in terms of net assets. If assets are greater than liabilities then the business has positive net assets. The greater the net assets then the greater the owner's capital interest.

Therefore, it is important to classify income and expenditure correctly in order to make a fair assessment of a business's performance and position. The options are as follows:

Cash received	either	income	in the profit and loss account,
	or	a liability	in the balance sheet.
Cash paid	either	an expense	in the profit and loss account,
	or	an asset	in the balance sheet.

2 DETERMINING WHETHER AN ITEM IS AN EXPENSE OR NOT

2.1 THE MATCHING (ACCRUALS) CONCEPT

Financial statements are prepared using basic principles known as the *fundamental accounting concepts.* One of these, the **accruals** (or **matching**) concept, is used to determine whether an item is an expense or not.

The **accruals concept** states that, in the profit and loss account, **costs** should be **matched** with the **revenues** that those costs helped to produce.

2.2 USING THE MATCHING CONCEPT TO DETERMINE WHETHER AN ITEM IS AN EXPENSE

It is normally quite clear when a sale has been earned, and it is therefore easy to decide which accounting period that sale should be recorded in. So, sales are accounted for first, and then all of the related costs are matched to those sales.

For example, the cost of stock is matched to the revenues it earns when it is sold. That is why unsold stock is carried forward at the year-end. They will then be charged against sales in the following year, when the related stock is sold.

Generally speaking, wages and salaries, heat, light and water, sundry expenses and so on are charged to the profit and loss account as they are incurred. These running costs (or *overheads*) help to generate sales from day to day, and so they are charged as they are incurred.

Fixed assets, such as plant and machinery, also comply with the accruals concept. The machine is paid for in one period, but it will help to generate income over many periods.

2.3 GUIDELINES FOR CLASSIFYING EXPENDITURE

Type of expenditure	Accounts category
Something that is used up within the period	Expense
Something that is sold within the period	Expense
Something that will last for more than one period	Asset
Expenditure for the owner's personal use	Drawings

An item that falls within the expense category is known as revenue expenditure, because it is set against the revenue (sales) produced by the business in the period.

The asset category is more involved and is explained below.

3 DIFFERENT TYPES OF ASSETS

3.1 CURRENT ASSETS

A **current asset** is an asset which will be converted into money soon within the normal course of the business's trading cycle. Normally it will be converted into cash within the next twelve months.

There are three items that have been looked at so far which fall into this sub-category:

- Stock will be sold in the near future
- Debtors will be collected in the near future
- Cash at bank is already money.

3.2 FIXED ASSETS

A **fixed asset** is an asset purchased not for resale, but for use within the business in the generation of profits over more than one accounting period.

Capital expenditure is expenditure on fixed assets.

Usually, the classification of an item will depend on the management's intentions. For example, if a furniture removal company buys a van, then it is probably going to be used in the business over many years for transporting furniture. Therefore it is a fixed asset.

If a motor dealership purchases a van then it is probably intending to sell it to a customer, so the van will be the current asset of stock. (However, from time to time the dealership may have to purchase a van for its own use – say for parts delivery – and these vans would then be fixed assets.)

4 TANGIBLE AND INTANGIBLE FIXED ASSETS

In this section two sub-categories of fixed assets will be introduced:

- tangible fixed assets
- intangible fixed assets.

Tangible fixed assets are assets that can be physically touched. For example:

- property
- vehicles

- machines
- tools
- office equipment.

Intangible fixed assets are assets that cannot be physically touched. These assets may not exist in a physical sense, but money has been spent on them and hopefully they will generate profits in the future. Examples of intangible fixed assets are:

- goodwill
- development costs

Goodwill arises when a businesses is bought. The amount paid for the business is often more than the market value of the physical assets within that business. The difference is known as goodwill. Goodwill represents reputation, the quality of the staff, customer contacts, and many, many other factors.

Development costs arise when money is spent on developing new products. These new products will hopefully create profitable sales in the future. You do not need to know the detailed rules for accounting for development costs.

Tangible and intangible assets will be discussed in more detail in the following chapters.

ACTIVITY 1

How would the following assets be classified in the balance sheet?

(a) New cars held by a motor dealership.

(b) A car owned by a driving school.

(c) Finished aeroplanes held by an aircraft manufacturer.

(d) Aeroplanes held by an airline.

(e) The costs incurred by an aircraft manufacturer when developing an improved version of an existing plane.

For a suggested answer, see the 'Answers' section at the end of the book.

SELF TEST QUESTIONS

		Paragraph
1	What is the accruals concept?	2.1
2	What is a current asset?	3.1
3	What is a fixed asset?	3.2
4	What is a tangible fixed asset?	4

KEY TERMS

Revenue expenditure – expenditure on goods and services where the benefits are used or obtained immediately, or within a short time after the purchase.

CHAPTER 4 : CAPITAL AND REVENUE EXPENDITURE

Accruals concept – the principle that revenue and costs are recognised as they are earned or incurred, are matched with one another, and dealt with in the profit and loss account of the period to which they relate, irrespective of the period of receipt or payment.

Capital expenditure – expenditure on items that will have a long-term use and long-term value for the business.

Fixed assets – items that are purchased for long-term use by a business.

Intangible fixed assets – assets that cannot be physically touched.

Tangible fixed assets – assets that can be physically touched.

Current assets – assets held for a short time (stock, debtors, cash and so on).

Chapter 5

RECORDING CAPITAL EXPENDITURE

This chapter explains how capital expenditure is recorded in the general ledger accounts, and why a fixed asset register is also needed.

CONTENTS

1 Tangible fixed assets
2 Accounting for the purchase of fixed assets
3 Setting up a fixed asset register
4 Recording in the fixed asset register
5 Reconciliation of the fixed asset register to the general ledger
6 A fixed asset count

KNOWLEDGE AND UNDERSTANDING

		Reference
1	How to use plant registers and similar subsidiary records	Item 12

PERFORMANCE CRITERIA

		Reference
1	Record relevant details relating to capital expenditure in the appropriate records.	Item A in element 5.1
2	Ensure that the organisation's records agree with the physical presence of capital items.	Item B in element 5.1
3	Correctly identify and record all acquisition and disposal costs and revenues in the appropriate records.	Item C in element 5.1
4	Ensure that the organisation's policies and procedures relating to the maintenance of capital records are adhered to.	Item G in element 5.1
5	Identify and resolve or refer to the appropriate person any lack of agreement between physical items and records.	Item H in element 5.1

6   Make suggestions for improvements in the way the organisation maintains its capital records where possible to the appropriate person.   Item I in element 5.1

LEARNING OUTCOMES

At the end of this chapter you should be able to:

- recognise capital expenditure and show which general ledger accounts it should go in

- account for the purchase of assets in the general ledger including the necessary VAT entries

- set up a fixed asset register with all the necessary details included

- record the purchase of assets in the register

- perform a monthly reconciliation of the register to the general ledger

- do a physical verification of assets and reconcile the results to the register

- show how the costs of fixed assets are shown in a set of financial statements.

1 TANGIBLE FIXED ASSETS

1.1 COSTS TO CAPITALISE

When money is spent on fixed assets, the expenditure is 'capitalised' in the balance sheet.

'Capitalised' means that costs have been recognised as an asset in the balance sheet rather than as a charge in the profit and loss account. All costs incurred in getting the new fixed asset to its current location and working condition can be capitalised. These costs should include:

- purchase price of the fixed asset

- delivery charges

- preparation of where the fixed asset will go (for example if a machine needs foundations)

- modifications to the fixed asset

- installation charges

- professional fees (architects, engineers, etc.)

Also, borrowing costs may be capitalised while an asset is being constructed. However, not many British companies do this.

All of these separate items of expenditure will be added up and treated as the cost of the fixed asset.

CHAPTER 5 : RECORDING CAPITAL EXPENDITURE

1.2 REPAIRS AND IMPROVEMENTS

A **repair** is expenditure incurred to return the fixed asset to its original working condition. Repairs do not create a new fixed asset, they merely restore old and damaged fixed assets. Therefore, repair costs must be charged straight to the profit and loss account. They must not be capitalised.

Improvements enhance a fixed assets earning capacity. For example, improvements to a machine might increase its volume of production, improve the quality of its output, or extend its working life. All of these will bring extra profits to the business. These costs must be capitalised.

The accounting treatment of each type of expenditure is as follows.

(a) **Repairs**

Repair expenditure is treated as an expense in the profit and loss account in the period when the fixed asset was repaired. It is shown under the heading 'Repairs'.

(b) **Improvements**

Improvement expenditure is treated as an addition to the cost of the fixed asset and is therefore included in the balance sheet along with the original cost of the fixed asset.

Where there is a mixture of both repair and improvement in an item of expenditure, then the expenditure is split between the profit and loss account and the balance sheet.

1.3 EXAMPLE

A business needed to repair one of its factory doors. While the builders were on site it was decided to widen these doors as well. Widening the doors would improve production and therefore increase profits.

The builders' final invoice (excluding VAT) was £10,000. Of this figure, £1,000 was the repair to the door, £9,000 for the widening of the doorway.

The double entry would be:

Debit	P&L	Repairs	£1,000	
Debit	B/S	Cost of factory	£9,000	
Credit	B/S	Trade creditors		£10,000

and in T-account form:

Repairs account

	£	
Creditors	1,000	

Factory cost account

	£	
Creditors	9,000	

Creditors account

			£
		Repairs/Fixed assets	10,000

2 ACCOUNTING FOR THE PURCHASE OF FIXED ASSETS

2.1 SETTING UP THE CORRECT LEDGER ACCOUNTS

Before a business accounts for the purchase of a fixed asset, it must decide how its fixed assets will be grouped together. Fixed assets are grouped together in the financial accounts because there would not be enough room to show every single asset separately.

Typical groupings are as follows:

- land and buildings
- furniture, fixtures and fittings (chairs, desks, shelving, lights, etc)
- office equipment (computers, typewriters etc)
- plant and machinery
- motor vehicles.

These groupings will become the ledger account headings for recording the cost of purchasing fixed assets.

2.2 BASIC DOUBLE ENTRY FOR FIXED ASSET COST

Having set up the necessary ledger accounts, the business will now record the cost of the fixed assets purchased.

Using the example of a machine costing £4,000, purchased on credit, the expenditure is recorded as follows:

Machine at cost

	£		
Creditors	4,000		

Trade creditors

			£
		Machine cost	4,000

2.3 DOUBLE ENTRY WITH VAT

Businesses registered for VAT can recover the input VAT on all purchases, whether for capital or revenue items. The only exception is for the VAT on cars. The examples below illustrate the double entry required.

Example 1   Normal rules for VAT

A VAT-registered business buys a delivery van. The price is £10,000 plus £1,750 VAT.

This transaction would then be recorded in the main ledger accounts as follows:

CHAPTER 5 : RECORDING CAPITAL EXPENDITURE

Motor vans at Cost

	£	
Creditors (PDB)	10,000	

VAT account

	£	
Fixed asset (PDB)	1,750	

Trade creditors

			£
		Machine cost (PDB)	11,750

Example 2   Irrecoverable VAT on cars

There is just one important exception in the treatment of VAT on fixed assets and that is VAT on motor cars. Although motor cars have VAT on them, VAT legislation says that a business cannot reclaim this VAT.

Therefore this un-reclaimable or irrecoverable VAT is included in the cost of the fixed asset.

If the above asset had been a motor car costing £11,750 including VAT, then the full £11,750 is shown as the cost of the car. The double entry would therefore be:

Motor car account

	£	
Creditors	11,750	

Creditors account

			£
		Motor car	11,750

Note: that the VAT on vans, trucks and other commercial vehicles can be recovered.

3   SETTING UP A FIXED ASSET REGISTER

3.1   THE NEED FOR A FIXED ASSET REGISTER

This chapter so far has concentrated on determining the cost of fixed assets, classifying them according to their type and then recording the cost in the relevant accounts.

When a fixed asset has been purchased, the cost has been recorded in the T accounts of the main ledger. However the only detail recorded in the general ledger will be the date of purchase, a purchase day book reference and the cost. Furthermore, when the T account is balanced up at the end of the year and the balance on the T account is carried down, even these details get lost as the individual cost is merged into an account total.

What is required, therefore, is a memorandum record for each individual fixed asset that will enable the business to maintain specific details about individual fixed assets. The fixed asset register is where all these individual records are kept.

3.2 LINK OF FIXED ASSET REGISTER TO THE MAIN LEDGER

As stated above, the fixed asset register is a memorandum ledger. It does not form part of the main ledger double entry system. It merely gives a detailed breakdown of the fixed asset category balances in the general ledger.

3.3 THE CONTENTS OF THE FIXED ASSET REGISTER

The layout of a fixed asset register depends on the organisation concerned and whether or not the fixed asset register is computerised. Information common to all fixed asset registers is listed below:

- An asset number. This is a unique number given to each individual asset and also put on the asset itself. This number is a means of identifying any fixed asset in the business and tracing it back to the fixed asset register.

- A description of the fixed asset.

- A location reference. This will indicate where the fixed asset can be found.

- A reference to the supplier. This will enable the fixed asset to be traced back to an invoice.

- A date of purchase.

- The useful life of the asset. How long the asset is expected to be used in the business before it is sold or scrapped.

- The type of depreciation method used. This will be covered in more detail later.

- The cost of the asset.

- The scrap value of the asset. This is how much the asset is expected to be worth at the end of its useful life.

- The accumulated depreciation to the beginning of the year. This will be covered in more detail later.

- The depreciation charge for the current year. This will be covered in more detail later.

- Net book value. This is the cost of the fixed asset less accumulated depreciation to date.

- Date disposed of. This is when the business gets rid of the fixed asset, it will be covered in more detail in the chapter on disposal of fixed assets.

- Disposal proceeds. This will be covered in more detail later.

CHAPTER 5 : RECORDING CAPITAL EXPENDITURE

An example of how this information can be arranged in a fixed assets register is shown below.

(Please be aware that there are other formats of fixed asset register.)

Fixed asset register

Asset number	Descrip-tion	Location	Supplier ref	Purchase date	Useful life	Dep method	Cost £	Scrap value £	Acc dep b/d £	Dep for year £	NBV £	Date of disposal	Disposal proceeds £

4 RECORDING ENTRIES IN THE FIXED ASSET REGISTER

All the information (except the accumulated depreciation figure and the disposal details) relating to a fixed asset should be recorded in the fixed asset register when the asset is purchased.

The accumulated depreciation and disposal information is recorded at a later stage in the lives of the assets.

If the information on the fixed asset changes then the new information must be recorded in the fixed asset register. The business will normally have procedures that ensure that the accounting department is made aware of any of these changes, to allow the updating of the fixed asset register.

Example

The assets detailed below were purchased by XYZ Ltd.

An IBM computer (asset number 13465), to be used in Accounts, from Computer Supplies Ltd for £1,500 on 30 November 20X4. The machine has a useful life of three years and an estimated scrap value of £300. It is to be depreciated on a straight line basis.

A mixing machine (asset number 24536) from Industrial Supplies Ltd to be used in Factory one, for £4,000. This has a useful life of five years and will be depreciated using the reducing balance method. The machine was purchased on 4 October 20X4 and is not expected to have any value at the end of its useful life.

Depreciation is the way in which a portion of the cost of an asset is charged to the profit and loss account each year. Depreciation, the straight line and reducing balance methods of depreciation, are explained in Chapter 7. For now all we need do is record the depreciation method used in the Fixed Asset Register.

Record this information in the fixed asset register.

Solution

Fixed asset register

Asset number	Descrip-tion	Location ref	Supplier ref	Purchase date	Useful life	Dep method	Cost £	Scrap value £	Acc dep b/d £	Dep for year £	NBV £	Date of disposal	Disposal proceeds £
13465	IBM computer	Accounts	CS Ltd	30/11/X4	3	SL	1,500	300					
24536	Mixing machine	Fact 1	IS Ltd	4/10/X4	5	RB	4,000	nil					

Note that some fixed asset registers have a separate page for each fixed asset so that information which changes annually may be updated. For example, depreciation is charged on assets annually. The register records each year's charge and the cumulative amount charged to date. This is known as accumulated depreciation.

ACTIVITY 1

Record the following fixed asset additions in the Fixed Asset Register for Robert & Co, a firm of builders.

23 June 20X4   Asset number 10907

A cement pump purchased from Plant Providers Ltd for £3,600 net. The cement pump will have a useful life of six years (4) and a scrap value of £400.

17 September 20X4   Asset number 10908

A digger purchased from Just Diggers Ltd for £23,000 net. It has a ten year useful life and a £3,000 scrap value.

Both assets will be depreciated using the straight line method. The assets will be used on site.

This activity covers performance criterion A in element 5.1.

For a suggested answer, see the 'Answers' section at the end of the book.

5 RECONCILIATION OF THE FIXED ASSET REGISTER TO THE MAIN LEDGER

5.1 THE NEED TO AGREE THE FIXED ASSET REGISTER AND THE MAIN LEDGER

The same information in respect of the cost of a fixed asset is recorded in the main ledger and the fixed asset register. In theory the total cost on the register and the ledger should agree.

In addition, the information recorded for accumulated depreciation is also the same on the main ledger and the fixed asset register and therefore this information should also agree.

However differences will occur if one is not updated or if different figures are recorded in each.

To ensure the accuracy of the accounting information, a regular reconciliation between the main ledger and the fixed asset register should take place.

5.2 HOW THE TWO ARE AGREED

Reconciling the main ledger and the fixed asset register is a matter of balancing the fixed asset main ledger accounts for cost and accumulated depreciation, adding up the cost and accumulated depreciation columns in the register and comparing the sets of figures.

If the sets of figures agree then the general ledger and the fixed asset register are probably accurate. If they do not agree however then some investigative work is needed to track down the difference.

5.3 FINDING DIFFERENCES BETWEEN THE TWO

This usually involves checking every single entry made since the last reconciliation in the ledger and the register, making sure entries in both have been recorded identically. The entries in the main ledger will have been posted from the Purchase Day Book or from the Cash Day Book. These postings should be checked. The entries in the Fixed Asset Register will be more detailed. The entry for each asset in the Fixed Asset Register should be checked against the individual invoices in the Purchase Day Book or payments in the Cash Book. Calculations may also need checking for accuracy.

5.4 ACCOUNTING FOR THE DIFFERENCES

If an entry in the fixed asset register is incorrect, then it is a simple matter of just correcting the entry in the fixed asset register.

If the main ledger is incorrect then the correction that will take place will depend on the type of error. This will be looked at in the chapter on the trial balance and correction of errors.

6 A FIXED ASSET COUNT

6.1 THE NEED FOR A FIXED ASSET COUNT ON A REGULAR BASIS

The above section looked briefly at the need for a reconciliation between the general ledger and the fixed asset register. That, however, is only half the story. There is also a need to make sure, on a regular basis, that the fixed assets shown on the fixed asset register actually exist and also that fixed assets that are being used by the business have been recorded on the fixed asset register.

A business, therefore, should undertake a count of all of its fixed assets and reconcile the count back to the fixed asset register.

6.2 PROCEDURES FOR A FIXED ASSET COUNT

In general, the following procedure is used:

1. A team of employees will be given a list of the fixed assets, taken from the fixed asset register, that they should expect to find at a location.

2. As a fixed asset is found, the asset number on the asset will be checked against the list of fixed assets to ensure the description is correct. Notes may also be made as to the condition of the asset.

3. The fixed asset will be marked as having been counted, probably by putting a coloured sticker on it.

4. If a fixed asset is found but no details can be found on the fixed asset register then the fixed asset will be added to the list. This asset will then be a cause for investigation.

5   When all the fixed assets in the location have been counted the fixed asset list will be reviewed and any items not marked as having been counted are therefore missing and need to be investigated.

6   The fixed asset list with either items not found or with missing items will be returned to the accounting department who will update the fixed asset register with these differences.

6.3 HOW TO ACCOUNT FOR THE DIFFERENCES

The differences between the fixed asset register and the fixed assets that are being used by the business can be caused by a variety of reasons. The fixed asset may have been recorded on the register incorrectly, or maybe the fixed asset has been stolen or sold.

Whatever the reason, the differences must be adjusted for in the fixed asset register and, because the fixed asset register has been reconciled to the fixed asset accounts in the general ledger, the differences must also be recorded in the general ledger.

(a) **Fixed assets that are missing**

The details of these fixed assets must be removed from the fixed asset register and also the cost and accumulated depreciation must be taken out of the fixed asset accounts and the net book value treated as an expense of the period when the fixed asset count was done.

(b) **Fixed assets found but not on register**

The details of these fixed assets will be added to the fixed asset register except that they will probably be recorded at zero cost. The cost of the fixed asset will probably have been incorrectly recorded as a profit and loss expense some time in the past. All differences must be reported to a manager. However small, they may be evidence of a weakness in the accounting system or a failure to follow the organisations policies and procedures. They may also alert management to theft or misuse of assets. If there are material differences between physical assets present and the accounting records, then a more formal system of recording fixed assets in the fixed asset register maybe required. However, the business still needs to record the fact that it owns the fixed asset regardless of whether management is adjusting for this item or not. Regular fixed asset counts should ensure that fixed assets are not omitted from the register for long periods of time before discovery.

CONCLUSION

This chapter covered the accounting for fixed assets, including the following stages:

- deciding in which category the fixed asset is to be recorded

- accounting for the cost

- recording fixed assets in the fixed asset register

- reconciling the fixed asset register and general ledger on a regular basis

- performing a fixed asset count on a regular basis.

CHAPTER 5 : RECORDING CAPITAL EXPENDITURE

SELF TEST QUESTIONS

Paragraph

1   A business spent £5,000 transporting a machine from its suppliers to Germany to their own factory in Manchester. Will this £5,000 be charged as an expense or capitalised?   1.1

2   Can repairs be capitalised?   1.2

3   A builder has just purchased a new pick-up truck and a new salon car. How will the VAT on these two items be accounted for?   2.3

4   Fixed assets are recorded in the Fixed Asset accounts in the General Ledger. Why does a business need to maintain a Fixed Asset Register as well?   3.1

5   Why do fixed asset counts take place?   6.1

KEY TERMS

Fixed asset register – a record of individual tangible assets.

Fixed asset count – a count of all of the business's fixed assets and its reconciliation with the fixed asset register.

Chapter 6

AUTHORISING AND FUNDING CAPITAL EXPENDITURE

This chapter explains the need to formally authorise capital expenditure and disposals. It also looks at the various sources of finance for capital expenditure.

CONTENTS

1 Capital expenditure

2 Funding capital expenditure

3 Accounting for finance leases and purchase agreements

4 Authorisation for the disposal of fixed assets

KNOWLEDGE AND UNDERSTANDING

		Reference
1	The methods of funding: part exchange deals	Item 14

PERFORMANCE CRITERIA

		Reference
1	Ensure that the records clearly show the prior authority for capital expenditure and disposal and the approved method of funding and disposal	Item E in element 5.1

LEARNING OUTCOMES

At the end of this chapter you should be able to:

- understand and be able to produce a capital expenditure authorisation form

- be aware of the funding alternatives available for the purchase of fixed assets

- understand the importance of the authorisation and approval of disposals of fixed assets.

1 CAPITAL EXPENDITURE AUTHORISATION

1.1 WHY CAPITAL EXPENDITURE NEEDS TO BE AUTHORISED

One of the largest items of expenditure in a business is the purchase of fixed assets. A fixed asset is also one of the few business assets open to misuse by employees purchasing fixed assets for their own use.

For these reasons it is important that a business makes sure that when an asset is purchased:

(a) it is for business purposes

(b) the business is really justified in purchasing the asset

(c) the business can afford it.

Most businesses ensure that these criteria are satisfied by means of a capital authorisation form to support all requests for capital expenditure.

1.2 CAPITAL EXPENDITURE AUTHORISATION FORMS

A capital authorisation form documents the management's approval for purchasing a fixed asset. It must be signed by the manager authorised to approve the expenditure.

The form normally details:

- a description of the fixed asset
- why the fixed asset is required
- evidence to justify this reason
- alternative quotes for the cost of the fixed asset
- the supplier recommended from the quotes and why that supplier has been chosen (see note 1)
- how the purchase of the fixed asset is to be funded (see next section)
- the requester's signature
- an authorised counter signatory (see note 2).

Notes:

1   The order will not always go to the supplier with the lowest quote. Other factors such as speed of delivery, reliability and customer care may mean a slightly more expensive quote is chosen.

2   Before the purchase of a fixed asset is allowed, the form will have to be signed by someone who agrees with the reasons for the purchase and has been given the authority by either the owner of the business or the board of directors of the company to purchase fixed assets. Usually, that person will have been given an approval limit, i.e. that person can sign requests up to a maximum specified amount. If the request is for a larger amount, the form will have to be passed to someone with a higher approval limit.

A typical capital expenditure authorisation form is shown below.

Capital expenditure authorisation

Description fixed asset

Reason for purchase including costs and benefits

List quotes for purchase of fixed assets (three required)

Supplier

Recommended supplier including reason for choice

Means of funding

Requestor's signature

Authorised by

2 FUNDING CAPITAL EXPENDITURE

2.1 INTRODUCTION

A business will not always have the spare cash needed to purchase new fixed assets. This section looks at the various sources of finance for capital expenditure.

(a) **Funding from retained profits (cash)**

Profits eventually generate cash. A profitable business may be able to purchase new fixed assets from the cash that it has generated. The business is said to be funding its capital expenditure from retained profits.

Retained profits are the cumulating profits made by a business, less any drawings taken out.

(b) **Funding by the introduction of capital**

With this method the capital expenditure is funded by the owner of the business introducing some more of their own money. An alternative is that the owner takes on a new partner who introduces some money into the business.

(c) **Funding by borrowing**

A bank will lend the business the money needed to purchase the fixed asset.

(d) **Funding by hire purchase**

For smaller items of capital expenditure it may be appropriate to purchase the fixed asset via a hire purchase (HP) agreement. With an HP agreement, a business has use of the fixed asset, but does not pay for the asset straight away. From the accounting point of view the business takes out a loan secured on the asset being purchased. The instalments will include an element of capital repayment and an interest charge. (The legal point of view is that the business has hired an asset and is paying rentals. The final rental payment includes a nominal amount to purchase the asset outright. Hence the name; hire-purchase.)

(e) **Funding by leasing (operating and finance)**

There are two types of lease; finance leases and operating leases

An **operating lease** is a straight forward rental, such as when you hire a car for a holiday or some machinery for the weekend. The lease period is only for a small fraction of the asset's total life, and the hire charge paid is only a small fraction of the total cost of the asset. These operating leases are treated as expenses in the profit and loss account. The cash paid will be charged straight to the P&L.

Finance leases are a sophisticated form of hire purchase. In some finance leases the user of the asset (the lessee) never actually gets to own the asset. However, with all finance leases the lessee will use the asset for the majority of the asset's life and the rentals paid will cover the cost of the asset.

(f) **Part exchange deals**

It is common for some old assets (particularly vehicles) to be traded-in to help fund the cost of a new asset. For example, suppose a business was purchasing a new van costing £17,000. If they traded in their old van at an agreed value of £5,000 then there would only be £12,000 to pay in cash.

3 ACCOUNTING FOR FINANCE LEASES AND PURCHASE AGREEMENTS

3.1 BASIC RULES

Assets held under finance leases and hire purchase agreements are accounted for in the same way.

- The assets will be capitalised at its normal selling price.
- The double entry will be to the credit of a loan account.
- The hire/lease payments will be split into two elements:
  - A capital repayment, reducing the balance of the "loan" in the balance sheet.
  - Interest payments that will be charged to the P&L as an expense.

CHAPTER 6 : AUTHORISING AND FUNDING CAPITAL EXPENDITURE

The accounting treatment is to assume that the finance lease or HP agreements are loans to purchase the assets.

3.2 EXAMPLE BASED ON AN HP AGREEMENT

The situation

On 1 January 20X5, Bricks & Co, an engineering business, acquired a new excavator under a hire purchase agreement. The normal list price was £18,000. The hire purchase terms were 36 monthly instalments of £550 each. The total amount payable under the HP agreement was £19,800.

Step 1   Calculating the finance charge

The extra £1,800 payable under HP represents the interest on the loan of £18,000 given to Bricks to buy the excavator. The interest charge will be spread over the 36 months of the loan, amounting to £50 pcm.

Step 2   Recognising the fixed asset and the loan

The fixed asset and the loan will be recognised at their fair value of £18,000.

The double entry is:

Debit   B/S   Fixed assets at cost   £18,000
Credit   B/S   Hire purchase loan   £18,000

Step 3   Monthly payments

Each monthly payment of £550 will be split between a capital and an interest element.

The £500 capital repayment will reduce the balance of the loan in the balance sheet.

The £50 interest payment will be charged to the profit and loss account.

The double entry is:

Debit   P&L   HP interest charge   £50
Debit   B/S   Hire purchase loan   £500
Credit   B/S   Cash   £550

At the end of the first month the ledger accounts will show the following entries:

Fixed assets at cost excavator

		£		
2	HP loan account	18,000		

Hire purchase loan account

		£			£
3	Bank and cash	500	2	Fixed assets	18,000

Bank and cash

				£
		3	HP instalment	550

Hire purchase interest charge

		£
3	Bank and cash	50

4 AUTHORISATION FOR THE DISPOSAL OF FIXED ASSETS

4.1 THE NEED FOR AUTHORISATION

A business may dispose of fixed assets for a variety of reasons. The assets may be worn out, technologically out of date, no longer used within the business or not productive enough. A business must have tight control over the disposal of fixed assets. These controls must ensure that:

- the disposal is properly documented
- written authorisation is obtained and kept on file
- only surplus fixed assets are disposed of
- a fair price is obtained for disposals.

There have been occasions when dishonest staff have sold assets to themselves at bargain prices.

4.2 METHOD OF DISPOSAL

If a fixed asset is to be disposed of then in most cases it will be sold to another party either as a working asset or for a scrap value. If there are a number of possible purchasers then the best complete deal should be determined. This will include consideration of not only the price offered for the asset but also other matters such as who bears any dismantling or delivery costs.

4.3 PART EXCHANGE DEALS

If an asset is to be part exchanged for a new asset then the entire deal must be considered before deciding which purchaser/supplier to choose. This will include not only the part exchange value placed upon the asset to be disposed of but also the cost of the new asset and other related costs and services.

CONCLUSION

This chapter has covered the practical aspects of fixed asset purchases including the following stages:

- obtaining authorisation for capital expenditure
- working out the cost of the fixed asset
- deciding on the method of funding
- authorisation and methods of disposal of fixed assets.

CHAPTER 6 : AUTHORISING AND FUNDING CAPITAL EXPENDITURE

SELF TEST QUESTIONS

		Paragraph
1	What information is found on a capital expenditure authorisation form?	1.2
2	Give four ways of funding capital expenditure.	2
3	What are the differences between a finance lease and an operating lease?	2
4	An instalment paid under a hire purchase agreement is split into two elements. What are they?	3.2

Chapter 7

DEPRECIATION

This chapter explains the purpose of depreciation in financial statements, and how depreciation is recorded in the general ledger accounts and fixed asset register.

CONTENTS

1. The purpose of depreciation
2. Methods of depreciation
3. Depreciation in the years of acquisition and disposal
4. Accounting for depreciation
5. Depreciation and the fixed asset register
6. Changes in depreciation

KNOWLEDGE AND UNDERSTANDING

		Reference
1	Methods of depreciation and when to use each of them: straight line; reducing balance	Item 10
2	The objectives of making provisions for depreciation and other purposes	Item 30

PERFORMANCE CRITERIA

		Reference
1	Correctly calculate and record depreciation charges and other necessary entries and adjustments in the appropriate records	Item D in element 5.1

LEARNING OUTCOMES

At the end of this chapter you should be able to:

- explain what depreciation is and its purpose
- know when, and when not to depreciate a fixed asset
- calculate depreciation using the straight line method
- calculate depreciation using the reducing balance method

- work out a depreciation charge for an accounting period
- account for depreciation
- account for a change in useful life of an asset
- account for a change in method of depreciation
- show how depreciation of fixed assets is presented in a set of financial statements.

1 THE PURPOSE OF DEPRECIATION

Fixed assets include items which will be used in the business for an extended period: an office building, an item of computer equipment, a delivery van, a machine used in the business's manufacturing operations, and so on. When a fixed asset is purchased by a business, the double entry is to debit a fixed asset account and credit either cash or a creditor account. The original cost of the asset is reported in the balance sheet.

So far so good, but we also need to recognise the cost of acquiring the asset in the profit and loss account. By definition, a fixed asset will remain in the business for several accounting periods. Some way must be found of allocating the cost of the asset to the accounting periods that will benefit from its use.

Depreciation is a method of charging a proportion of a fixed asset's original cost to the profit and loss account each year to match the profits that the asset earns.

1.1 WHAT IS DEPRECIATION?

Depreciation is the measure of the cost or revalued amount of a fixed asset that has been consumed during an accounting period.

The definition suggests that a fixed asset is eventually 'consumed', i.e. it has no further value. This consumption may arise because of any of the following factors.

- **Use** – e.g. plant and machinery or motor vehicles are eventually used so much that they are not fit for further use.
- **Passing of time** – e.g. a ten year lease of property eventually expires when the ten years have passed.
- **Obsolescence** through technology and market changes – e.g. plant and machinery of a specialised nature can quickly become obsolete and will need to be replaced by more modern equivalents.
- **Depletion** – e.g. the extraction of material from a quarry.

It is important to remember that depreciation does not represent the fall in value of an asset. Fixed assets are held for use, not for resale, and so their market values are not relevant. The net book value left in the balance sheet after depreciation has been charged does not represent market values. As a separate exercise fixed assets may be revalued to reflect changes in their market values, but this is not part of the Unit 5 syllabus.

1.2 DEPRECATION AND ACCRUALS

Depreciation is based on the accruals concept. Costs are matched to the benefits that they help to create. Because a fixed asset will help to generate profits over a number of periods, then its cost is capitalised and spread over those periods.

1.3 WHICH FIXED ASSETS SHOULD BE DEPRECIATED?

All fixed assets with a finite life must be depreciated. Because nothing lasts forever, all fixed assets should be depreciated. The only exception to this rule is freehold land. Land lasts forever, and so it should not be depreciated, unless it is being used as a mine or quarry in which case the land will eventually be consumed.

2 METHODS OF DEPRECIATION

2.1 ESTIMATION

The depreciation charge is merely an estimate of the amount of the cost of the asset that has been consumed during the year. The exact amount of depreciation can only be calculated with hindsight when an asset is sold.

The basic rule is that an asset should be depreciated down to its **residual value** over its **useful economic life**. These will be estimated when an asset is acquired.

Residual value is an estimate of the disposal value of an asset at the end of its useful life. For many assets this is assumed to be £Nil. However, there are some assets, like cars, that will probably still have a healthy second-hand value even when they are no longer of any use to the business.

Useful economic life is the length of time that the business intends to profitably use a fixed asset. It is normally a lot less than the total life span of the asset. For example, a prestige car hire firm will probably only keep its cars for two or three years. After that time their customers will be unwilling to hire them and the running costs will tend to increase. The car hire firm will then sell off these cars, even though they may still have ten or so good years of life left in them.

There are two common ways in which these ideas are applied; straight-line depreciation and reducing balance depreciation.

2.2 STRAIGHT-LINE DEPRECIATION

This method of depreciation assumes that the fixed asset wears out in equal amounts over its useful life. The annual figure for depreciation is found by using the following formula:

$$\text{Annual depreciation} = \frac{(\text{cost} - \text{residual value})}{\text{useful life}}$$

This figure can also be expressed as a percentage of the cost of the fixed asset which is then applied to the cost of the fixed asset every year.

$$\text{Annual percentage depreciation on cost} = \frac{\text{annual depreciation}}{\text{cost of fixed asset}} \times 100$$

Example

A fixed asset has a cost of £12,500, an estimated life of 4 years and an estimated residual value of £2,500 at the end of that life. If the straight line method of calculating depreciation is adopted:

$$\text{Annual depreciation} = \frac{(12{,}500 - 2{,}500)}{4}$$

$$= £2{,}500 \text{ pa}$$

$$\text{Annual percentage depreciation cost} = \frac{2{,}500}{12{,}500} \times 100$$

$$= 20\%$$

2.3 REDUCING BALANCE

The reducing balance method assumes that the fixed asset is used more in the earlier years of its useful life than in later years, so larger depreciation charges are made in the early years.

The annual depreciation under the reducing balance method is calculated by applying a percentage to the net book value (cost less accumulated depreciation) of the fixed asset as at the start of the year (the end of the previous year).

In the first year the percentage is applied to the original cost of the fixed asset but in subsequent years it is applied to the asset's **net book value** (alternatively known as **written down value**). The net book value (NBV) or written down value (WDV) of a fixed asset is its original cost less the accumulated depreciation on the asset to date

Example

A fixed asset, purchased for £20,000, is expected to have a useful economic life of 4 years. The reducing balance method of depreciation is to be used, the appropriate percentage rate being 20%.

Method

1. Record the original cost (purchase price)
2. Calculate the depreciation for year 1 by multiplying the cost by 20%
3. Take away the first year's depreciation charge from the cost of the fixed asset to get the net book value (NBV) at the end of Year 1. This is the opening balance for the following year. Now go back to Step 2.

		Depreciation calculation	*Balance sheet* £
Year 1	Original cost		20,000
	Depreciation @ 20% on cost	£20,000 × 20%	(4,000)
	Closing net book value		16,000
Year 2	Depreciation @ 20% on opening net book value	£16,000 × 20%	(3,200)
	Closing net book value		12,800
Year 3	Depreciation @ 20% on opening net book value	£12,800 × 20%	(2,560)
	Closing net book value		10,240
Year 4	Depreciation @ 20% on opening net book value	£10,240 × 20%	(2,048)
	Closing net book value		8,192

CHAPTER 7 : DEPRECIATION

3 DEPRECIATION IN THE YEARS OF ACQUISITION AND DISPOSAL

3.1 BASIC RULES

Depreciation must be charged on all fixed assets (except for land). There are two ways in which this can be achieved:

1 Traditional method for manual accounting systems and exams.	•	Charge a full year's depreciation in the year of acquisition.
	•	Charge no depreciation in the year of disposal. This will be adjusted for through the profit or loss on disposal.
2 Exact method used by computerised systems.	•	On acquisition, charge depreciation from the month of acquisition on a time apportioned basis.
	•	In the year of disposal, charge depreciation up to the month of disposal on a time apportioned basis.
	•	There will still be a profit or loss on disposal to calculate.

In the past some business did not charge depreciation in the year of acquisition. This is contrary to accounting standards and it is also illegal.

The examples below are both based upon an asset costing £12,000 being depreciated over five years. It was purchased on 1st May 20X0 and disposed of on 30th November 20X4.

3.2 EXAMPLE OF FULL CHARGE IN THE YEAR OF ACQUISITION, NONE IN THE YEAR OF DISPOSAL

			P&L charge £
20X0	12,000 / Five years	Full charge in year of acquisition	2,400
20X1			2,400
20X2			2,400
20X3			2,400
20X4			nil

In 20X4 the profit or loss on disposal will automatically adjust for the remaining cost of the asset. This will in effect be the depreciation charge for that year.

3.3 EXAMPLE OF THE TIME APPORTIONED METHOD

			P&L charge £
20X0	12,000 / Five years	For 8 months	1,600
20X1		Full year	2,400
20X2		Full year	2,400
20X3		Full year	2,400
20X4		For 11 months	2,200

There will still be a profit or loss on disposal in 20X4, which will automatically adjust for the remaining cost of the asset.

ACTIVITY 1

Billy Blue runs a decorating business. He has a 31 March Year-End. On 1 January 20X7 he purchased a new paint sprayer for £1,900. The sprayer should last for ten years, but Billy intends to use it for two years and then sell it. Its residual value after two years is £500, and after ten years the residual value will be £Nil.

Task

Calculate the depreciation charges for the years-ending 31 March 20X7 and 20X8 under each of the following situations:

(a) Straight line depreciation with a full year's charge in the year of acquisition.

(b) Straight line depreciation on a time apportioned basis.

(c) Depreciated on a 60% reducing balance basis, with a full year's charge in the year of acquisition.

For a suggested answer, see the 'Answers' section at the end of the book.

4 ACCOUNTING FOR DEPRECIATION

4.1 PROVISION ACCOUNTING

In accounting there are two meanings for the term 'provision':

- The reduction in the balance sheet value of an asset
- The recognition of a probable liability that may become payable in the future.

In this chapter we are concerned with the 'provision for depreciation' that reduces the balance sheet value of a fixed asset. Taking the example in 3.3 above, the balance sheet value of the asset at the end of 20X0 will be calculated and disclosed as follows:

Balance sheet	£
Cost	12,000
Less provision for depreciation	(1,600)
Net book value	10,400

4.2 DOUBLE ENTRY FOR DEPRECIATION IN THE FIRST YEAR

The double entry for depreciation follows the principle that when a fixed asset is purchased its cost is shown as an asset and as that asset is 'used up', a chunk of the cost is transferred to become an expense which is matched against sales in the profit and loss account.

However, as noted above, rather than the cost of the fixed asset being reduced, a provision is set off against the cost.

The double entry to record the depreciation for 20X0 in our example is:

			Dr	Cr
			£	£
Debit	P&L	Depreciation charge	1,600	
Credit	B/S	Provision for depreciation		1,600

4.3 DOUBLE ENTRY FOR DEPRECIATION IN SUBSEQUENT YEARS

Each year's profit and loss account will suffer the annual depreciation charge. This will be added to the provision for depreciation in the balance sheet, and so the provision will increase annually and the net book value will decrease.

Example

This example will be based on 4.4 above. We will follow through the first three years of the asset's life, showing how the depreciation will be recorded in the ledger accounts. We will also show how the cost and depreciation of the asset will be disclosed in the balance sheet.

P&L   Depreciation charge

		£
20X0	Provision for depreciation	1,600
20X1	Provision for depreciation	2,400
20X2	Provision for depreciation	2,400

B/S   Provision for depreciation

	£			£
		20X0	P&L charge	1,600
c/d	1,600			1,600
	1,600			
		20X1	b/f	1,600
			P&L charge	2,400
c/d	4,000			
	4,000			4,000
		20X2	b/f	4,000
			P&L charge	2,400
c/d	6,400			
	6,400			6,400
		20X3	b/f	6,400

The presentation in the balance sheet will be as follows:

	20X0	20X1	20X2
	£	£	£
Cost	12,000	12,000	12,000
Less provision for depreciation	(1,600)	(4,000)	(6,400)
Net book value	10,400	8,000	5,600

The depreciation charge in the profit and loss will be categorised as an operating expense.

5 DEPRECIATION AND THE FIXED ASSET REGISTER

5.1 INTRODUCTION

The fixed asset register records details of depreciation of each fixed asset. The required depreciation for the year is worked out for each asset and entered into the 'depreciation for the year' column.

In practice, it is the sum of these calculations of depreciation for each asset that is used in the depreciation double entry in the general ledger.

This figure is then added to the 'accumulated depreciation brought down' figure and the result is taken away from cost to get the fixed asset's net book value.

Example

Using the information in the following fixed asset register, write in the depreciation for the year and work out the net book value at the end of 20X6.

Fixed asset register

Asset number	Description	Location ref	Supplier ref	Purchase date	Useful life	Dep method	Cost £	Scrap value £	Acc dep b/d £
13465	IBM computer	Accounts	CS Ltd	1/1/X4	4	SL	1,500	300	600
24536	Mixing machine	Fact 1	IS Ltd	31/12/X4	5	SL	4,000	nil	800
55681	Volvo car	D Denis	VFG Ltd	30/6/X6	5	SL	15,000	5,000	

Step 1 Work out the depreciation for the year for each asset based on the cost, useful life and scrap value

IBM computer = $\dfrac{(£1,500 - £300)}{4 \text{ years}}$ = £300 per annum

Mixing machine = $\dfrac{(£4,000)}{5 \text{ years}}$ = £800 per annum

Volvo car = $\dfrac{(£15,000 - £5,000)}{5 \text{ years}}$ = £2,000 per annum

But notice the Volvo was only purchased half way through the year and therefore only requires six months depreciation charged on it, that is:

£2,000 × 6/12 months = £1,000

CHAPTER 7 : DEPRECIATION

Step 2 Write in the depreciation for the year

Fixed asset register

Asset number	Description	Location ref	Supplier ref	Purchase date	Useful life	Dep method	Cost £	Scrap value £	Acc dep b/d £
13465	IBM computer	Accounts	CS Ltd	1/1/X4	4	SL	1,500	300	600
24536	Mixing machine	Fact 1	IS Ltd	31/12/X4	5	SL	4,000	nil	800
55681	Volvo car	D Denis	VFG Ltd	30/6/X6	5	SL	15,000	5,000	

Step 3 Work out the net book value for each asset

IBM computer	£	£
Cost		1,500
Depreciation brought down	600	
Depreciation in the year	300	
Depreciation carried down		(900)
Net book value		**600**

Mixing machine	£	£
Cost		4,000
Depreciation brought down	800	
Depreciation in the year	800	
Depreciation carried down		(1,600)
Net book value		**2,400**

Volvo	£	£
Cost		15,000
Depreciation brought down	-	
Depreciation in the year	1,000	
Depreciation carried down		(1,000)
Net book value		**14,000**

Step 4 Write the net book value into the fixed asset register

Fixed asset register

Asset number	Description	Location ref	Supplier ref	Purchase date	Useful life	Dep method	Cost £	Scrap value £	Acc dep b/d £	Dep for year £	NBV £	Date of disposal	Disposal proceeds £
13465	IBM computer	Accounts	CS Ltd	1/1/X4	4	SL	1,500	300	600	300	600		
24536	Mixing machine	Fact 1	IS Ltd	31/12/X4	5	SL	4,000	nil	800	800	2,400		
55681	Volvo car	D Denis	VFG Ltd	30/6/X6	5	SL	15,000	5,000		1,000	14,000		

Note: the fixed asset register will start afresh in the following year with updated accumulated depreciation figures as shown below:

	Acc depn b/d £	Dep for year £	NBV £
	900 (600+300)		
	1,600 (800+800)		
	1,000 (0+1,000)		

6 CHANGES IN DEPRECIATION

6.1 CHANGE IN USEFUL ECONOMIC LIFE

FRS 15 requires businesses regularly to review the period over which an asset is being depreciated i.e. to review the useful economic life. If a business decides that the asset life requires revision because the asset will be used for a shorter or longer period than originally estimated, this should be taken account of in current and future depreciation charges.

The basic rule is that the net book amount is written off over the revised remaining economic life.

6.2 CHANGE IN THE METHOD OF DEPRECIATION

FRS 15 allows a change in the method of calculating depreciation **only** if the new method gives a fairer presentation of the results and financial position of the business. If this is so, the net book amount is written off over the remaining useful economic life using the new method, commencing with the period in which the change is made.

CONCLUSION

This chapter has looked at the following areas in respect of depreciation.

- the reason why fixed assets are depreciated in financial accounts
- the various methods available for calculating depreciation
- accounting for depreciation
- the way depreciation is shown in the financial accounts.

Depreciation is a very important accounting topic and therefore will be frequently examined. It is vital that this chapter has been fully understood before moving on to further chapters.

SELF TEST QUESTIONS

Paragraph

1	What is depreciation?	1.1
2	What are the two main depreciation methods?	2
3	At what value are fixed assets carried in the balance sheet?	4

KEY TERMS

Depreciation - the measure of the cost or revalued amount of a fixed asset that has been consumed during an accounting period.

Residual value - an estimate of the disposal value of an asset at the end of its useful life. For many assets this is assumed to be £Nil.

Useful economic life - the length of time that the business intends to profitably use a fixed asset.

Net book value (NBV) or written down value (WDV) - of a fixed asset is its original cost less the accumulated depreciation on the asset to date.

Chapter 8

DISPOSAL OF FIXED ASSETS

This chapter explains how disposals are accounted for in the main ledger and the fixed asset register.

CONTENTS

1 The basics
2 Disposal and part exchange
3 Disposals and the fixed asset register
4 Showing disposals of fixed assets in financial accounts

KNOWLEDGE AND UNDERSTANDING

		Reference
1	The accounting treatment for capital items sold, scrapped or otherwise retired from service	Item 11

PERFORMANCE CRITERIA

		Reference
1	Correctly identify and record all acquisition and disposal costs and revenues in the appropriate records	Item C in element 5.1
2	Correctly calculate and record the profit and loss on disposal in the appropriate records	Item F in element 5.1

LEARNING OUTCOMES

At the end of this chapter you should be able to:

- account for a basic disposal of a fixed asset
- account for a disposal of a fixed asset where a part-exchange has taken place
- record the disposal in the fixed asset register.

MAINTAINING FINANCIAL RECORDS AND PREPARING ACCOUNTS : UNIT 5

1 THE BASICS

1.1 WHAT NEEDS TO BE ACHIEVED

When a business purchases a fixed asset, it is usually with the intention that it will be used over a long period of time. However, at any time in a fixed asset's useful life the asset may be disposed of or sold.

There are four elements to a disposal of a fixed asset:

- the cost of the fixed asset in the main ledger fixed asset account
- the accumulated depreciation on that fixed asset in the general ledger provision for depreciation account
- the amount of money that is received if the fixed asset is sold
- the resulting profit or loss from the disposal of the fixed asset.

At the time of the disposal the ledger accounts record the cost of the fixed asset and its corresponding accumulated depreciation. Combined these give a net book value for the fixed asset.

The difference between the net book value and the proceeds of disposal will be the profit or loss on disposal. The proceeds are normally cash, but they may also include trade in allowances or other benefits.

1.2 ACCOUNTING FOR A DISPOSAL

The accounting for a disposal has to follow the above logic. The steps therefore are as follows:

Step 1 Set up a T-account called 'disposal of fixed asset'. This will be used to record all aspects of the disposal

Step 2 Remove the cost of the asset from its main ledger account

    Dr   Disposal of fixed asset account
    Cr   Fixed asset cost account

Step 3 Remove the accumulated depreciation on the fixed asset from its main ledger account

    Dr   Accumulated depreciation
    Cr   Disposal of fixed asset account

Step 4 Bring down the balance on the disposal of fixed asset account. This represents the net book value of the asset sold

Step 5 Account for the sale proceeds of the disposal

    Dr   Cash at bank account
    Cr   Disposal of fixed asset account

Step 6 Balance the disposal account and work out the profit or loss.

CHAPTER 8 : DISPOSAL OF FIXED ASSETS

Example

A machine is currently recorded in the books of a business with a cost of £10,000 and accumulated depreciation of £3,000.

The machine is sold for £8,000. Account for the disposal.

Step 1 Remove the cost of the fixed asset from it general ledger account.

Machine account (BS)

	£		£
Balance b/d	10,000	Disposal a/c	10,000

Disposal of fixed assets account (P&L)

	£		£
Machine cost	10,000		

Step 2 Remove the accumulated depreciation on the fixed asset from its general ledger account.

Machine account (BS)

	£		£
Balance b/d	10,000	Disposal a/c	10,000

Disposal of fixed assets account (P&L)

	£		£
Machine cost	10,000	Machine provision for dep'n a/c	3,000

Machine provision for depreciation account (BS)

	£		£
Disposals a/c	3,000	Balance b/d	3,000

Step 3 Bring down the balance on the disposal of fixed asset account.

Disposal of fixed assets account (P&L)

	£		£
Machine cost	10,000	Machine provision for dep'n	3,000
		Balance c/d	7,000
	10,000		10,000
Balance b/d	7,000		

Step 4 Account for the sale proceeds of the disposal.

Disposal of fixed assets account (P&L)

	£		£
Machine cost	10,000	Machine provision for dep'n	3,000
		Balance c/d	7,000
	10,000		10,000
Balance b/d	7,000	Cash at bank a/c (sale proceeds)	8,000

Cash at bank account (BS)

	£		£
Disposals a/c	8,000		

Step 5 Balance the disposal account and work out the profit or loss.

Disposal of fixed assets account (P&L)

	£		£
Machine cost	10,000	Machine provision for dep'n	3,000
		Balance c/d	7,000
	10,000		10,000
Balance b/d	7,000	Cash at bank a/c (proceeds)	8,000
Profit on disposal (p&l)	1,000		
	8,000		8,000

1.3 JOURNAL FOR A FIXED ASSET DISPOSAL

Using the above example as an illustration, the journal for a fixed asset disposal would be as follows:

Account	Dr	Cr	Description
Fixed asset disposal	10,000		'Get rid' of the asset out of the machine
Machine at cost		10,000	account and dispose of it into Fixed Asset Disposals.
Fixed asset disposal		3,000	'Get rid' of any depreciation to date on the
Machine: provision for depreciation	3,000		disposed asset.
Cash at bank	8,000		Enter any proceeds on sale of the fixed
Fixed asset disposal		8,000	asset.
Fixed asset disposal	1,000		With any profit on disposal.
P&L: Profit on Disposal		1,000	

ACTIVITY 1

On 1 January 20X1 Zenith Ltd bought an asset costing £39,000. It was expected to have a five year life and a residual value of £4,000. The asset was sold for £12,300 during 2004. Zenith has a 31 December year-end and charges a full year's depreciation in the year of acquisition and none in the year of disposal.

Tasks

(a) Prepare the T accounts to record the disposal of this asset.

(b) Draft the Journal to record this transaction.

For a suggested answer, see the 'Answers' section at the end of the book.

CHAPTER 8 : DISPOSAL OF FIXED ASSETS

2 DISPOSALS AND PART EXCHANGE

2.1 INTRODUCTION

Sometimes when a new fixed asset is purchased, the fixed asset that it is replacing is given in part-exchange. This is particularly common with motor vehicles. The new asset will have a list price which, instead of being satisfied in full by a cash payment will be satisfied partly by cash and partly in the form of the old asset. In this way the purchase of the new asset and the disposal of the old asset are linked.

2.2 ACCOUNTING FOR PART EXCHANGE

In terms of the disposal of the old asset, the same principles apply as before. However, the proceeds of disposal of the old asset are the part-exchange value (see definition below) given against the cost of the new asset.

For the new fixed asset, the main thing to remember is that the figure recorded in the fixed asset cost account is the full list price of the asset, comprising cash and the part exchange value.

Example

A car has a list price of £8,000. An older car is offered in part-exchange and as a result the business only pays £6,000 for the new car.

The part-exchange value is calculated as:

	£
List price	8,000
Less: part-exchange value	(2,000)
Cash paid	6,000

The steps in accounting for a disposal of a fixed asset with a part-exchange are as follows:

Step 1 Set up a T-account called 'disposal of fixed asset'

Step 2 Remove the cost of the old fixed asset from its general ledger account

    Dr   Disposal of fixed asset account
    Cr   Fixed asset cost account

Step 3 Remove the accumulated depreciation on the old fixed asset from its general ledger account

    Dr   Accumulated depreciation
    Cr   Disposal of fixed asset account

Step 4 Bring down the balance on the disposal of fixed asset account

(Note: the above steps are identical to the basic disposal of a fixed asset.)

Account for the disposal proceeds of the old asset, which is linked with the purchase of the new asset:

			£	£
Debit	B/S	Fixed assets at cost	8,000	
Credit	P&L	Disposal of fixed assets		2,000
Credit	B/S	Cash at Bank		6,000

MAINTAINING FINANCIAL RECORDS AND PREPARING ACCOUNTS : UNIT 5

This double entry deals neatly with both the purchase of the new asset at its full cost of £8,000 and the disposal of the old asset.

Step 5 Balance up the disposal account and work out the profit or loss

This is the same final step as in the basic disposal.

Example

Hammer Ltd is to buy a new motor van, which has a list price of £9,000. The new van is to replace a van which cost £7,500 four years ago, and has accumulated depreciation of £6,000 on it.

Hammer Ltd will pay the motor van dealer £7,000 for the new van and therefore the part exchange value is (£9,000 – £7,000) £2,000.

Step 1 Set up a T account called 'disposal of fixed assets.

Step 2 Remove the cost of the fixed asset from its general ledger account.

Van account (BS)

	£		£
Balance b/d	7,500	Disposal a/c	7,500

Disposal of fixed assets account (P&L)

	£		£
Van at cost	7,500		

Step 3 Remove the accumulated depreciation on the fixed asset from its general ledger account.

Disposal of fixed assets account (P&L)

	£		£
Van at cost	7,500	Provision for depreciation	6,000

Van provision for depreciation account (BS)

	£		£
Balance b/d	6,000	Disposal a/c	6,000

Step 4 Bring down the balance on the disposal of fixed assets account.

Disposal of fixed assets account (P&L)

	£		£
Van at cost	7,500	Provision for depreciation	6,000
		Balance c/d	1,500
	7,500		7,500
Balance b/f	1,500		

CHAPTER 8 : DISPOSAL OF FIXED ASSETS

Step 5 Account for the disposal proceeds of the old asset, and the purchase of the new asset.

Disposal of fixed assets account (P&L)

	£		£
Van at cost	7,500	Provision for deprecation	6,000
		Balance c/d	1,500
	7,500		7,500
Balance b/f	1,500		
		Proceeds: Part-exchange	2,000

Cash at bank account (BS)

	£		£
		Cost of fixed asset	7,000

Fixed asset cost account (BS)

	£		£
Balance b/d	7,500	Disposal a/c	7,500
Cost of fixed asset: Part-exchange	2,000		
Cost of fixed asset: Cash	7,000	Balance c/d	9,000
	9,000		9,000
Balance b/f	9,000		

Disposal of fixed assets account (P&L)

	£		£
Van at cost	7,500	Provision for deprecation	6,000
		Balance c/d	1,500
	7,500		7,500
Balance b/f	1,500		
		Proceeds: Part-exchange	2,000
Profit on disposal	500		
	2,000		2,000

ACTIVITY 2

In 20X3 Armand Ltd bought an elevator for £45,000. It was to have a twenty year life and a £5,000 residual value. In 20X9 Armand decided to upgrade their elevator for a new one with a list price of £99,000. This will have a useful life of thirty years and a residual value of £9,000. The supplier will give Armand a £20,000 trade in allowance on their old elevator. Armand charges a full year's depreciation in the year of acquisition and none in the year of disposal.

Task

Prepare the following accounts for the year-ending 31 December 20X9:

- Elevators at cost
- Provision for depreciation on elevators
- Disposals account.

For a suggested answer, see the 'Answers' section at the end of the book.

MAINTAINING FINANCIAL RECORDS AND PREPARING ACCOUNTS : UNIT 5

3 DISPOSALS AND THE FIXED ASSET REGISTER

3.1 PROCEDURES NEEDED FOR FIXED ASSET DISPOSALS

When a fixed asset is disposed of its specific cost and depreciation must be taken out of the general ledger fixed asset accounts and put into the disposal account. In practice, this information is obtained from the fixed asset register. When a fixed asset is to be disposed of, authorisation for the disposal will be obtained on a fixed asset disposal authorisation form. This form will be passed to the accounting department who will find the fixed asset on the fixed asset register.

A journal will then be raised to remove the cost and depreciation from the general ledger fixed asset accounts and transfer them to the disposal account.

The sale proceeds will be recorded in the cash receipts book and posted to the general ledger in the normal way.

3.2 RECORDING THE DISPOSAL IN THE FIXED ASSET REGISTER

To maintain the integrity of the fixed asset register, the disposal must be recorded therein. The details recorded are:

- date the fixed asset was disposed of
- the sale proceeds.

This will show that the fixed asset is no longer owned by the company.

3.3 EXAMPLE

Fixed asset number 23675 was disposed of on 31 May 20X3 for £300.

Fixed asset register

Asset Number	Description	Useful life	Dep'n method	Cost £	Acc'd Dep'n £	NBV £	Date of disposal	Disposal Proceeds £
15687	Delivery van	3	SL	8,000	6,000	2,000		
21475	Machine	10	SL	20,000	17,000	3,000		
23675	**Car**	**5**	**SL**	**10,000**	**9,000**	**1,000**	**31 May 20X3**	**300**
35897	Desk	25	SL	250	30	220		

4 SHOWING DISPOSALS OF FIXED ASSETS IN FINANCIAL ACCOUNTS

4.1 THE PROFIT AND LOSS ACCOUNT

The profit or loss on disposal of a fixed asset is taken to the profit and loss account. A loss will be listed with expenses, normally alongside the depreciation charge. A profit may be included with sundry income, listed after gross profit or is sometimes shown as a negative expense. All are acceptable treatments.

CHAPTER 8 : DISPOSAL OF FIXED ASSETS

CONCLUSION

This chapter on disposals has covered the final part of accounting for fixed assets. There are some potentially difficult aspects; the way to get the double entry right is to learn the steps for a basic disposal, learn the extra steps for a part-exchange disposal and then practise the entries. The understanding will develop as confidence in the accounting grows. Note that in the workbook you will be given the opportunity to try other formats of the fixed asset register layout.

SELF TEST QUESTIONS

		Paragraph
1	How do you account for the disposal of a fixed asset?	1.2
2	How do you account for a part-exchange disposal?	2.2
3	On a disposal, which details are recorded in the fixed asset register?	3.2

KEY TERMS

Depreciation – the measure of the costs or revalued amount of the economic benefits of the tangible fixed asset that have been consumed during the period.

Consumption of assets – includes wearing out, using up or other reduction in the useful economic life of a tangible fixed asset.

Chapter 9

THE TRIAL BALANCE

This chapter explains how to extract a trial balance from the main ledger, and how it can be used to detect and correct any errors that might have arisen in the ledger accounts during the year. The trial balance forms the foundation for the extended trial balance which is looked at in a later chapter.

CONTENTS

1. The trial balance
2. Types of error in double entry
3. Suspense accounts and the trial balance
4. Correction of errors and clearing the suspense account

KNOWLEDGE AND UNDERSTANDING

		Reference
1	The method of closing off revenue accounts	Item 17
2	How to identify and correct different types of error	Item 19
3	The function and form of a trial balance and an extended trial balance	Item 27

PERFORMANCE CRITERIA

		Reference
1	Correctly prepare reconciliations for the preparation of final accounts	Item A in element 5.2
2	Identify any discrepancies in the reconciliation process and either take steps to rectify them or refer them to the appropriate person	Item B in element 5.2
3	Accurately prepare a trial balance and open a suspense account to record any imbalance	Item C in element 5.2
4	Establish the reasons for any imbalance and clear the suspense account by correcting the errors, or reduce them and resolve outstanding items to the appropriate person	Item D in element 5.2
4	Correctly identify, calculate and record appropriate adjustments	Item F in element 5.2
5	Make the relevant journal entries to close off the revenue accounts in preparation for the transfer of balances to the final accounts	Item G in element 5.2

MAINTAINING FINANCIAL RECORDS AND PREPARING ACCOUNTS : UNIT 5

6   Identify and resolve or refer to the appropriate person   Item D in element 5.3
    discrepancies, unusual features or queries

LEARNING OUTCOMES

At the end of this chapter you should be able to:

- extract a trial balance from the main ledger
- correct different types of error
    - errors of commission
    - errors of principle
    - errors of omission
- explain the purpose of a suspense account
- clear a suspense account balance.

1 THE TRIAL BALANCE

1.1 INTRODUCTION

The trial balance is a memorandum listing of all the ledger account balances by name. To extract the trial balance, all of the ledger accounts in the main ledger are balanced-off, and the balances copied to the trial balance. If the double entry procedures have been carefully followed, then the trial balance should show that the total of the debit balances agrees with the total of the credit balances.

Example

The general ledger accounts of Avalon as at 31 December 20X4 are noted below. Balance the accounts, bring down the balances and show all the balances in a trial balance.

Cash at bank account

Date	Details	£	Date	Details	£
(1)	Capital	1,000	(2)	Motor car	400
(4)	Sales	300	(3)	Purchases	200
(8)	Debtors	100	(7)	Creditors	200
(11)	Loan	600	(9)	Drawings	75
			(10)	Rent	40
			(12)	Insurance	30

Capital account

Date	Details	£	Date	Details	£
			(1)	Cash at bank	1,000

Motor car account

Date	Details	£	Date	Details	£
(2)	Cash at bank	400			

CHAPTER 9 : THE TRIAL BALANCE

Purchases account

Date	Details	£	Date	Details	£
(3)	Cash at bank	200			
(5)	Creditors	400			

Sales account

Date	Details	£	Date	Details	£
			(4)	Cash at bank	300
			(6)	Debtors	250

Creditors account

Date	Details	£	Date	Details	£
(7)	Cash at bank	200	(5)	Purchases	400

Debtors account

Date	Details	£	Date	Details	£
(6)	Sales	250	(8)	Cash at bank	100

Drawings account

Date	Details	£	Date	Details	£
(9)	Cash at bank	75			

Rent account

Date	Details	£			£
(10)	Cash at bank	40			

Loan account

Date	Details	£	Date	Details	£
			(11)	Cash at bank	600

Insurance account

Date	Details	£	Date	Details	£
(12)	Cash at bank	30			

Step 1 Balance each account and bring down the balances.

Cash at bank account

Date	Details	£	Date	Details	£
(1)	Capital	1,000	(2)	Motor car	400
(4)	Sales	300	(3)	Purchases	200
(8)	Debtors	100	(7)	Creditors	200
(11)	Loan	600	(9)	Drawings	75
			(10)	Rent	40
			(12)	Insurance	30
				Balance c/d	1,055
		2,000			2,000
	Balance b/d	1,055			

Capital account

Date	Details	£	Date	Details	£
			(1)	Cash at bank	1,000

Motor car account

Date	Details	£	Date	Details	£
(2)	Cash at bank	400			

Purchases account

Date	Details	£	Date	Details	£
(3)	Cash at bank	200		Balance c/d	600
(5)	Creditors	400			
		600			600
	Balance b/d	600			

Sales account

Date	Details	£	Date	Details	£
	Balance c/d	550	(4)	Cash at bank	300
			(6)	Debtors	250
		550			550
				Balance b/d	550

Creditors account

Date	Details	£	Date	Details	£
(7)	Cash at bank	200	(5)	Purchases	400
	Balance c/d	200			
		400			400
				Balance b/d	200

Debtors control account

Date	Details	£	Date	Details	£
(6)	Sales	250	(8)	Cash at bank	100
				Balance c/d	150
		250			250
	Balance b/d	150			

Drawings account

Date	Details	£	Date	Details	£
(9)	Cash at bank	75			

Rent account

Date	Details	£	Date	Details	£
(10)	Cash at bank	40			

CHAPTER 9 : THE TRIAL BALANCE

Loan account

Date	Details	£	Date	Details	£
			(11)	Cash at bank	600

Insurance account

Date	Details	£	Date	Details	£
(12)	Cash at bank	30			

Step 2 Prepare the trial balance showing each of the balances in the ledger accounts.

Avalon
Trial balance as at 31 December 20X4

Account	Debit £	Credit £
Cash at bank	1,055	
Capital		1,000
Motor car	400	
Purchases	600	
Sales		550
Creditors		200
Debtors	150	
Drawings	75	
Rent	40	
Loan		600
Insurance	30	
	2,350	2,350

Note: A trial balance is simply a memorandum listing of all the ledger account balances. It is *not* part of the double entry e.g. cash is not being credited with £1,055 and the trial balance debited with £1,055. It merely summarises the net result of all the debits and credits that have been made during the period.

ACTIVITY 1

Carlo Argenti set up in business as a silversmith on 1 February 2005.

The transactions for the first month of trade were as follows:

Date	Transaction
1	Started business with £4,500 in the bank and £2,000 cash.
2	Bought goods on credit from the following suppliers: Pewter £533, Tin £687, Ring £354.
3	Purchased raw materials from various suppliers paying £867 in cash and £2,000 by cheque.
4	Paid rent in cash £100.
5	Bought office supplies for £109 paying by cheque.
6	Sold goods on credit as follows: Smart £475, Trendy £500, Cool £1,240.
7	Paid wages in cash: £230.

10	Returned £345 worth of goods to Tin. A credit note was received by Argenti in respect of these items.
11	Paid rent in cash £100.
13	Trendy returned goods worth £80. Argenti issued a credit note in respect of these items.
15	Sold goods on credit to the following customers: Smart £470, Cool £956.
16	Paid Auric Decorators £265 cash to paint the offices.
18	Wrote a £1,276 cheque to Midas Media Ltd in full and final settlement for an opening advertising campaign run by them.
19	Paid rent by cheque: £200.
20	Bought a pick-up truck on credit from Bakkie Ltd for £2,250. The depreciation charge for February will be £80.
21	Paid £65 cash for oil and petrol for the truck.
23	Paid wages in cash: £290.
24	Received a £750 cheque from Cool in part payment of his outstanding balance. On the same day Smart settled his account in full also by cheque.
27	Paid off Pewter and Bakkie in full by cheque.
28	Total cash sales during the month were £2,962. Carlo Argenti took £300 per week from the till for his own personal use.
28	Closing stock was counted and valued at £1,630.

Tasks

1 Enter all of the transactions in the appropriate ledger accounts.

2 Balance off the accounts at the end of February.

3 Extract a Trial Balance and ensure that it balances.

This activity covers performance criteria C and F in element 5.2.

For a suggested answer, see the 'Answers' section at the end of the book.

2 TYPES OF ERROR IN DOUBLE ENTRY

2.1 INTRODUCTION

The trial balance checks to see whether there have been any errors in the accounting system. However, it is limited in that it will only pick up errors in double entry because, as long as the debits and credits are equal, the trial balance will balance. This section looks at the various types of error that could occur and whether the trial balance would be affected.

2.2 ERROR OF COMMISSION

An error of commission is where a transaction has been recorded in the correct *category* of account, but in the wrong account.

For example, the purchase of a computer should get recorded in the tangible fixed asset account, office equipment. If the purchase was recorded in the motor vehicles account then this is the correct type of account (tangible fixed assets) but the wrong account within this category.

2.3 ERROR OF PRINCIPLE

An error of principle is where the transaction is recorded in completely the wrong category of account. For example the receipt of a loan should be recognised as a liability in the balance sheet. If it were recorded as income in the profit and loss account then this is an error of principle.

If a sale (P&L) were to be recorded as a trade creditor (B/S) then this would also be an example of an error of principle.

These types of errors will require a transfer of a transaction between accounts.

To deal with errors of commission and principle:

Step 1 Set up the T account affected by the error and put in the balances from the trial balance.

Step 2 Perform the double entry required to remove the transaction from one account to the other.

Step 3 Produce the required journal.

2.4 ERROR OF OMISSION

This error is where a transaction has been completely missed out of the accounting system and therefore will not require a suspense account entry.

The steps to deal with this type of error are identical to the transactions posted to the wrong account error except that the accounts affected may not yet exist in the trial balance and thus new ones may need to be created.

2.5 COMPENSATING ERROR

Compensating errors occur when two transactions have been recorded incorrectly, but by coincidence they are both incorrect by the same amount and cancel one another out. These errors are very difficult to locate.

2.6 ORIGINAL ENTRY ERRORS

Original entry errors are where there has been an error in the posting of the amounts of the transaction. These entries can take two forms:

1   the wrong amounts for both the debit and the credit entry
2   different amounts for the debit and the credit.

An example of the first is where £4.00 is misread as £400 and so entered on both the debit and the credit side of the correct accounts.

The second is a result of a breakdown in the double entry and would occur when £3,200 was debited to one account and £2,300 (the first two figures having been transposed) is credited to another account.

MAINTAINING FINANCIAL RECORDS AND PREPARING ACCOUNTS : UNIT 5

ACTIVITY 2

Which of the above errors (2.2 to 2.6) would lead to an imbalance on the trial balance?

This activity covers performance criterion D in element 5.2.

For suggested answer, see the 'Answers' section at the end of the book.

2.7 SUMMARY

All the errors mentioned above need to be corrected before financial accounts are produced. The correction is via the journal.

The correction of the errors requires a sound knowledge of what the correct entry should be and then, having determined that, the required journal to put the entry right.

The section on suspense accounts and error correction highlights the need for this knowledge of the correct entries.

Large, unusual or suspicious errors should be notified to a manager, even if you have corrected them. They may be symptomatic of a weakness in the accounting system of a wider problem in the organisation.

3 SUSPENSE ACCOUNTS AND THE TRIAL BALANCE

3.1 INTRODUCTION

A suspense account is a multi-purpose account that is used to record errors in the accounting system and also to record entries where the bookkeeper is not sure where the entries should be recorded.

It takes the form of a T-account, but does not attach to either the profit and loss account or the balance sheet because the balance on the account should be cleared by the time the financial statements are prepared.

3.2 USE OF A SUSPENSE ACCOUNT WHEN UNSURE ABOUT AN ENTRY

Some transactions are quite difficult to record. When such a transaction occurs, the bookkeeper should always maintain the double entry by recording the unknown entry in the suspense account.

For example, suppose money is received by the business for the sale of an asset. The correct entries are:

    Dr   Cash at bank

    Cr   Disposal account

However, if the bookkeeper does not know what the credit entry is the credit should be posted to the suspense account:

    Dr   Cash at bank

    Cr   Suspense account

The entry will then be cleared out by the person producing the financial accounts:

    Dr   Suspense account
    Cr   Disposal account

3.3 ERROR SUSPENSE ENTRIES

Suspense account entries from errors arise from a variety of sources but all have one common theme, that there has been a breakdown in the double entry. This means that the trial balance will not balance without the creation of an entry in a suspense account. Two categories of error which may give rise to suspense account entries are considered below.

3.4 INCORRECT EXTRACTION OF THE TRIAL BALANCE

When a trial balance is produced, debit balances should go under the debit column and credit balances should go under the credit column. If all the other double entry has been correct, the trial balance will balance.

If one of the debit balances is written on the wrong side (i.e. on the credit side) then the trial balance will no longer balance.

There are a few account balances that often cause a problem. These are mentioned below, along with a reminder of which side the account balances should go on.

Account	Side of trial balance
Drawings	debit
Discounts received	credit
Discounts allowed	debit
Opening stock	debit
Cash at bank account	debit
Overdraft	credit
Bad (doubtful) debts provision	credit
Provision for depreciation	credit
Closing stock	should not be an entry at all!(see below)

Note: The entry for closing stock is a final adjustment made to the trial balance before the financial statements are produced and therefore it would not normally appear in the trial balance.

Example

The trial balance below is incorrect. Re-create the trial balance with the balances on the correct side.

MAINTAINING FINANCIAL RECORDS AND PREPARING ACCOUNTS : UNIT 5

Incorrect trial balance

Account	Debit £	Credit £	
Fixed assets		20,000	wrong side!
Current assets	45,000		
Current liabilities		10,000	
Long term liabilities		5,000	
Owner's capital		30,000	
Drawings	5,000		
Profit		25,000	
	50,000	90,000	
Imbalance	40,000		
	90,000	90,000	

This imbalance would normally be put into a suspense account. However, no double entry is required to correct this suspense account entry as it only arises because the 'memorandum' trial balance is incorrect, not the underlying accounts. By re-drafting the trial balance correctly, the suspense entry would disappear.

Correct trial balance

Account	Debit £	Credit £
Fixed assets	20,000	
Current assets	45,000	
Current liabilities		10,000
Long term liabilities		5,000
Owner's capital		30,000
Drawings	5,000	
Profit		25,000
	70,000	70,000

3.5 THE POSTING FROM THE DAY BOOKS IS INCORRECT

In the chapter on day books and personal ledger accounting, it was seen that the totals of the columns of the day books formed the double entry. If there has been a breakdown in this double entry then a suspense account entry will follow.

The breakdown in double entry can occur from:

- one side of the entry being totally missed out; or

- a transposition error in the figures of one of the entries.

Using the purchase day book as an example:

Summary of purchase day book

Total £	VAT £	Purchases £	Other £
50,000	15,000	30,000	5,000

CHAPTER 9 : THE TRIAL BALANCE

Creditors	VAT	Purchases	Other expenses
50,000	15,000	missed out	5,000

The total has been posted correctly, as have the VAT and other expenses. However the purchases figure has been missed. If the T-accounts were balanced up and a trial balance produced, the debits and the credits would not balance and a suspense account entry would be required until the error is discovered and corrected.

Note: If an exam question states that the total of, for example, the repair column has not been posted, then assume that the creditors ledger column has been posted correctly and therefore there has been a breakdown in the double entry.

Ordinarily, an incorrect posting to the individual account in the debtors or creditors personal ledger from a day book would not affect the general ledger double entry. The reason for this is that it is still assumed that the total of the control account column is correct.

However, if the business does not maintain control accounts then the individual posting will affect the double entry.

Note: In an exam, if the question says that control accounts are not maintained, then any incorrect posting to an individual account will create a suspense account entry.

3.6 CREATING A SUSPENSE ACCOUNT FROM A TRIAL BALANCE

A step that often proves troublesome is the creation of the initial entry in the suspense account from the trial balance.

An imbalancing trial balance will be presented and the task is to set up a suspense account. This is a straightforward task as long as one thing is remembered:

The suspense account entry is required to bring the smaller total up to the larger total.

Example

An imbalancing trial balance is provided.

Step 1 Total up each side of the trial balance.

Step 2 Add an amount to the smaller total to make it equal to the larger total.

Incorrect trial balance

Account	Debit	Credit
Fixed assets	20,000	
Current assets	45,000	
Current liabilities		10,000
Long term liabilities		5,000
Owner's capital		30,000
Drawings	5,000	
Profit		15,000
	70,000	60,000

MAINTAINING FINANCIAL RECORDS AND PREPARING ACCOUNTS : UNIT 5

Suspense account		10,000	Brings the credit side up to £70,000
		70,000	70,000

Step 3 Put the entry into the suspense account.

Suspense account

	£		£
		Balance b/d	10,000

ACTIVITY 3

Tasks

(a) Classify the errors listed below.

(b) Identify which errors will affect the suspense account.

(c) Suggest how these errors might be discovered in practice.

1 A sales invoice for £500 was entered as a Credit Note onto the Purchase Day Book. On the same day a Credit Note for £500 from a supplier was entered into the Sales Day Book.

2 An invoice for £950 in respect of repairs made to the office interior has been posted to cleaning by mistake.

3 An invoice has been entered into the Sales Day Book twice.

4 A cash sale for £75 was made without raising an invoice. The cash was locked in the petty cash tin but it has not been entered into the Petty Cash Book.

5 A £15,000 business loan received from a friend of the proprietor has been credited to Capital.

6 The Purchase Day Book has been correctly added-up and cross-cast. However, when the Total of £56,789 was posted to the Purchase Ledger control Account the clerk accidentally entered £57,689 in the PLCA.

For suggested answer, see the 'Answers' section at the end of the book.

ACTIVITY 4

The following trial balance has been incorrectly extracted from the books of F Manning and Co. Re-draft the trial balance, find the suspense account balance and set up a suspense account.

CHAPTER 9 : THE TRIAL BALANCE

Incorrect Trial Balance

Account	Debit £	Credit £
Motor vehicles	15,000	
Office equipment	10,000	
Opening stock	30,000	
Debtors	20,000	
Bank	12,000	
Creditors		45,000
Loan		20,000
Capital		5,000
Sales		100,000
Purchases	45,000	
Expenses	23,000	
Drawings		10,000
	155,000	180,000

This activity covers performance criterion C in element 5.2.

For a suggested answer, see the 'Answers' section at the end of the book.

4 CORRECTION OF ERRORS AND CLEARING THE SUSPENSE ACCOUNT

4.1 INTRODUCTION

Correcting suspense accounts is potentially the most difficult problem that can arise in an exam (and real life) situation. It requires not only a sound grasp of bookkeeping principles but also a degree of logic.

However the best approach to solving the suspense account problem is to focus on what the correct entries should be in the accounts and not on the clearing of the suspense account. Only when the correct entries have been ascertained will the suspense account be considered.

4.2 TECHNIQUE

The technique to clear a suspense account is:

Step 1 Work out what the correct entry should have been.

This is best done in T-account format.

Step 2 Work out what entries have been made.

Take the entries made in the exam question and put them into T-accounts.

Step 3 Compare the accounts in steps one and two and work out the required entry to correct the entry that has been made.

Step 4 Complete the double entry to the suspense account.

MAINTAINING FINANCIAL RECORDS AND PREPARING ACCOUNTS : UNIT 5

Having decided what entry is required in step three, just make the other half of the double entry to the suspense account.

Step 5 Produce a journal showing the correcting entries.

Sometimes a question requires the clearing of the suspense account via a journal. In this case write out the journal when all the entries have been worked out.

Example

A trial balance has created a debit suspense account balance of £40,000.

It has been discovered that the purchases total of the purchase day book, £20,000, has been credited to the purchases account.

Step 1 Work out what the correct entry should have been.

Purchases		Creditors	
20,000			20,000

Step 2 Identify the incorrect entries that have been made.

Purchases		Creditors	
	20,000		20,000

Note: Assume creditors posted correctly.

Step 3 To make the purchase account in Step two look like the purchase account of Step one, a £40,000 debit is required. This is made up of a £20,000 debit to cancel out the incorrect credit, plus a £20,000 debit to put in the correct entry.

Purchases		Creditors	
40,000	20,000		20,000

Step 4 Opposite entry to the suspense account.

Purchases		Suspense	
40,000	20,000	b/d 40,000	**40,000**

116

CHAPTER 9 : THE TRIAL BALANCE

Step 5	Dr	Purchases	40,000
	Dr	Suspense	40,000

ACTIVITY 5

Joe Ltd has just prepared its trial balance. The debit side totalled £345,678 and the credit side totalled £296,050.

The following errors have been noted:

(i) Sundry cash sales of £23,456 were debited to the sales returns account.

(ii) The purchase day book total for sundry expense was posted to the general ledger as £53,124 instead of £35,124.

(iii) Sales invoices totalling £10,000 had not been entered into the sales day book.

(iv) A cheque payment of £15,284 for rent had been entered into the total column of the cash payments book but left out of the analysis columns. The cash book clerk had forgotten to cross-cast the cash book for that particular month.

Tasks

1   Prepare and clear the suspense account.

2   Prepare the journals to correct these errors.

This activity covers performance criteria D and E in element 5.2.

For a suggested solution, see the 'Answers' section at the end of the book.

CONCLUSION

This chapter has covered the production of the trial balance from balances brought down on the main ledger accounts.

The errors that can occur in recording transactions were classified according to their nature with one specific type leading to the creation of a suspense account.

As mentioned earlier, the trial balance forms the basis for the extended trial balance (ETB). The ETB incorporates adjustments for closing stock, accruals & prepayments, and bad & doubtful debts. Therefore, before we look at the ETB we will look at the year-end adjustments that need to be made for stock, accruals, prepayments and debts. These are covered in the next few chapters.

SELF TEST QUESTIONS

		Paragraph
1	What is a trial balance?	1.1
2	Name and explain five types of error in double entry?	2
3	What are the two forms of original entry errors?	2.6
4	What is a suspense account?	3.1

KEY TERMS

Trial balance – a memorandum listing of all the main ledger account balances. If the records have been correctly maintained the sum of the debit balances will equal the sum of the credit balances.

Error of omission – occurs where no entry of a transaction has been made at all

Error of commission – occurs where an amount has been correctly posted but to the wrong account, although it is the right type of account.

Error of principle – occurs where an item is incorrectly classified by the bookkeeper and posted to the wrong type of account.

Error of entry – occurs where an incorrect amount is posted to both the accounts in question.

Compensating error – occurs where two or more errors cancel out each other.

Suspense account - a multi-purpose account that is used to record errors in the accounting system and also to record entries where the bookkeeper is not sure where the entries should be recorded.

Chapter 10

STOCK

This chapter explains how to value stock. This involves calculating its cost, its net realisable value, and then valuing the stock at the lower of these two values.

CONTENTS

1 Introduction

2 The meaning of stock

3 The components of cost of an item of stock

4 Stock cost valuation

5 The value of stock in the balance sheet

6 Accounting for stock

7 Transactions on a 'sale or return' basis

KNOWLEDGE AND UNDERSTANDING

		Reference
1	The basic principles of stock valuation, including those relating to cost or net realisable value and to what is included in cost	Item 29

LEARNING OUTCOMES

At the end of this chapter you should be able to:

- describe what is meant by stock
- apply the components of cost to an item of stock
- apply the correct cost valuation to stock
- calculate the value at which stock is shown in the balance sheet
- account for stock
- account for stock transactions on a sale or return basis.

1 INTRODUCTION

Accounting for stock is a multi stage process.

Firstly the business must decide exactly what is meant by the 'cost of the stock'.

The cost of stock will always be changing, so secondly, the business must decide which cost value at what point in time will be used to value stock.

Having put a value on the cost of the stock, the next step is to decide whether the stock will be sold for a price less than cost. If so, then the stock is valued at below cost.

Finally, having gone through the process of actually valuing stock, the business must then reflect that stock value in the accounting records.

2 THE MEANING OF STOCK

2.1 INTRODUCTION

Stock is counted and valued at the end of an accounting period, usually at the end of the year. The stock value is carried forward into the next year's accounts and charged against the following year's sales, which is when it will be sold.

Before looking at the various methods and techniques surrounding stock valuation, it is important to clarify exactly what is meant by the stock of a business.

Raw materials

Definition Materials and components purchased by a business for incorporation into manufactured products.

Work in progress

Definition Raw materials that have had further work done on them, but have not been competed at the point of valuation.

So the business would have purchased some raw materials and then would have incurred further cost in getting those raw materials to their semi finished state. Those further costs would have consisted of:

- labour
- appropriate overheads.

Finished goods

Definition Goods purchased or produced that are ready for sale (re-sale).

So, for example, in a supermarket the goods on the shelves would be classified as finished goods because they have been purchased and are ready for immediate resale.

Contrast the supermarket stock with a computer manufacturing company where the finished goods are a result of the business buying raw materials and incurring cost in assembling those raw materials.

3 THE COMPONENTS OF COST OF AN ITEM OF STOCK

Having distinguished the types of stock, the next step is to determine what is meant by the cost of stock.

The cost of stock

Definition All expenditure incurred in the normal course of business in bringing an item of stock to its present location and condition. The expenditure should include the cost of purchase and the cost of doing further work on the raw materials (cost of conversion).

Cost of purchase

The cost of purchase includes:

- the purchase price
- transport and handling costs
- Less: trade discounts.

Note that the discounts refer to trade discounts, that is a discount for buying in bulk or being a regular customer. It does **not** refer to settlement discounts which are given for an early payment of an invoice.

Cost of conversion

Costs of conversion are only applicable to raw materials that have had some further work done to them.

The costs of conversion include:

- direct labour costs (the staff working directly on the raw materials)
- direct expenses (e.g. drills used to make holes in a bit of metal)
- production overheads (e.g. supervisory labour, factory rent and rates).

The inclusion of production overheads is a potentially difficult area because the overhead is not directly related to production levels and therefore the business must find some way of allocating those overheads to the stock.

For example, suppose a business normally produces 100,000 units per year of a product. Production overheads for the year are £300,000. The allocation would therefore be:

£300,000 ÷ 100,000 units = £3 per unit

If there had been a fire in the factory during the year and as a result only 50,000 units had been produced then the allocation might be recalculated as:

£300,000 ÷ 50,000 units = £6 per unit

(Remember that overheads would remain fixed at £300,000 regardless of production.)

It will be seen later on that a higher stock value leads to increased profit and thus it appears very unreasonable that a fire in the factory should lead to an increased stock valuation and thus increased profit.

Conclusion The allocation of production overheads is based on the normal levels of activity of the business, that is usual production levels taking one year with the next.

So, in the example above, the allocation of production overheads is always based on 100,000 units.

4 STOCK COST VALUATION

4.1 INTRODUCTION

Ideally, an exact cost would be found for every single item of stock and every single item sold. In some cases where items have a specific identifying serial number this is possible. However, in general, most businesses have a stockroom full of identical products all purchased or manufactured at different points in time and therefore with different costs.

In the absence of a specific cost for each item, the business has to decide which cost at what point in time is going to be used to value stock.

Conclusion The rule that must be followed is that whichever method is used, it must give a good approximation to the true cost of the stock.

This section shows the most common methods for determining which cost value to use when valuing stock.

4.2 FIRST IN FIRST OUT (FIFO)

Definition A method of estimating cost which assumes that stock is used or sold in the same order that it is purchased or produced by the business. Therefore, the stock that is left at the end of the year is the most recently purchased or produced stock.

Example of FIFO

XYZ Ltd purchases and sells the following items in January:

		Units	£ per unit
1 Jan	purchases	100	£5
3 Jan	sells	10	
15 Jan	purchases	200	£6
30 Jan	sells	170	

What is the value of closing stock and what is the value of the units sold?

FIFO assumes that all the stock purchased on 1 January is sold first, so that the items sold on 30 January are assumed to be the 90 units left from the 1 January purchase, plus 80 of the units purchased on 15 January.

Therefore the stock left on 31 January represents the remaining 120 units purchased on 15 January and is valued at:

120 units @ £6 = £720

The value of the goods sold is:

100 units @ £5 + 80 units @ £6 = £980

4.3 LAST IN LAST OUT (LIFO)

Definition A method of estimating cost which assumes that the stock that is used or sold is the latest stock to be purchased or produced by the business. Therefore, the stock that is left is not the most recently purchase or produced stock.

Example of LIFO

Using the same example as above.

		Units	£ per unit
1 Jan	purchases	100	£5
3 Jan	sells	10	
15 Jan	purchases	200	£6
30 Jan	sells	170	

What is the value of closing stock and what is the value of the units sold?

LIFO assumes that the sales on 3 January are from the goods purchased on 1 January, but that the sales on 30 January are from the goods purchased on 15 January. Therefore, the balance left on 31 January represents the remaining 30 units purchased on 15 January, plus 90 of the 100 units purchased on 1 January and is valued at:

30 units @ £6 + 90 units @ £5 = £630

The value of the goods sold is:

170 units @ £6 + 10 units @ £5 = £1,070

4.4 WEIGHTED AVERAGE

Definition A method of estimating cost which assumes that all stock purchased or produced and, therefore all costs, are mixed together. Goods sold and stock unsold are valued at an average of all purchase prices.

The 'weighted' part of this average valuation reflects that different quantities at different prices are purchased.

Example of weighted average

Using the same example as above.

		Units	£ per unit
1 Jan	purchases	100	£5
3 Jan	sells	10	
15 Jan	purchases	200	£6
30 Jan	sells	170	

What is the value of closing stock and what is the value of the units sold?

MAINTAINING FINANCIAL RECORDS AND PREPARING ACCOUNTS : **UNIT 5**

		Units	£ per unit	Value £
1 Jan	purchases	100	5	500
3 Jan	sells	(10) @ avge $\frac{500}{100}$	5	(50)
	balance	90	5	450
15 Jan	purchases	200	6	1,200
	balance	290		1,650

Average $(90 \times 5) + (200 \times 6) = 1,650$

30 Jan	sells	(170) @ avge $\frac{1,650}{290}$	5.69	(967)
	balance	120	5.69	683

From the table above:

The balance left at 31 January is valued at £683

The value of goods sold is (50 + 967) £1,017

Note: All three methods are valid but do show a different result.

ACTIVITY 1

Charles Smart runs a sweet shop. At the year-end (December) he had 236 boxes of Mercury Bars on hand. These had been purchased over the previous few months as follows:

Date of purchase	Number of boxes	Price per Box
5 November	53	£35
23 November	57	£36
3 December	78	£38
17 December	99	£40
31 December	65	£34

Calculate the cost of his closing stock using the FIFO method.

For a suggested answer, see the 'Answers' section at the end of the book.

5 THE VALUE OF STOCK IN THE BALANCE SHEET

5.1 INTRODUCTION

Having determined the cost of stock there is one more check to perform before a final valuation can be placed on the stock to ensure compliance with the prudence concept.

Prudence concept says that revenue and profits are not anticipated, but are included in the profit and loss account only when realised in the form either of cash or of other assets. Provision is made for all known liabilities (expenses and losses).

CHAPTER 10 : STOCK

In broad outline, if an item of stock cost more than it is going to sell for, a loss will be incurred. The prudence concept says that this loss must be accounted for straight away. The way this is done is to calculate the net realisable value of stock and to apply the following important rule from SSAP 9.

Stock is valued in the balance sheet at the lower of cost and net realisable value.

5.2 NET REALISABLE VALUE

Definition   Net realisable value of stock is the estimated sales proceeds less all costs to completion and all selling, marketing and distribution costs.

	£	£
Selling price		x
Less: Trade discounts	(x)	
All further costs to completion	(x)	
All marketing, selling and distribution costs	(x)	
		(x)
Net realisable value		xx

Where the item of stock is a finished good, this definition ensures that all costs of selling the product are taken into account, such as discounts, marketing and delivery costs.

The definition also caters for stock that is not yet complete, where it would be incorrect to compare the cost of that stock with its selling price because most costs will be incurred later on to complete the item of stock.

Conclusion   The net realisable value calculation is saying 'Will the stock sell for more than it will eventually cost?' If not, then the loss must be accounted for straight away.

5.3 NET REALISABLE VALUE COMPARED TO COST

When following the rule of valuing stock at the lower of cost and net realisable value, the valuation must be done on an item by item basis.

It is incorrect to total up the whole of the costs of the items of stock and then total up all the net realisable values of the items of stock, compare the two and take the lower.

Example

Calculate the correct total valuation of the following items of stock:

	Cost	Notes
Item A	£2,000	Finished item to be sold for £3,500. No other costs are anticipated.
Item B	£500	Finished item to be sold for £600. Selling costs will be £50 and a 10% trade discount needs to be given on the selling price to sell the item.

Item C	£1,500	Part completed item that will eventually be sold for £2,500 after further work costing £600. Selling costs will be £200.		
Item D	£1,000	Part completed item that will sell for £1,500. Costs to complete the item will be £600 whilst selling costs will be negligible.		

Solution

	Cost	NRV calculation	NRV £	Valuation £
Item A	£2,000	selling price	3,500	2,000
Item B	£500	£600-£60-£50	490	490
Item C	£1,500	£2,500-£600-£200	1,700	1,500
Item D	£1,000	£1,500-£600	900	900
Total				4,890

ACTIVITY 2

Charles Smart runs a sweet shop. His annual stock count in December revealed a few seasonal items of stock which would have to be reduced in price in the new year. These were as follows:

Range	Number of boxes	Cost	Normal retail price	Expected selling price
Venus	35	£5.30	£8	£4
Earth	54	£5.70	£9	£6
Saturn	85	£7.80	£11	£8
Pluto	47	£9.90	£14	£8
Jupiter	72	£6.50 (8.50)	£10	£8

Calculate the balance sheet value of his closing stock.

For a suggested answer, see the 'Answers' section at the end of the book.

6 ACCOUNTING FOR STOCK

6.1 INTRODUCTION

The final step in dealing with stock is to perform the accounting for that stock. In earlier chapters we avoided the problem of stock by recording all purchases in the year in a purchases account, and all sales in a sales account, as is done in practice. Stock needs only to be recorded at the year end when an adjustment is made to the accounts for stock that is left.

The business will ascertain its year end stock figure by performing a stock count. The quantities counted for each type of stock are valued as described in the sections that follow. The year end adjustment is then made as set out as follows:

CHAPTER 10 : STOCK

6.2 ACCOUNTING FOR STOCK WHERE THERE IS CLOSING STOCK ONLY

During the year, purchases are recorded in the general ledger using the following double entry (ignoring VAT):

Dr   Purchases account
Cr   Creditors account or cash at bank account with the cost of goods purchased

The purchases account records all the goods bought which are available for sale during the year. If all the goods are sold, leaving no closing stock, then the cost of goods sold in the profit and loss account will simply be the balance on the purchases account.

However, if there are any closing stocks at the year end, an adjustment will be required to achieve two aims:

1   the stock value should be deducted from purchases to give the cost of goods actually sold in the profit and loss account

2   the unsold goods should be shown in the balance sheet as a current asset, stock.

The necessary adjustment requires two ledger accounts. The first records the asset for display in the balance sheet, whilst the second records the stock value(s) to adjust purchases in the profit and loss account.

The double entry to record the closing stock adjustment is:

Dr   Stock account (in the balance sheet)
Cr   Stock account (in the profit and loss account)

The profit and loss account will show the cost of goods sold as follows:

	£	£
Sales		x
Less: Cost of goods sold	x	
Purchases	(x)	
Less: Closing stock		(x)
		x

Example

Reflect the following transactions in T-account format and prepare an extract from the profit and loss account (assume a sales figure of £180,000)

Year 1 - purchases paid from bank account   £90,000

Year 1 - closing stock at valuation   £20,000

Step 1   Record the purchases during the year.

Purchases account

	£		£
Cash at bank	90,000		

127

MAINTAINING FINANCIAL RECORDS AND PREPARING ACCOUNTS : **UNIT 5**

Cash at bank account

	£		£
		Purchases	90,000

Step 2 Record the closing stock at the year end.

Stock account (balance sheet)

	£		£
Closing stock	20,000		

Stock account (profit and loss)

	£		£
		Closing stock	20,000

Step 3 Transfer purchases and closing stock to the profit and loss account.

Purchases account

	£		£
Cash at bank	90,000	P&L a/c	90,000

Stock account (profit and loss)

	£		£
P&L a/c	20,000	Closing stock	20,000

Step 4 Prepare the profit and loss account (assuming a sales figure of £180,000).

Profit and loss account

		£	£
Sales			180,000
Less: Cost of goods sold			
Purchases		90,000	
Less: Closing stock		20,000	
			70,000
Gross profit			110,000

6.4 ACCOUNTING FOR STOCK WHERE THERE IS OPENING AND CLOSING STOCK

The section above dealt with closing stock only. This will be the case where a business is at the end of its first year of trading. At any other year end there will be both opening stock (last year's closing stock) and the current year's closing stock.

The opening stock and purchases in the year represent what the business has available to sell in the year. This figure is then reduced by the value of the closing stock to find out what the business has actually sold.

The accounting entries necessary to reflect the above are as follows:

    Dr   Purchases account

    Cr   Cash at bank account or trade creditors

CHAPTER 10 : STOCK

with the cost of goods purchased:

- Dr Stock account (in the profit and loss account)
- Cr Stock account (in the balance sheet)

with the opening stock. This will be cleared out to the profit and loss account adding the opening stock to purchases as the cost of goods available for sale:

- Dr Stock account (in the balance sheet)
- Cr Closing stock account (in the profit and loss account)

with the closing stock, as in the last example.

Having recorded the entries in the relevant T-accounts, it will then be necessary to show the resulting cost of goods sold in the profit and loss account.

The format of the cost of goods sold calculation in the profit and loss account is:

	£	£
Sales		x
Less: Cost of goods sold		
Opening stock	x	
Purchases	x	
	x	
Less: Closing stock	(x)	
		(x)
Gross profit		xx

To get to this point, the T accounts are balanced off and the balances are slotted into the relevant position.

Example

Reflect the following transactions in T-account format and prepare an extract from the profit and loss account (assume a sales figure of £150,000)

Year 2 - opening stock (year 1 closing)	£20,000
Year 2 - purchases on credit	£110,000
Year 2 - closing stock at valuation	£40,000

Step 1 Record the purchases during the year.

Purchases account

	£		£
Creditors	110,000		

Step 2 At the year end transfer opening stock (balance sheet) to stock (profit and loss) and clear this to the profit and loss account.

Stock account (balance sheet)

	£		£
Balance b/d (opening stock)	20,000	Transfer to stock (profit and loss)	20,000

Stock account (profit and loss)

	£		£
Transfer from stock (bal sheet)	20,000	P&L a/c (opening stock)	20,000

Creditors control account

	£		£
		Purchases in year	110,000

Step 3 Record the closing stock.

Stock account (balance sheet)

	£		£
Balance b/d	20,000	Transfer to stock (profit and loss)	20,000
Closing stock	40,000		

Stock account (profit and loss)

	£		£
Transfer from stock (bal sheet)	20,000	P&L a/c (opening stock)	20,000
		Closing stock	40,000

Step 4 Record the closing stock.

Stock account (profit and loss)

	£		£
Transfer from stock (bal sheet)	20,000	P&L a/c (opening stock)	20,000
P&L a/c (closing stock)	40,000	Closing stock	40,000
	60,000		60,000

Purchases account

	£		£
Creditors	110,000	P&L a/c	110,000
	110,000		110,000

Creditors control account

	£		£
Balance c/d	110,000	Purchases	110,000
	110,000		110,000
		Balance b/d	110,000

Stock account (balance sheet)

	£		£
Balance b/d	20,000	Transfer to P&L a/c	20,000
Closing stock	40,000	Balance c/d	40,000
	60,000		60,000
Balance b/d	40,000		

CHAPTER 10 : STOCK

Step 5 Prepare the profit and loss accounting (assume a sales figure of £150,000).

	£	£
Sales		150,000
Less: Cost of goods sold		
Opening stock	20,000	
Purchases	110,000	
	130,000	
Less closing stock	(40,000)	
		(90,000)
		60,000

7 TRANSACTIONS ON A 'SALE OR RETURN' BASIS

Consider the following scenario: a manufacturer, A Ltd sells goods to a retailer, B Ltd, who then sells them on to a customer, Mr C. In the normal course of events, ownership of the goods will be transferred from A Ltd to B Ltd to Mr C, and B Ltd will be obliged to pay A Ltd for the goods irrespective of whether or not he finds a customer such as Mr C. Consequently, if B Ltd has the goods in stock at its financial year end, they will be counted, valued and included in B Ltd's closing stock.

However, if A Ltd and B Ltd do business on a sale or return basis, A Ltd will retain ownership of the goods transferred to the premises of B Ltd until they are sold to Mr C. In addition, B Ltd will only have to pay A Ltd for the goods when they are sold to Mr C. Of course, when Mr C buys the goods from B Ltd, he will become their owner and will have to pay B Ltd.

Note:

- The purchase and sale of goods acquired on a sale or return basis are both recorded at the time of sale.

- Goods held on a sale or return basis should not be included in the closing stock of the holder, but the original supplier who still retains ownership.

CONCLUSION

This chapter on stock has seen how the cost of stock needs to be determined, either by FIFO, LIFO or weighted average. Once the correct valuation is achieved, a final check is needed to make sure the cost does not exceed the net realisable value of the stock on an item by item basis.

When a correct valuation has been placed on the stock quantities counted at the year end, the value is then accounted for and a trading account is produced from the information.

SELF TEST QUESTIONS

Paragraph

1	Define raw materials.	2.2
2	Define work in progress.	2.3

3	Define finished goods.	2.4
4	Define the cost of stock.	3
5	Explain the FIFO method of valuing stock.	4.2
6	Explain the LIFO method of valuing stock.	4.4
7	What is the rule in SSAP 9 for valuing stock?	5.1
8	Define net realisable value.	5.2

KEY TERMS

Raw materials - materials and components purchased by a business for incorporation into manufactured products.

Work in progress - raw materials that have had further work done on them, but have not been competed at the point of valuation.

Finished goods - goods purchased or produced that are ready for sale (re-sale).

Cost of stock - all expenditure incurred in the normal course of business in bringing an item of stock to its present location and condition. The expenditure should include the cost of purchase and the cost of doing further work on the raw materials (cost of conversion).

First in first out (FIFO) - a method of estimating cost which assumes that stock is used or sold in the same order that it is purchased or produced by the business. Therefore, the stock that is left at the end of the year is the most recently purchased or produced stock.

Last in first out (LIFO) - A method of estimating cost which assumes that the stock that is used or sold is the latest stock to be purchased or produced by the business. Therefore, the stock that is left is not the most recently purchase or produced stock.

Weighted average - A method of estimating cost which assumes that all stock purchased or produced and, therefore all costs, are mixed together. Goods sold and stock unsold are valued at an average of all purchase prices.

Net realisable value - net realisable value of stock is its estimated sales proceeds less all costs to completion and all selling, marketing and distribution costs.

Chapter 11

ACCRUALS AND PREPAYMENTS

This chapter explains the purpose of accruals and prepayments, how they are calculated and how they are accounted for.

CONTENTS

1 Introduction
2 The accruals concept
3 Accrued expenses
4 Prepaid expenses
5 Expenses with prepaid and accrued elements
6 Miscellaneous income
7 Prepayments and accruals in the financial statements

KNOWLEDGE AND UNDERSTANDING

		Reference
1	The accounting treatment of accruals and prepayments	Item 15

PERFORMANCE CRITERIA

		Reference
1	Correctly identify, calculate and record appropriate adjustments	Item E in element 5.2
2	Make the relevant journal entries to lose off the revenue accounts in preparation for the transfer of balances to the final account	Item F in element 5.2

LEARNING OUTCOMES

At the end of this chapter you should be able to:

- explain the meaning of the accruals or matching concept

MAINTAINING FINANCIAL RECORDS AND PREPARING ACCOUNTS : UNIT 3

- understand the practical implications of the accruals concept for items of expense and miscellaneous income
- calculate the amounts that should appear in the profit and loss account and balance sheet where there are accruals or prepayments of expenses and items of income
- carry out the double entry required to account for accrued and prepaid expenses and miscellaneous income
- present accruals and prepayments in the balance sheet

1 INTRODUCTION

The amount charged to the profit and loss account should reflect the amount of goods and services consumed, rather than those goods and services paid for. This is the accruals concept. As a result the balance sheet recognises creditors, accruals, and prepayments in order to ensure that the correct amount has been charged to the P&L.

Likewise, income is claimed as it is earned, not as it is received. As a result the balance sheet recognises trade debtors (for sales made on credit) and accrued income (where customers have paid in advance for goods or services yet to be delivered).

Calculating these adjustments can form the whole of an exam question, or more commonly, form a part of a larger question.

2 THE ACCRUALS CONCEPT

2.1 A FUNDAMENTAL ACCOUNTING CONCEPT

As already seen, the accruals concept states that income and expenses should be matched together and dealt with in the profit and loss account for the period to which they relate regardless of the period in which the cash was actually received or paid. Therefore all of the expenses involved in making the sales for a period should be matched with the sales income and dealt with in the period in which the sales themselves are accounted for.

Examples

- If the rental due on a business's factory is £5,000 every quarter then the annual rental expense will be £20,000 whatever the pattern of cash payments for the rental is.

- If a business has an accounting year to 31 December 20X2 and during that year has paid £1,000 of electricity bills and has outstanding a bill for the quarter from 1 October to 31 December 20X2 of £300 then the electricity expense incurred by the business is £1,300 for the year to 31 December 20X2.

- If in the previous example the outstanding bill had been for the period from 1 November 20X2 to 31 January 20X3 then an estimate of the electricity expense for the year to 31 December 20X2 would be

    $£1,000 + (\frac{2}{3} \times 300) = £1,200$

- If a business with an accounting year end of 31 December 20X2 pays for 18 months of insurance on its buildings on 1 January 20X2 at a total cost of £3,000 then the insurance expense for the year to 31 December 20X2 would be

    $\frac{12}{18} \times £3,000 = £2,000$

CHAPTER 11 : ACCRUALS AND PREPAYMENTS

3 ACCRUED EXPENSES

3.1 INTRODUCTION

Definition   An accrual is an item of expense that has been incurred during the accounting period but has not been paid at the period end.

In order to ensure that all expenses incurred in a period have been included in the profit and loss account the accountant must ensure that the expense accounts include not only those items that have been paid for during the period but also any outstanding amounts. In some instances an invoice will have been received for any such outstanding amounts by the time the accounts are prepared and therefore the accrual can be accurately calculated. Otherwise, the accrual will need to be estimated from previous years and earlier invoices.

3.2 EXAMPLE WITH NO OPENING ACCRUAL

John Simnel's business has an accounting year end of 31 December 20X2. He rents factory space at a rental cost of £5,000 per quarter payable in arrears. During the year to 31 December 20X2 his cash payments of rent have been as follows:

	£
31 March (for quarter to 31 March 20X2)	5,000
29 June (for quarter to 30 June 20X2)	5,000
2 October (for quarter to 30 September 20X2)	5,000

The final payment due on 31 December 20X2 for the quarter to that date was not paid until 4 January 20X3.

It should be quite clear that the rental expense for John Simnel's business for the year to 31 December 20X2 is £20,000 (4 × £5,000) even though the final payment for the year was not made until after the year end. It should also be noted that at 31 December 20X2 John Simnel's business owes the landlord £5,000 of rental for the period from 1 October to 31 December 20X2.

Solution

Step 1   Bring down any opening balance on the account. In this example there is no opening balance. The significance of this step will become apparent in the next example.

Step 2   Record cash payments in the Factory rent account.

Factory rent

20X1		£	20X1		£
31 Mar	Cash at bank	5,000			
29 Jun	Cash at bank	5,000			
2 Oct	Cash at bank	5,000			

Step 3   The charge to the profit and loss account that is required at 31 December 20X2 is £20,000 and this is entered into the account on the credit side (the debit side is the expense in the profit and loss account).

MAINTAINING FINANCIAL RECORDS AND PREPARING ACCOUNTS : UNIT 3

Factory rent

20X2		£	20X2		£
31 Mar	Cash at bank	5,000			
29 Jun	Cash at bank	5,000			
2 Oct	Cash at bank	5,000			
			31 Dec	P&L a/c	20,000

Step 4 In order for the account to balance, a further debit entry of £5,000 is required.

- This will be the balance carried down on the account, the accrual.

- The double entry is to debit the account above the total with £5,000 and credit the account below the total.

- This gives a brought down credit balance representing the amount owed to the landlord for the final quarter's rent.

Factory rent

20X1		£	20X1		£
31 Mar	Cash at bank	5,000			
29 Jun	Cash at bank	5,000			
2 Oct	Cash at bank	5,000			
31 Dec	Bal c/d	5,000	31 Dec	P&L a/c	20,000
		20,000			20,000
			20X2		
			1 Jan	Bal b/d	5,000

- By this method the correct expense has been charged to the profit and loss account under the accruals concept, £20,000, and the amount of £5,000 owed to the landlord has been recognised as a credit balance on the account.

- This credit balance would be listed in the balance sheet under the heading of current liabilities and described as an accrual.

Note that steps 2 and 3 above may be performed in reverse order depending on personal preference and sometimes, the information given.

3.3 EXAMPLE WITH AN OPENING ACCRUAL

During the year to 31 December 20X3 John Simnel's rental charge remained the same and his payments were as follows:

	£
4 January (for quarter to 31 December 20X2)	5,000
28 March (for quarter to 31 March 20X3)	5,000
28 June (for quarter to 30 June 20X3)	5,000
4 October (for quarter to 30 September 20X3)	5,000
23 December (for quarter to 31 December 20X3)	5,000

CHAPTER 11 : ACCRUALS AND PREPAYMENTS

Step 1   Bring down the opening balance on the account, in this case an accrual of £5,000.

Factory rent

20X3		£	20X3		£
			1 Jan	Bal b/d	5,000

Step 2   Record the cash payments.

Factory rent

20X3		£	20X3		£
4 Jan	Cash at bank	5,000	1 Jan	Bal b/d	5,000
28 Mar	Cash at bank	5,000			
28 Jun	Cash at bank	5,000			
4 Oct	Cash at bank	5,000			
23 Dec	Cash at bank	5,000			

Step 3   Calculate the closing accrual. There is no accrued expense to be carried forward this year since the amount die for the final quarter of the year was paid before the year end.

Step 4   Balance the account. The balancing figure is the factory rent expense of £20,000 (4 × £5,000) which is transferred to the profit and loss account.

Factory rent

20X3		£	20X3		£
4 Jan	Cash at bank	5,000	1 Jan	Bal b/d	5,000
28 Mar	Cash at bank	5,000			
28 Jun	Cash at bank	5,000			
4 Oct	Cash at bank	5,000			
23 Dec	Cash at bank	5,000	31 Dec	P&L a/c (bal fig)	20,000
		25,000			25,000

Note that steps 3 and 4 were performed in reverse order in comparison with the previous example.

Note: The accounting treatment of an accrued expense is to debit the expense account, thereby increasing the expense in the profit and loss account and carry this balance forward as a creditor, an accrual, in the balance sheet.

ACTIVITY 1

John Ball is a sole trader with a 30 June year-end. His purchase ledger for the year-ending 30 June 20X8 includes all invoices dated up to an including 30 June 20X8. Any invoice received after that was posted to the July (or subsequent) purchase ledger. Estimate the closing accruals for the following items:

(a) An electricity bill for £900 for the three months to 31 August 20X8.

(b) Water bill for £780 for the quarter to 31 July 20X8.

(c) Sewerage bill for £642 for the quarter to 31 May 20X8. When the annual accounts were being prepared no further bills had been received, although John Ball had continued to use the service.

MAINTAINING FINANCIAL RECORDS AND PREPARING ACCOUNTS : UNIT 3

(d) John Ball also uses gas supplied through a gas main. The meter reading on the last invoice received before the year-end was 23645 units; on 30 June the meter read 24098 units. Gas costs 10 pence per unit.

This activity covers performance criterion E in element 5.2.

For a suggested answer, see the 'Answers' section at the end of the book.

ACTIVITY 2

James Bell has a December year-end. Prepare the T accounts for the following expense headings and calculate the annual profit and loss charge.

(a) Electricity. Invoices totalling £697 were received and posted to the ledgers during the year. The opening accrual was £172 and the closing accrual is £238.

(b) Rates. Invoices totalling £756 were received and posted to the ledgers during the year. The opening accrual was £365 and the closing accrual is £28.

This activity covers performance criterion E in element 5.2.

For a suggested answer, see the 'Answers' section at the end of the book.

4 PREPAID EXPENSES

4.1 INTRODUCTION

As well as ensuring that all of the expenses incurred in the period appear in the profit and loss account the accountant must also ensure that no items of expense that relate to future periods, but have already been paid for, are shown as expenses of the current period.

Definition A prepayment is an item of expense that has been paid during the current accounting period but will not be incurred until the next account period.

4.2 EXAMPLE WITH NO OPENING PREPAYMENT

John Simnel pays insurance on the factory that he rents and this is paid in advance. His payments during 20X1 for this insurance were as follows:

	£
1 January (for three months to 31 March 20X2)	800
28 March (for six months to 30 September 20X2)	1,800
2 October (for six months to 31 March 20X3)	1,800

The insurance expense for the year to 31 December 20X2 can be calculated as follows:

	£
1 January to 31 March 20X2	800
1 April to 30 September 20X2	1,800
1 October to 31 December 20X2 ($\frac{3}{6} \times 1,800$)	900
	3,500

CHAPTER 11 : ACCRUALS AND PREPAYMENTS

The remaining £900 that was paid on 2 October which is not to be charged to the profit and loss account for the year to 31 December 20X2 is a prepaid expense. It is an amount that has been paid in advance to the insurance company and as such it has the characteristics of a debtor, the insurance company effectively owing the £900 back to John Simnel at 31 December 20X2.

Solution

Step 1   Bring down any opening balance on the expense account. In this example the balance is £nil.

Step 2   Enter the cash payments into the Factory insurance account.

Factory insurance

20X2		£	20X2	£
1 Jan	Cash at bank	800		
28 Mar	Cash at bank	1,800		
2 Oct	Cash at bank	1,800		

Step 3   The charge to the profit and loss account calculated above as £3,500 is then entered into the account.

Step 4

- In order for the account to balance a further credit entry of £900 is required.

- The double entry is to credit the account above the total with £900 and put the debit entry in below the total at 21 Jan 20X3.

- This is the prepayment that is to be carried down and will appear as a bought down debit balance or debtor.

Factory insurance

20X2		£	20X2		£
1 Jan	Cash at bank	800	31 Dec	P&L a/c	3,500
28 Mar	Cash at bank	1,800	31 Dec	Bal c/d	900
2 Oct	Cash at bank	1,800			
		4,400			4,400
20X3					
1 Jan	Bal b/d	900			

- This has given the correct charge to the profit and loss account of £3,500 for the year to 31 December 20X2 and has recognised that there is a debtor or prepayment of £900 at 31 December 20X2.

- The £900 balance will appear in the balance sheet in current assets under the heading of prepayments. Prepayments appear just below debtors, or may be included with debtors and described as debtors and prepayments.

4.3 EXAMPLE WITH OPENING PREPAYMENT

In writing up expense accounts care must be taken to remember to include any opening balances on the account which were accruals or prepayments at the end of the previous year. For example, John Simnel pays his annual rates bill of £4,000 in

MAINTAINING FINANCIAL RECORDS AND PREPARING ACCOUNTS : UNIT 3

two equal instalments of £2,000 each on 1 April and 1 October each year. His rates account for the year to 31 December 20X2 would therefore look like this:

Rates

20X2		£	20X2	£
1 Jan	Bal b/d ($\frac{3}{6} \times 2,000$)	1,000		
1 April	Cash	2,000	31 Dec P&L a/c (bal fig)	4,000
1 Oct	Cash	2,000	31 Dec Bal c/d ($\frac{3}{6} \times 2,000$)	1,000
		5,000		5,000

Note that at 1 January 20X2 there is an opening debit balance on the account of £1,000. This is the three months rates from 1 January 20X1 to 31 March 20X2 that had been paid for on 1 October 20X1. You were not specifically told this opening balance but would be expected to work it out from the information given.

Note: The treatment of a prepaid expense is to credit the expense account with the amount of the prepayment, thereby reducing the expense to be charged to the profit and loss account, and to carry the balance forward as a debtor, a prepayment, in the balance sheet.

ACTIVITY 3

John Ball is a sole trader with a 30 June year-end. His purchase ledger includes all invoices dated up to an including 30 June 20X8. Estimate the closing prepayments for the following items:

(a) An insurance invoice for £2,136 paid in January 20X8 for the year to 28 February 20X9.

(b) £7,800 rent for the quarter to 31 July 20X8 paid in April 20X8.

This activity covers performance criterion E in element 5.2.

For a suggested answer, see the 'Answers' section at the end of the book.

ACTIVITY 4

James Bell has a December year-end. Prepare the T accounts for the following expense headings and calculate the annual P&L charge.

(a) Insurance. Invoices totalling £7,295 were received and posted to the ledgers during the year. The opening prepayment was £3,672 and the closing prepayment is £4,107.

(b) Rent. Invoices totalling £19,540 were received and posted to the ledgers during the year. The opening prepayment was £3,908 and the closing prepayment is £2,798.

This activity covers performance criterion E in element 5.2.

For a suggested answer, see the 'Answers' section at the end of the book.

CHAPTER 11 : ACCRUALS AND PREPAYMENTS

5 EXPENSES WITH PREPAID AND ACCRUED ELEMENTS

Some expenses may have both brought down and carried down accruals and prepayments. An example might use a telephone expense as the telephone bill will comprise two elements. There will be a charge for the rental of the telephones and lines which is paid in advance, and a further charge for calls made, paid in arrears.

Example

The details of John Simnel's telephone bills for 20X2 are as follows:

	£
Quarterly rental payable in advance on 1 February, 1 May, 1 August and 1 November each year	60
Calls paid in arrears for previous three months to:	
1 February 20X2	120
1 May 20X2	99
1 August 20X2	144
1 November 20X2	122
1 February 20X3	132

His telephone account for the year to 31 December 20X2 is to be written up.

Solution

Step 1 Calculate and enter the opening balances for accruals or prepayments at the beginning of the year in the telephone account.

- The opening debit balance represents the prepayment of the rental at 31 December 20X1. On 1 November 20X1 a payment of £60 would have been made to cover the period from 1 November 20X0 to 31 January 20X2. The amount of the 20X2 expense paid in 20X1 is therefore $\frac{1}{3} \times £60 = £20$.

- The opening credit balance represents the calls made in November and December 20X1 that were not paid for until 1 February 20X2. This can be approximated as $\frac{2}{3} \times £120 = £80$.

Telephone

20X2		£	20X2		£
1 Jan	Bal b/d	20	1 Jan	Bal b/d	80

Step 2 Enter the cash payments made during the year.

Telephone

20X2		£	20X2		£
1 Jan	Bal b/d	20	1 Jan	Bal b/d	80
1 Feb	Cash - rental	60			
1 Feb	Cash - calls	120			
1 May	Cash - rental	60			
1 May	Cash - calls	99			
1 Aug	Cash - rental	60			
1 Aug	Cash - calls	144			
1 Nov	Cash - rental	60			
1 Nov	Cash - calls	122			

Step 3 Calculate and enter the closing accruals and prepayments.

- There is a closing prepayment of telephone rental. £60 was paid on 1 November 20X2 for the following three months rental. This covers November and December 20X2 as well as January 20X3. The prepayment is the amount that relates to January 20X3 = $\frac{1}{3} \times £60 = £20$.

- The accrued expense at 31 December 20X2 is for November and December's calls that will not be paid

Step 4 Enter the profit and loss account charge as the balancing figure in the account.

Telephone

20X2		£	20X2		£
1 Jan	Bal b/d	20	1 Jan	Bal b/d	80
1 Feb	Cash - rental	60			
1 Feb	Cash - calls	120			
1 May	Cash - rental	60			
1 May	Cash - calls	99			
1 Aug	Cash - rental	60			
1 Aug	Cash - calls	144			
1 Nov	Cash - rental	60			
1 Nov	Cash - calls	122	31 Dec	P&L a/c (bal fig)	733
31 Dec	Bal c/d (accrual)	88	31 Dec	Bal c/d (prepayment)	20
		833			833
20X3			20X3		
1 Jan	Bal b/d (prepayment)	20	1 Jan	Bal b/d (accrual)	88

The profit and loss account expense that was included in the account as a balancing figure could be proved although this is not generally necessary in actual questions.

CHAPTER 11 : ACCRUALS AND PREPAYMENTS

	£
Rental charge for 1 January to 31 December 20X2 (4 × 60)	240
Calls:	
1 January to 31 January 20X2 ($\frac{1}{3} \times 120$)	40
1 February to 30 April 20X2	99
1 May to 31 July 20X2	144
1 August to 31 October 20X2	122
1 November to 31 December 20X2 ($\frac{2}{3} \times 132$)	88
	733

6 MISCELLANEOUS INCOME

In addition to accrued and prepaid expenses some organisations also have sources of miscellaneous income which may also be received in advance or arrears. The key to understanding the entries in income accounts is that, in comparison with expense accounts, they are the opposite way round.

Example

John Simnel sublets part of his factory space for a quarterly rental in advance of £900. The payments are due on 1 March, 1 June, 1 September and 1 December each year and are always paid on time.

The rent receivable account for the year to 31 December 20X2 will show both an opening and a closing balance of rental paid in advance of ($\frac{2}{3} \times £900$) = £600.

Income received in advance is effectively a creditor. The opening and closing balances will therefore be credit balances brought down.

The cash received in the year will be credit entries in the rent receivable account (debit in the cash account).

The income which will be credited to the profit and loss account (debit the rent receivable account) will be £3,600 (4 × £900).

Rental receivable

20X2		£	20X2		£
			1 Jan	Bal b/d	600
			1 Mar	Cash at bank	900
			1 June	Cash at bank	900
31 Dec	P&L a/c	3,600	1 Sept	Cash at bank	900
31 Dec	Bal c/d	600	1 Dec	Cash at bank	900
		4,200			4,200
			20X3		
			1 Jan	Bal b/d	600

The £600 credit balance brought down at 31 December 20X2 would be shown in the balance sheet as a creditor and described as income received in advance or deferred income.

ACTIVITY 5

Jane Bolt is preparing her accounts for the year-ending 31 December 20X6. She has two sources of miscellaneous income; franchising and rents. Prepare the T accounts for these items and calculate the annual income to be claimed in the P&L.

(a) Franchising. £56,364 of franchise income was received during the year. £14,726 related to income earned in 20X5, and she estimates that there is a further £28,645 receivable in respect of 20X6. (This was all received in January and February 20X7.)

(b) Rent. Invoices totalling £74,936 were issued and posted to the ledgers during the year. £23,985 of these invoices relates to periods in 20X7. In 20X5 £17,625 of invoices were issued in respect of rent periods in 20X6.

This activity covers performance criterion E in element 5.2.

For a suggested answer, see the 'Answers' section at the end of the book.

7 PREPAYMENTS AND ACCRUALS IN THE FINANCIAL STATEMENTS

7.1 THE BALANCE SHEET

A balance on an income or expense account represents a prepayment or an accrual and will be shown in the balance sheet with all other account balances. They appear under the headings current assets and current liabilities as they tend to be short term in nature. The extract from a balance sheet, below, shows their usual positions.

	£	£
Current assets		
Stock		x
Debtors	x	
Less: Provision for doubtful debts	(x)	
Prepayments		x
Cash at bank		x
Cash in hand		x
		x
		x
Current liabilities		
Creditors	x	
Accruals and deferred income	x	
		(x)
NET CURRENT ASSETS		x

7.2 THE PROFIT AND LOSS ACCOUNT

Accruals or prepayments of income and expenditure do not appear separately in the trading and profit and loss account. The amount transferred to the profit and loss account for expenses and income is, of course, affected by a prepayment or an accrual, though. An accrual has the effect of increasing the charge for an expense and a prepayment will reduce the charge. Similarly, income received in advance (or deferred income) will decrease the income credited to the profit and loss account and income due (or in arrears) will increase the amount credited.

CONCLUSION

Adjustments for accruals and prepayments for items of expense and miscellaneous income are necessary in order to accord with the fundamental accounting concept of accruals or matching whereby income and expenses of the business are matched and dealt with in the accounting period to which they relate regardless of the accounting period in which the related cash is received or paid.

An accrual is an expense of the period that has been incurred but not paid for by the year end. The accrual will increase the charge for the expense in the profit and loss account and be shown as a creditor, and described as an accrual, in the balance sheet at the year end.

A prepayment is an item of expense that has been paid for in the current year but relates to the next accounting period. A prepayment will reduce the expense for the year shown in the profit and loss account and will be shown as a debtor, and described as a prepayment, in the balance sheet at the year end.

If an item of income is received in advance then this will reduce the income credited to the profit and loss account and be shown as a creditor in the balance sheet as the amount is effectively due back to the payer at the year end. If an item of income due has not been received then this will increase the income to be shown in the profit and loss account and be shown as a debtor in the balance sheet at the year end.

SELF TEST QUESTIONS

Paragraph

1	Define an accrual.	3.1
2	Define a prepayment.	4.1
3	Does an accrual have the effect of increasing or decreasing an expense?	7.2

KEY TERMS

Accruals or **matching concept** states that costs and revenues should be matched one with the other and dealt with in the accounting period to which they relate.

Accrual - an item of expense that has been incurred during the accounting period but has not been paid at the period end

Prepayment - prepayment is an item of expense that has been paid during the current accounting period but will not be incurred until the next account period.

Chapter 12

BAD AND DOUBTFUL DEBTS

This chapter explains the purpose of the bad debt provision, and how the provision is calculated and recorded.

CONTENTS

1 Sales and accounting concepts

2 Bad debts

3 Doubtful debts

4 Bad debts recovered

KNOWLEDGE AND UNDERSTANDING

		Reference
1	How to make and adjust provisions	Item 20

PERFORMANCE CRITERIA

		Reference
1	Correctly identify, calculate and record appropriate adjustments	Item F in element 5.2

LEARNING OUTCOMES

At the end of this chapter you should be able to:

- understand the meaning of the terms bad debt and doubtful debt

- explain the accounting treatment of a bad debt written off

- explain the ledger entries for setting up a provision for doubtful debts and for both increasing and decreasing that provision

- explain the ledger entries for a bad debt recovered

MAINTAINING FINANCIAL RECORDS AND PREPARING ACCOUNTS : **UNIT 5**

- understand the financial statement presentation for bad debts and doubtful debt provisions.

1 SALES AND ACCOUNTING CONCEPTS

1.1 INTRODUCTION

If a sale is for cash then the customer pays for the goods immediately at the time the sale is made and will probably take the goods away with him or arrange for them to be delivered. If a sale is on credit terms then the customer will probably take the goods but not pay for them until later. Instead, the customer will be sent an invoice detailing the goods and their price and the normal payment terms. This will tell the customer when he is expected to pay for those goods.

1.2 ACCRUALS OR MATCHING CONCEPT

Under the accruals or matching concept a sale is included in the ledger accounts at the time that it is made. For a cash sale this will be when the cash or cheque is paid by the customer and the double entry will be:

    Dr   Cash at bank account
    Cr   Sales account

For a sale on credit the sale is made at the time that the invoice is sent to the customer and therefore the accounting entries are made at that time as follows:

    Dr   Debtors account
    Cr   Sales account

When the customer eventually settles the invoice the double entry will be:

    Dr   Cash at bank account
    Cr   Debtors account

This then clears out the balance on the debtors account.

1.3 PRUDENCE CONCEPT

The prudence concept states that sales and profit should not be included in the profit and loss account until the cash has been received or there is reasonable certainty that the cash will be received. In contrast, losses should be recognised in the profit and loss as soon as they are foreseen and considered reasonably certain.

The problem that businesses face with credit sales is that of the collectability of the amounts owing on sales invoices. If a customer is declared bankrupt or disappears without trace before the amount is paid then it is unlikely that the amounts due will be paid. If a customer is having financial difficulties or is in liquidation then there may be some doubt as to his eventual ability to pay.

For this reason, the application of the prudence concept means that some adjustment needs to be made to reflect this actual or potential loss. The required adjustments are looked at in this chapter.

2 BAD DEBTS

2.1 INTRODUCTION

Definition   A bad debt is a debt which is considered to be uncollectable.

If a debt is considered to be uncollectable then it is prudent to remove it totally from the accounts and to charge the amount as an expense to the profit and loss account. **The**

CHAPTER 12 : BAD AND DOUBTFUL DEBTS

original sale remains in the accounts as this did actually take place. The debtor, however, is removed and an expense is charged to the profit and loss account for bad debts.

The double entry required to achieve these effects is:

Dr Bad debts expense account
Cr Debtors account

Example

Abacus & Co have total debtors at the end of their accounting period of £45,000. Included in this total is an amount of £790 owed by James Scott who has been declared bankrupt and £1,240 due from Peter Campbell who has totally disappeared.

Solution

Step 1 Enter the opening balance in the debtors account. As debtors are an asset then this will be on the debit side of the ledger account.

Debtors

	£		£
Opening balance	45,000		

Step 2 As the two debts are considered to be irrecoverable then they must be removed from debtors by a credit to the debtors account and a corresponding debit entry to a bad debts expense account.

Debtors

	£		£
Opening balance	45,000	Bad debts expense - J Scott	**790**
		Bad debts expense - P Campbell	**1,240**

Bad debts expense

	£		£
Debtors - J Scott	**790**		
Debtors - P Campbell	**1,240**		

Step 3 The debtors account must now be balanced and the closing balance (of £42,970 in this case) would appear in the balance sheet as the debtors figure at the end of the period.

Debtors

	£		£
Opening balance	45,000	Bad debts expense - J Scott	790
		Bad debts expense - P Campbell	1,240
		Balance c/d	**42,970**
	45,000		45,000
Balance b/d	42,970		

Step 4 Finally the bad debts expense account should be balanced and the balance written off to the profit and loss account as an expense of the period.

Bad debts expense

	£		£
Debtors - J Scott	790	P&L a/c	**2,030**
Debtors - P Campbell	1,240		
	2,030		2,030

Note: When a debt is considered to be bad then it is written out of the accounts completely by removing it from debtors and charging the amount as an expense to the profit and loss account in the period in which the debt was determined as bad.

3 DOUBTFUL DEBTS

3.1 INTRODUCTION

Definition A doubtful debt is an amount owing to the business, the collectability of which is uncertain.

A doubtful debt is one about which there is some cause for concern but which is not yet definitely irrecoverable. Therefore, although it is prudent immediately to recognise the possible expense of not collecting the debt in the profit and loss account, it would also be wise to keep the original debt in the accounts in case the debtor does in fact pay up.

This is achieved by the following double entry:

Dr Bad debts expense

Cr Provision for doubtful debts account

The debt is not removed from debtors; instead a provision is set up which is a credit balance. This is netted off against debtors in the balance sheet to give a net figure for debtors that are probably recoverable.

3.2 TYPES OF DOUBTFUL DEBT

There are two types of amount that are likely to be considered as doubtful debts in an organisation's accounts.

(a) **Specific provisions**

There will be some specific debts where the debtor is known to be in financial difficulties and therefore the amount owing from that debtor may not be recoverable. The provision to be made against such a debtor is known as a specific provision.

(b) **General provisions**

The past experience and history of a business will indicate that not all of its debts will be recoverable in full. It may not be possible to indicate the precise debtors that will not pay but an estimate may be made that a certain percentage of debtors is likely not to pay its debts. The provision made against this percentage of debtors is known as a general provision.

CHAPTER 12 : BAD AND DOUBTFUL DEBTS

3.3 GENERAL PROVISION FOR DOUBTFUL DEBTS

Example

On 31 December 20X1 Jake Williams had debtors of £10,000. From past experience Jake estimated that 3% of these debtors were likely never to pay their debts and he therefore wished to make a general doubtful debt provision against this amount.

During 20X2 Jake made sales on credit totalling £100,000 and received cash from his debtors of £94,000. He still considered that 3% of the closing debtors were doubtful and should be provided against.

During 20X3 Jake made sales of £95,000 and collected £96,000 from his debtors. At 31 December 20X3 Jake still considered that 3% of his debtors were doubtful and should be provided against.

Solution

Step 1   Enter the balance on the debtors account at 31 December 20X1.

Debtors

20X1		£	20X1		£
31 Dec		10,000			

Step 2   Set up a provision against 3% of £10,000, £300, by debiting the bad debts expense account and crediting the provision for doubtful debts account.

Bad debts expense

20X1		£	20X1	£
31 Dec	Provision for doubtful debts	300		

Provision for doubtful debts

20X1	£	20X1		£
		31 Dec	Bad debts expense	300

Step 3   Balance the three accounts.

Debtors

20X1		£	20X1		£
31 Dec		10,000	31 Dec	Bal c/d	10,000
		10,000			10,000
20X2					
1 Jan	Bal b/d	10,000			

Bad debts expense

20X1		£	20X1		£
31 Dec	Provision for doubtful debts	300	31 Dec	P&L a/c	300
		300			300

151

The £300 charge is the expense for the period to be included in the 20X1 profit and loss account.

Provision for doubtful debts

20X1		£	20X1		£
31 Dec	Bal c/d	300	31 Dec	Bad debts expense	300
		300			300
			20X2		
			1 Jan	Bal b/d	300

This credit balance of £300 is netted off against the debtors at the end of 20X1 in order to indicate the amount of debtors that are doubtful.

An extract from the balance sheet at 31 December 20X1 would be as follows:

	£
Current assets	
Debtors	10,000
Less: Provision for doubtful debts	(300)
	9,700

Step 4 Write up the debtors account for 20X2 and balance it off to find the debtors figure at 31 December 20X2.

Debtors

20X2		£	20X2		£
1 Jan	Bal b/d	10,000	31 Dec	Cash	94,000
31 Dec	Sales	100,000	31 Dec	Bal c/d	16,000
		110,000			110,000
20X3					
1 Jan	Bal b/d	16,000			

Step 5 Set up the provision required of 3% of £16,000, £480. Remember that there is already an opening balance on the provision account of £300. Therefore, in order to end 20X2 with a total balance on the provision account of £480, only a further £180 will need to be charged to the bad debts expense account for the period.

Bad debts expense

20X2		£	20X2		£
31 Dec	Provision for doubtful debts	180	31 Dec	P&L a/c	180
		180			180

CHAPTER 12 : BAD AND DOUBTFUL DEBTS

Provision for doubtful debts

20X2		£	20X2		£
			1 Jan	Bal b/d	300
31 Dec	Bal c/d	480	31 Dec	Bad debts expense	180
		480			480
			20X3		
			1 Jan	Bal b/d	480

Step 6 The extract from the balance sheet at 31 December 20X2 would be as follows:

	£	£
Current assets		
Debtors	16,000	
Less: Provision for doubtful debts	(480)	
		15,520

Note: When a provision for doubtful debts is first set up, the full amount of the provision is charged to the profit and loss account for the period. In subsequent years if the provision required increases then it is only necessary to charge the increase in the provision over the period to the profit and loss account.

Step 7 Write up the debtors account for 20X3. Balance off the account to find the debtors at 31 December 20X3.

Debtors

20X3		£	20X3		£
1 Jan	Bal b/d	16,000	31 Dec	Cash	96,000
31 Dec	Sales	95,000	31 Dec	Bal c/d	15,000
		111,000			111,000
20X4					
1 Jan	Bal b/d	15,000			

Step 8 Set up the provision required at 31 December 20X3 of 3% of £15,000, £450. This time there is already an opening balance on the provision for doubtful debts account of £480.

The provision is to be reduced and this is done by **debiting** the provision account with the amount of the decrease required (£480 – £450 = £30) and **crediting** the bad debts expense account.

The credit on the bad debts expense account is transferred to the profit and loss account for the period as a negative expense and is described as 'decrease in doubtful debts provision'.

Provision for doubtful debts

20X3		£	20X3		£
31 Dec	Bad debts expense	30			
31 Dec	Bal c/d	450	1 Jan	Bal b/d	480
		480			480
			20X4		
			1 Jan	Bal b/d	450

Bad debts expense

20X3		£	20X3		£
31 Dec	P&L a/c	30	31 Dec	Provision for doubtful debts	30
		30			30

Step 9 The extract from the balance sheet at 31 December 20X3 would be as follows:

	£	£
Current assets		
Debtors	15,000	
Less: Provision for doubtful debts	(450)	
		14,550

Note: If the provision for doubtful debts is to be decreased from one period end to another then the provision for doubtful debts account will be debited with the amount of the decrease and the bad debts expense account will be credited. Note only the difference in the bad debt provision from one year to the next is posted.

3.5 SPECIFIC PROVISION FOR DOUBTFUL DEBTS

Example

Steven Saunders has debtors of £11,200 at his year end of 31 May 20X4. Of these he decides that there is some doubt as to whether or not he will receive a sum of £500 from Peter Foster and he also wishes to provide against the possibility of not receiving 2% of his remaining debtors.

At 1 June 20X3 Steven Saunders had a balance on his provision for doubtful debts account of £230.

Solution

Step 1 Calculate the provision for doubtful debts required at 31 May 20X4

	£
Specific provision against Peter Foster's debt	500
General provision against remaining debtors	
(£11,200 – 500) × 2%	214
Total provision required	714

CHAPTER 12 : BAD AND DOUBTFUL DEBTS

Step 2 Write up the provision for doubtful debts account putting in the opening balance of £230 and the closing balance required of £714. The increase in provision required of £484 is debited to the bad debts expense account.

Provision for doubtful debts

20X3/4	£	20X3/4	£
31 May Bal c/d	714	1 June Bal b/d	230
		31 May Bad debts expense	484
	714		714
		20X4/X5	
		1 June Bal b/d	714

Bad debts expense

20X3/4	£	20X3/4	£
31 May Provision for doubtful debts	484	31 May P&L a/c	484
	484		484

ACTIVITY 1

Andrew Lock is preparing his annual accounts as at June 20X9. The balance on the Sales Ledger Control Account is £78,635. Included in this figure are £2,385 of customers whose debts are now deemed to be irrecoverable. Andrew has already written off £1,234 of debts during the year. In addition, Andrew wishes to create a specific provision of £3,250 against certain customers who he knows to be in financial difficulties and a general provision of 3% on the remainder of the debtors. The opening provision for doubtful debts in July 20X8 was £4,300.

Tasks

(a) Adjust the sales ledger control account in respect of the bad debts.

(b) Calculate the provision for doubtful debts and prepare the T account for the provision.

(c) Prepare the P&L expense account for bad and doubtful debts.

(d) Show the trade debtor balance that will appear in the balance sheet.

This activity covers performance criterion E in element 5.2.

For a suggested answer, see the 'Answers' section at the end of the book.

4 BAD DEBTS RECOVERED

4.1 INTRODUCTION

There is a possible situation where a debt is written off as bad in one accounting period, and all or part of the money due is then unexpectedly received in a subsequent accounting period.

MAINTAINING FINANCIAL RECORDS AND PREPARING ACCOUNTS : UNIT 5

4.2 DOUBLE ENTRY

When a debt is written off the double entry is:

Dr   Bad debts expense account (an expense in the profit and loss account)

Cr   Debtors account (removing the debtor from the accounts)

If the debtor pays up in a subsequent accounting period, then the double entry is as follows:

Dr   Cash account

Cr   Bad debts expense account

as the debit and the credit to the debtors account cancel each other out.

CONCLUSION

Having studied this chapter you should now understand the reason for considering the collectability of debts and the accounting concepts that are relevant to this area: matching and prudence.

A bad debt is a debt that is considered irrecoverable and the double entry for writing off a bad debt is:

Dr   Bad debts expense account

Cr   Debtors account

A provision for doubtful debts is set up when there is some doubt as to whether all of the debts of the business will be recovered in full. This may be a specific provision if certain specific debts are known to be in doubt or a general provision based upon a certain percentage of debtors at the year end.

Unlike a bad debt write off, the double entry for a provision for doubtful debts does not entail removing the debtor from the debtors account. Instead the double entry is:

Dr   Bad debts expense account

Cr   Provision for doubtful debts account

for an increase in the required provision, or:

Dr   Provision for doubtful debts account

Cr   Bad debts expense account

with a decrease in the required provision.

The balance on the provision account is netted off against the balance on the debtors account in the balance sheet at the end of the accounting period, under the heading of current assets.

Finally you should be able to account for cash received from a debt that has been written off in a previous accounting period. This is recognised as sundry income by crediting the bad debts expense account:

Dr   Cash account

Cr   Bad debts expense account

CHAPTER 12 : BAD AND DOUBTFUL DEBTS

SELF TEST QUESTIONS

		Paragraph
1	Define bad debts.	2.1
2	Define doubtful debts.	3.1
3	Explain two types of provision for bad debts.	3.2
4	What is the double entry for writing off a bad debt and what for subsequent cash received?	4.2

KEY TERMS

Bad debt - a debt which is considered to be uncollectable.

Doubtful debt - an amount owing to the business, the collectability of which is uncertain.

Chapter 13

THE EXTENDED TRIAL BALANCE

The extended trial balance is a worksheet which takes an initial trial balance, makes all the year end adjustments and then produces a draft balance sheet and profit and loss account.

The extended trial balance is a core topic of the intermediate stage of the AAT qualification. This chapter therefore looks at how to produce an extended trial balance.

CONTENTS

1. Proforma extended trial balance
2. From trial balance to extended trial balance
3. Period end adjustments
4. Accruals and prepayments
5. Stock and the extended trial balance
6. Completing the extended trial balance

KNOWLEDGE AND UNDERSTANDING

		Reference
1	The function and form of a trial balance and an extended trial balance	Item 27

LEARNING OUTCOMES

At the end of this chapter you should be able to:

- prepare a proforma extended trial balance with the correct columns
- transfer balances from the trial balance to the extended trial balance
- correctly enter any required year end adjustments into the extended trial balance
- adjust for any accruals and prepayments
- deal with closing stock correctly
- total the extended trial balance and identify the profit or loss figure for the period

MAINTAINING FINANCIAL RECORDS AND PREPARING ACCOUNTS : UNIT 5

1 PROFORMA EXTENDED TRIAL BALANCE

1.1 WHAT AN EXTENDED TRIAL BALANCE LOOKS LIKE

An extended trial balance can be seen below.

Extended trial balance at 31 December 20X2

Account	Trial balance		Ref	Adjustments		Profit and loss		Balance sheet	
	Dr	Cr		Dr	Cr	Dr	Cr	Dr	Cr
	£	£		£	£	£	£	£	£

The layout is explained below.

(a) Account - the first column is used to list all the ledger accounts in the main ledger (general ledger).

(b) Trial balance - the next two columns are used to list the balances on all the main ledger accounts. The balance on an account is put into either the debit column or the credit column, and these columns are therefore the figures that appear in the initial trial balance.

(c) Ref and adjustments - these sections are used to record any period-end adjustments to the trial balance made via journals. The journal reference is entered in the 'ref' column so that the figures in the adjustment section can be traced back to source documentation. A double entry is performed for each adjustment using the debit and credit columns.

(d) Profit and loss – these columns are used to enter account balances that belong in the profit and loss account.

(e) Balance sheet – these columns are used to enter account balances that belong in the balance sheet.

An extended trial balance is prepared by working from left to right.

- First we enter the account names and the account balances for an initial trial balance

- We then have the information to prepare the profit and loss account and balance sheet

- Next, we make various year end adjustments

- Finally we can then enter the balances in the profit and loss account and balance sheet columns.

Note: It is of vital importance that the debit column total and credit column total of the trial balance and adjustments sections balance before moving on to the next sections.

ACTIVITY 1

Take a piece of A4 paper, turn it sideways and prepare a proforma extended trial balance from memory.

There is no feedback to this activity.

CHAPTER 13 : THE EXTENDED TRIAL BALANCE

2 FROM TRIAL BALANCE TO EXTENDED TRIAL BALANCE

The starting point for any extended trial balance is the initial trial balance. An initial trial balance is extracted from the main ledger (general ledger) and is a list of all balances in the main ledger accounts. The total of debit balances and total of credit balances must be equal. If the double entry has broken down somewhere, then the trial balance will not be in balance and a suspense account will be needed. In this instance correct the suspense account first so that the initial trial balance does balance.

Example

The following balances have been extracted from the books of XYZ, a small shower manufacturing firm.

	Dr £	Cr £
Capital account		12,000
Opening stock	15,000	
Sales		100,000
Purchases	40,000	
Rent and rates	10,000	
Drawings	12,000	
Electricity	2,000	
Motor van cost	8,000	
Motor van accumulated depreciation		4,000
Bank balance	4,500	
Trade debtors	20,000	
Trade creditors		21,000
Sundry expenses	500	
Wages and salaries	25,000	
	137,000	137,000

MAINTAINING FINANCIAL RECORDS AND PREPARING ACCOUNTS : UNIT 5

Step 1   Draw up a proforma extended trial balance using the account names given.

Extended Trial balance at 31 December 20X2

Account	Trial balance Dr £	Trial balance Cr £	Ref	Adjustments Dr £	Adjustments Cr £	Profit and loss Dr £	Profit and loss Cr £	Balance sheet Dr £	Balance sheet Cr £
Capital account									
Stock									
Sales									
Purchases									
Rent and rates									
Drawings									
Electricity									
Motor van cost									
Motor van provision for depreciation									
Bank balance									
Trade debtors									
Trade creditors									
Sundry expenses									
Wages and salaries									

Step 2   Put in the figures from the trial balance.

Extended trial balance at 31 December 20X2

Account	Trial balance Dr £	Trial balance Cr £	Ref	Adjustments Dr £	Adjustments Cr £	Profit and loss Dr £	Profit and loss Cr £	Balance sheet Dr £	Balance sheet Cr £
Capital account		12,000							
Stock	15,000								
Sales		100,000							
Purchases	40,000								
Rent and rates	10,000								
Drawings	12,000								
Electricity	2,000								
Motor van cost	8,000								
Motor van provision for depreciation		4,000							
Bank balance	4,500								
Trade debtors	20,000								
Trade creditors		21,000								
Sundry expenses	500								
Wages and salaries	25,000								
	137,000	137,000							

ACTIVITY 2

Set up an extended trial balance for PG Trading from the following draft trial balance. It is necessary to create and correct a suspense account first.

PG Trading Trial balance as at 31 December 20X6

Account	Dr £	Cr £
Capital account		63,000
Stock (see below)		
Sales		150,000
Purchases	105,000	
Rent and rates	15,000	
Drawings		18,000
Electricity	3,000	
Motor van cost	12,000	
Motor van provision for depreciation		6,000
Bank balance	6,750	
Trade debtors	30,000	
Trade creditors		31,500
Sundry expenses	750	
Wages and salaries	37,500	
	210,000	268,500

The bookkeeper is not sure what to do with £22,500 of opening stock. From his studies he can vaguely remember that there is a stock figure in the trial balance, but he cannot remember which one, so he has left it out.

For a suggested answer, see the 'Answers' section at the end of the book.

3 PERIOD END ADJUSTMENTS

Period end adjustments are accounting adjustments to the initial trial balance which are needed to prepare the period end financial accounts. They include items such as bad debt provisions and write offs, depreciation adjustments, disposals of fixed assets and correction of mis-postings.

Period end adjustments have already been explained in previous chapters. The purpose of this section is to demonstrate how those adjustments are shown in the extended trial balance.

Example

Using the example extended trial balance in section 2.2 earlier, produce the journals and make the following adjustments to the trial balance:

(a) a depreciation charge for the year of £500

(b) a bad debt write off amounting to £1,000

(c) an adjustment for drawings of £200 included in sundry expenses.

MAINTAINING FINANCIAL RECORDS AND PREPARING ACCOUNTS : UNIT 5

Step 1 Produce the journal entries.

		Dr £	Cr £
(a)	Depreciation expense	500	
	Provision for depreciation		500
	Being depreciation for the year		
(b)	Bad debts expense	1,000	
	Trade debtors		1,000
	Being the write off of a bad debt		
(c)	Drawings	200	
	Sundry expenses		200
	Being the transfer of an incorrect posting		

Step 2 Enter the adjustments on to the extended trial balance.

Step 3 Check the debit and credit columns balance but do not enter the totals yet.

Note: The total of the debit and credit columns must balance, that is, the double entry has been maintained. If the column totals are not checked at this point and the columns do not balance there are two main effects. Firstly, the extended trial balance will not balance and secondly, it is a major headache trying to find out what has gone wrong at a later stage. Whilst it appears a little slower working through methodically, it will be a lot quicker than having to go back through the whole extended trial balance to find errors when it does not balance at the final stage.

Extended trial balance at 31 December 20X2

Account	Trial balance Dr £	Trial balance Cr £	Ref	Adjustments Dr £	Adjustments Cr £	Profit and loss Dr £	Profit and loss Cr £	Balance sheet Dr £	Balance sheet Cr £
Capital account		12,000							
Stock	15,000								
Sales		100,000							
Purchases	40,000								
Rent and rates	10,000								
Drawings	12,000		c	200					
Electricity	2,000								
Motor van cost	8,000								
Motor van provision for depreciation		4,000	a		500				
Bank balance	4,500								
Trade debtors	20,000		b		1,000				
Trade creditors		21,000							
Sundry expenses	500		c		200				
Wages and salaries	25,000								
Depreciation expenses			a	500					
Bad debt expense			b	1,000					
	137,000	137,000		1,700	1,700				

CHAPTER 13 : THE EXTENDED TRIAL BALANCE

ACTIVITY 3

Start with your corrected initial trial balance for PG Trading that you prepared in Activity 2.

PG Trading needs to make the following year end adjustments to the trial balance:

1   a bad debt of £1,500 is to be written off

2   depreciation of £750 is to be charged

3   a mis-posting of £300 to rent and rates that should have been wages is to be corrected.

Task

Add these adjustments to the extended trial balance.

For a suggested answer, see the 'Answers' section at the end of the book.

4 ACCRUALS AND PREPAYMENTS

4.1 INTRODUCTION

In practice, accruals and prepayments are often shown as separate adjustments with their own columns in the extended trial balance. However, in your exam, they are included with other year end adjustments. Their treatment warrants separate attention only because it is slightly different in the extended trial balance compared with the ledger accounts. If anything, it is more straightforward.

4.2 HOW TO ENTER ACCRUALS INTO THE EXTENDED TRIAL BALANCE

We need an extra line in the extended trial balance for accruals. In the extended trial balance accruals are entered in the debit column on the accruals line. The total of all the accruals is entered in the credit column on the accruals line. This credit entry for the expense account affected will eventually give the accruals figure in the balance sheet.

Example

Continuing with the example in section 4.2, the following accruals are needed at the year end:

    Electricity   £150

    Sundry expenses £50

Step 1   Write in accruals in the debit adjustments column on the appropriate account line.

Step 2   Total up the accruals and enter the amount in the credit adjustments column opposite a new account heading 'Accruals' (The reference column just shows the references for the new entries.)

MAINTAINING FINANCIAL RECORDS AND PREPARING ACCOUNTS : UNIT 5

Extended trial balance at 31 December 20X2

Account	Trial balance Dr £	Trial balance Cr £	Ref	Adjustments Dr £	Adjustments Cr £	Profit and loss Dr £	Profit and loss Cr £	Balance sheet Dr £	Balance sheet Cr £
Capital account		12,000							
Stock	15,000								
Sales		100,000							
Purchases	40,000								
Rent and rates	10,000								
Drawings	12,000			200					
Electricity	2,000		d	150					
Motor van cost	8,000								
Motor van provision for depreciation		4,000			500				
Bank balance	4,500								
Trade debtors	20,000				1,000				
Trade creditors		21,000							
Sundry expenses	500		d	50	200				
Wages and salaries	25,000								
Depreciation expenses				500					
Bad debt expense				1,000					
Accruals			d		200				
	137,000	137,000		1,900	1,900				

4.3 HOW TO ENTER PREPAYMENTS INTO THE TRIAL BALANCE

We now need another extra line in the extended trial balance for ~~accruals~~. PREPAYMENT.

Prepayments are listed individually in the credit adjustments column for the expense account affected. This will form the credit side of the account line of the double entry. Total prepayments are placed in the new account line, 'Prepayments', in the debit column. This debit will eventually appear in the balance sheet as 'Prepayments'.

Example

Carrying on the same example, a prepayment of rent of £800 is required. Again the reference column only shows the reference for the new entries.

CHAPTER 13 : THE EXTENDED TRIAL BALANCE

Extended trial balance at 31 December 20X2

Account	Trial balance Dr £	Trial balance Cr £	Ref	Adjustments Dr £	Adjustments Cr £	Profit and loss Dr £	Profit and loss Cr £	Balance sheet Dr £	Balance sheet Cr £
Capital account		12,000							
Stock	15,000								
Sales		100,000							
Purchases	40,000								
Rent and rates	10,000		e		800				
Drawings	12,000			200					
Electricity	2,000			150					
Motor van cost	8,000								
Motor van provision for depreciation		4,000			500				
Bank balance	4,500								
Trade debtors	20,000				1,000				
Trade creditors		21,000							
Sundry expenses	500			50	200				
Wages and salaries	25,000								
Depreciation expenses				500					
Bad debt expense				1,000					
Accruals					200				
Prepayments			e	800					
	137,000	137,000		2,700	2,700				

Note: When all the accruals and prepayments have been entered, total up the columns and make sure they balance.

ACTIVITY 4

PG Trading requires accruals for wages of £225 and for sundry expenses of £75. In addition, rates are prepaid by £1,200.

Show the necessary entries in the extended trial balance stated in the earlier activity.

For a suggested answer, see the 'Answers' section at the end of the book.

5 STOCK AND THE EXTENDED TRIAL BALANCE

5.1 INTRODUCTION

In the chapter on stock it was shown that the period end requires an adjustment to account for the **closing stock** as follows:

    Dr   stock account (balance sheet)

    Cr   stock account (profit and loss account)

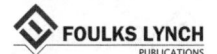

MAINTAINING FINANCIAL RECORDS AND PREPARING ACCOUNTS : UNIT 5

An entry is also required to transfer last year's closing stock, now forming this year's opening stock to the profit and loss account:

Dr   stock (profit and loss account) and then cleared to P&L a/c

Cr   stock (balance sheet)

The required adjustments in the extended trial balance are to record these debits and credits.

5.2 ENTERING CLOSING STOCK INTO THE EXTENDED TRIAL BALANCE

In the extended trial balance the closing stock entries are made in the adjustment column. A new account is required called Stock (profit and loss). Remember, the stock account appearing in the initial trial balance is the stock (balance sheet) account.

Example

XYZ's closing stock was valued at £17,000.

Step 1   Write the new stock (profit and loss) account in the account column.

Step 2   Make the closing stock entry in the adjustment columns (The reference column only shows the reference for the new entries.)

Extended trial balance at 31 December 20X2

Account	Trial balance Dr £	Trial balance Cr £	Ref	Adjustments Dr £	Adjustments Cr £	Profit and loss Dr £	Profit and loss Cr £	Balance sheet Dr £	Balance sheet Cr £
Capital account		12,000							
Stock	15,000		f	17,000					
Sales		100,000							
Purchases	40,000								
Rent and rates	10,000				800				
Drawings	12,000			200					
Electricity	2,000			150					
Motor van cost	8,000								
Motor van provision for depreciation		4,000			500				
Bank balance	4,500								
Trade debtors	20,000				1,000				
Trade creditors		21,000							
Sundry expenses	500			50	200				
Wages and salaries	25,000								
Depreciation expenses				500					
Bad debt expense				1,000					
Accruals					200				
Prepayments				800					
Stock (profit and loss)			f		17,000				
	137,000	137,000		19,700	19,700				

168

CHAPTER 13 : THE EXTENDED TRIAL BALANCE

5.3 OPENING STOCK AND THE EXTENDED TRIAL BALANCE

For extended trial balance purposes, the opening stock can be cleared to the stock (profit and loss) account as an adjustment.

Example

Extended trial balance at 31 December 20X2

Account	Trial balance Dr £	Trial balance Cr £	Ref	Adjustments Dr £	Adjustments Cr £	Profit and loss Dr £	Profit and loss Cr £	Balance sheet Dr £	Balance sheet Cr £
Capital account		12,000							
Stock	15,000		g	17,000	15,000				
Sales		100,000							
Purchases	40,000								
Rent and rates	10,000				800				
Drawings	12,000			200					
Electricity	2,000			150					
Motor van cost	8,000								
Motor van provision for depreciation		4,000			500				
Bank balance	4,500								
Trade debtors	20,000				1,000				
Trade creditors		21,000							
Sundry expenses	500			50	200				
Wages and salaries	25,000								
Depreciation expenses				500					
Bad debt expense				1,000					
Accruals					200				
Prepayments				800					
Stock (profit and loss)			g	15,000	17,000				
	137,000	137,000		34,700	34,700				

Note that the stock (profit and loss) account shows the opening and closing stock figures that will be cleared to the profit and loss account.

ACTIVITY 5

Task

Continue the extended trial balance for PG Trading from the previous activity where the opening stock was £22,500. The closing stock for PG Trading is £25,500.

For a suggested answer, see the 'Answers' section at the end of the book.

6 COMPLETING THE EXTENDED TRIAL BALANCE

6.1 INTRODUCTION

The final step in preparing an extended trial balance is to complete the profit and loss and balance sheet columns.

6.2 EXTENDING THE ACCOUNT BALANCES ACROSS THE TRIAL BALANCE

Extending the account balances across the extended trial balance requires two skills:

(a) knowledge of which accounts go into the profit and loss account and which accounts go into the balance sheet.

(b) careful addition (casting).

6.3 RULES TO APPLY

1 The account balance for capital, assets and liabilities go in the balance sheet columns. The Stock (balance sheet) account is an asset item. The Accruals and Prepayments accounts are balance sheet assets.

2 The account balances for income and expenses and the Stock (profit and loss account) balances are profit and loss items.

3 Add the figures for each account in the trial balance and adjustment columns, and enter them in either the profit and loss columns or balance sheet columns as appropriate.

4 A debit balance in the initial trial balance column and a debit balance in an adjustments column are added together. Similarly, a credit balance in two columns are added. A debit balance is subtracted from a credit balance (or vice versa), depending on which balance is bigger.

5 The stock (profit and loss) entries in the adjustments column are not subtracted one from the other. Both figures are entered in the profit and loss columns.

The best way to demonstrate these rules is by example.

CHAPTER 13 : THE EXTENDED TRIAL BALANCE

Example

Extended trial balance at 31 December 20X2

Account	Trial balance Dr £	Trial balance Cr £	Ref	Adjustments Dr £	Adjustments Cr £	Profit and loss Dr £	Profit and loss Cr £	Balance sheet Dr £	Balance sheet Cr £
Capital account		12,000							12,000
Stock	15,000			17,000 15,000 15000				17,000	
Sales		100,000					100,000		
Purchases	40,000					40,000			
Rent and rates	10,000				800	9,200		12 200 12,200	
Drawings	12 000			200					
Electricity	2,000			150		2,150			
Motor van cost	8,000							8,000	
Motor van provision for depreciation		4,000			500				4,500
Bank balance	4,500							4,500	
Trade debtors	20,000				1,000			19,000	
Trade creditors		21,000							21,000
Sundry expenses	500			50	200	350			
Wages and salaries	25,000					25,000			
Depreciation expenses				500		500			
Bad debt expense				1,000		1,000			
Accruals					200				200
Prepayments				800				800	
Stock (profit and loss)				15,000	17,000	17,000	15,000		
	137,000	137,000		34,700	34,700				

Capital account

Capital accounts is a balance sheet account with only one credit entry (in the trial balance column), therefore carry that figure across to the credit column of the balance sheet section.

Stock

The stock account is the balance sheet stock therefore the final figure will go into the balance sheet. There are three entries on the stock line:

Trial balance debit	£15,000
Debit adjustment	£17,000
Credit adjustment	£15,000

Treating a debit as a 'plus' and a credit as a 'minus', add across the various columns. If the result is a plus then the account balance is a debit, whilst a minus would mean a credit balance.

Cross casting this line:

15,000 + 17,000 – 15,000 = £17,000

So the final balance is a debit balance of £17,000 in the balance sheet column.

MAINTAINING FINANCIAL RECORDS AND PREPARING ACCOUNTS : UNIT 5

Sales and purchases

Single figures in the profit and loss account figures.

Rent and rates

This is a profit and loss account item with more than one figure. Following the same procedure as for the stock:

10,000 – 800 = £9,200

Continue to cross cast the remaining account lines, except for stock (profit and loss) to confirm that they follow the same procedure.

Stock (profit and loss)

Rather than cross casting this line, transfer each figure to the profit and loss account, as both will be shown separately. This is the exception to the rule.

ACTIVITY 6

Cross cast the extended trial balance you produced in Activity 5 for PG Trading, ensuring that each balance is correctly placed in either the balance sheet or profit and loss account columns. Then, cast the remaining columns which, at this stage, will not balance.

For a suggested answer, see the 'Answers' section at the end of the book.

6.4 FINDING THE PROFIT AND LOSS FOR THE PERIOD

Having completed the profit and loss and balance sheet columns, the final step of the extended trial balance is to find the profit or loss for the period.

The steps for doing this are as follows.

Step 1	Add up the credit column of the profit and loss section.
Step 2	Add up the debit column of the profit and loss section.
Step 3	Take the debit away from the credit.
	If there are more credits than debits, a profit has been made, whereas an excess of debits over credits means a loss has been incurred.
	This makes sense, because if the income (credit) is bigger than the expenses (debit) a profit is made.
Step 4	Insert the figure to make the two balances equal.
Step 5	If a profit has been made (more credits) a balancing figure will be required in the debit column. A loss (more debits) would go as a balancing figure on the credit side.
Step 6	Cast the two balance sheet columns.
Step 7	Insert the same profit (or loss) figure as a balancing figure in the balance sheet. However, this time the profit figure goes as a balancing figure on the credit side whereas a loss would have to sit on the debit side.

Note: Do not worry unduly about which side the profit figure or loss figure goes on. If the double entry has been maintained it will be obvious where the resultant figure lives.

CHAPTER 13 : THE EXTENDED TRIAL BALANCE

Example

Extended trial balance at 31 December 20X2

Account	Trial balance Dr £	Trial balance Cr £	Ref	Adjustments Dr £	Adjustments Cr £	Profit and loss Dr £	Profit and loss Cr £	Balance sheet Dr £	Balance sheet Cr £
Capital account		12,000							12,000
Stock	15,000			17,000	15,000			17,000	
Sales		100,000					100,000		
Purchases	40,000					40,000			
Rent and rates	10,000				800	9,200			
Drawings	12,000			200				12,200	
Electricity	2,000			150		2,150			
Motor van cost	8,000							8,000	
Motor van provision for depreciation		4,000			500				4,500
Bank balance	4,500							4,500	
Trade debtors	20,000				1,000			19,000	
Trade creditors		21,000							21,000
Sundry expenses	500			50	200	350			
Wages and salaries	25,000					25,000			
Depreciation expenses				500		500			
Bad debt expense				1,000		1,000			
Accruals					200				200
Prepayments				800				800	
Stock (profit and loss)				15,000	17,000	15,000	17,000		
	137,000	137,000		34,700	34,700	93,200	117,000	61,500	37,700
Profit						23,800			23,800
						117,000	117,000	61,500	61,500

ACTIVITY 7

Find the profit or loss for PG Trading by completing the extended trial balance.

For a suggested answer, see the 'Answers' section at the end of the book.

CONCLUSION

This chapter covers a very important aspect of accounting both from a practical and exam perspective. It has covered the translation of the trial balance, via adjustments, accruals and prepayments to a draft set of accounts from which the financial statements may be produced. Mastering the extended trial balance, so that the mechanics of the exercise are second nature, requires practice. The workbook exercises provide this practice. Finally, try to begin to understand what is happening with the extended trial balance when doing the exercises.

MAINTAINING FINANCIAL RECORDS AND PREPARING ACCOUNTS : **UNIT 5**

SELF TEST QUESTIONS

		Paragraph
1	What is an extended trial balance?	1
2	What account comes into use where the double entry has broken down and the trial balance will not balance?	2
3	Define period end adjustments.	3
4	How are accruals entered into the extended trial balance?	4
5	What accounting entry is needed to deal with closing stock?	5
6	How would you deduce the profit or loss for the period from the extended trial balance?	6

KEY TERMS

Extended trial balance - a worksheet which takes an initial trial balance, makes all the year end adjustments and then produces a draft balance sheet and profit and loss account.

Period end adjustments - accounting adjustments to the initial trial balance which are needed to prepare the period end financial accounts. They include items such as bad debt provisions and write offs, depreciation adjustments, disposals of fixed assets and correction of mis-postings.

Accrual - an item of expense that has been incurred during the accounting period but has not been paid at the period end

Prepayment - prepayment is an item of expense that has been paid during the current accounting period but will not be incurred until the next account period.

Closing stock - the goods purchased and not sold by the period end. Closing stock appears on the balance sheet as an asset.

Opening stock - goods sold but not purchased in the period, but in an earlier period. Opening stock appears in the profit an loss account.

Chapter 14

PRODUCING THE ACCOUNTS

This chapter covers the final stage of the accounts production process. The information in the Extended Trial Balance is extracted and presented in the approved format for sole traders.

CONTENTS

1 Introduction
2 Error and suspense account adjustments
3 Accounting adjustments
4 Technique for producing a set of financial accounts from a trial balance

KNOWLEDGE AND UNDERSTANDING

		Reference
1	The structure of the organisational accounts of sole traders and partnerships	Item 6
2	The need to present accounts in the correct form	Item 7
3	The form of final accounts of sole traders and partnerships	Item 8
4	How to draft year-end final accounts of sole traders and partnerships	Item 21
5	The function and form of accounts for income and expenditure	Item 26
6	The function and form of a profit and loss account and balance sheet for sole traders and partnerships	Item 28

PERFORMANCE CRITERIA

		Reference
1	Prepare final accounts of sole traders in proper form from the trial balance.	Item A in element 5.3

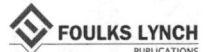

MAINTAINING FINANCIAL RECORDS AND PREPARING ACCOUNTS : UNIT 5

LEARNING OUTCOMES

At the end of this chapter you should be able to:

- make the required adjustments to the trial balance
- prepare a set of financial accounts from a trial balance

1 INTRODUCTION

The next two sections describe the two main groups of adjustments that are usually required at the year end. There is no new learning in this section; it is a consolidating exercise, summarising the knowledge gained from the preceding chapters. The main groups of adjustments are:

- error and suspense account adjustments
- accounting adjustments.

2 ERROR AND SUSPENSE ACCOUNT ADJUSTMENTS

2.1 INTRODUCTION

The chapter on the trial balance looked at the various types of errors that might occur in an accounting system. This section is a very brief reminder of those errors. Exam questions will often require adjustment to the trial balance for these types of errors with supporting journal entries.

Transactions posted to the wrong account

There are two types of error in this category:

- error of commission
- error of principle.

Both require the incorrect postings to be transferred from the incorrect account to the correct account via a journal.

A transaction has not been recorded at all

This error is known as an error of omission and its correction necessitates the posting of the complete double entry.

Compensating errors

Where two entirely separate errors have been made but both are incorrect by the same amount, then these are known as compensating errors.

Suspense account creating errors

These errors are known as original entry errors and result in the creation of a suspense account.

CHAPTER 14 : PRODUCING THE ACCOUNTS

They can occur from:

- an incorrect trial balance
- transposing figures when making one half of a double entry
- only posting one side of a double entry
- casting (addition) errors on an account.

The first error requires the re-drafting of the trial balance, whereas the last three require the setting up of a suspense account and clearing it via the method described in the chapter on the trial balance and suspense accounts.

3 ACCOUNTING ADJUSTMENTS

3.1 STOCK

The stock figure shown in the trial balance is last year's closing stock which forms this year's opening stock. It will be a debit balance because it was shown as a current asset in last year's balance sheet. The figure has remained unaltered during the year as all stock movements are recorded as sales (at selling price) and purchases (at cost). It is only at the year end that the stock adjustment is made.

In practice, the stock is counted and valued before the adjustment can be made. In a question the notes to the trial balance will state what the current year's closing stock is.

To deal with this entry:

Step 1 Set up the two accounts specified in the chapter on stock.

- stock - profit and loss account
- stock - balance sheet

Step 2 Put the stock figure per the trial balance on the debit side of the stock - balance sheet account. This will become the opening stock in the profit and loss account, so transfer it to the stock-profit and loss account.

Dr   Stock - profit and loss

Cr   Stock - balance sheet

with opening stock.

Step 3 Clear the opening stock in the stock - profit and loss account to P&L.

Step 4 Record the year's closing stock.

Dr   Stock - balance sheet

Cr   Stock - profit and loss

with closing stock.

Step 5 Clear the closing stock in the stock - profit and loss account to P&L.

MAINTAINING FINANCIAL RECORDS AND PREPARING ACCOUNTS : UNIT 5

3.2 FIXED ASSET ADJUSTMENTS - DEPRECIATION AND DISPOSALS

There is usually a requirement to work out the depreciation charge for the year from information given in the notes. In addition there may well be a disposal of a fixed asset to deal with as well.

Step 1   Set up the required T-accounts:

- fixed asset cost
- fixed asset provision for depreciation
- disposal account
- depreciation expense.

Step 2   Put in the balances from the trial balance.

The proceeds from the disposal may need searching for in the trial balance and there will not be any entries for depreciation expense.

Step 3   Work out the depreciation on the disposal and post the disposal entries (see chapter on fixed asset disposals).

Step 4   Work out the depreciation on the remaining fixed assets and post the entries to the T-accounts.

3.3 BAD DEBTS

A bad debt adjustment may have to be made to the trial balance. This may take the form of a bad debt write off and a change in the provision for doubtful debts.

Step 1   Set up the required T-accounts.

- debtors ledger control
- provision for doubtful debts
- bad debt expense.

Step 2   Put in the balances from the trial balance.

Step 3   Write off the bad debt.

Step 4   Work out the required doubtful debt provision carried down and account for any increase or decrease with a double entry from the provision for doubtful debts to the bad debt expense account.

3.4 ACCRUALS AND PREPAYMENTS

Most trial balance questions require some entries for accruals and prepayments. For each expense which is prepaid or requires an accrual, set up a T-account and follow the usual steps.

Step 1   Bring down any opening balance representing a prepayment (debit balance) or accrual (credit balance) from the previous year end.

Step 2   Record any cash payments during the year as a debit entry in the expense account.

CHAPTER 14 : PRODUCING THE ACCOUNTS

Step 3 Calculate the closing accrual or prepayment and carry down the balance.

Step 4 The balancing figure will be the charge to the profit and loss account.

Remember that sundry income accounts are the opposite way round from expense accounts. Income received in advance is a credit balance whilst income in arrears is a debit balance. Cash received during the year will be a credit entry in the income account.

3.5 SUMMARY

There appears to be a lot to think about with this type of question. However, the next section will outline a disciplined approach to the questions that will demonstrate some of these techniques. It will also show that the key to answering the question is to take each adjustment as a separate mini exercise and not to get overwhelmed with all the adjustments at once.

4 TECHNIQUE FOR PRODUCING A SET OF FINANCIAL ACCOUNTS FROM A TRIAL BALANCE

In exam questions, moving from a trial balance to the balance sheet and profit and loss account generally involves three steps:

Step 1 Working out the double entries for the adjustments.

Step 2 Working out the effect of these entries on the balances in the trial balance.

Step 3 Slotting the adjusted balances into the balance sheet and profit and loss account.

The following example illustrates how this is achieved.

Example

The trial balance of Jason and Co at 31 May 20X6 is as follows:

	£	£
Capital		15,258
Drawings	5,970	
Purchases	73,010	
Returns inwards	1,076	
Returns outwards		3,720
Discounts	1,870	965
Credit sales		96,520
Cash sales		30,296
Customs duty	11,760	
Carriage inwards	2,930	
Carriage outwards	1,762	
Salesman's commission	711	
Salesman's salary	3,970	
Office salaries	7,207	
Bank charges	980	
Loan interest	450	
Light and heat	2,653	
Sundry expenses	2,100	
Rent and rates	7,315	

MAINTAINING FINANCIAL RECORDS AND PREPARING ACCOUNTS : UNIT 5

Printing and postage	2,103	
Advertising	1,044	
Bad debts	1,791	
Provision for doubtful debts		437
Stock	7,650	
Debtors	10,760	
Creditors		7,411
Cash at bank	2,534	
Cash in hand	75	
New delivery van (less trade-in)	2,200	
Motor expenses	986	
Furniture and equipment:		
Cost	8,000	
Depreciation at 1 June 20X5		2,400
Old delivery van:		
Cost	2,100	
Depreciation at 1 June 20X5		1,000
Loan account at 9% (repayable in five years)		5,000
	163,007	163,007

You ascertain the following information:

(a) Closing stock has been valued for accounts purposes at £8,490.

(b) The motor van was sold on 1 June 20X5 and traded in against the cost of a new van. The trade-in price was £1,000 and the cost of the new van was £3,200.

(c) Depreciation on the straight line basis is to be provided at the following annual rates:

Motor vans 20%

Furniture and equipment 10%

(d) 5% of the closing debtors total is estimated to be doubtful.

Assessment tasks – prepare:

1 ledger accounts to record the transactions listed in (a) to (d) above

2 a trading and profit and loss account for the year ended 31 May 20X6

3 a balance sheet as at 31 May 20X6.

Solution

Step 1   Work through the adjustments.

T-accounts have been asked for: these will help you to work out the double entries and find the new balances on accounts.

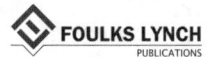

CHAPTER 14 : PRODUCING THE ACCOUNTS

(a) **Closing stock**

Stock account (profit and loss)

	£		£
Transfer from balance sheet	7,650	P&L a/c (opening stock)	7,650
P&L a/c (closing stock)	8,490	Accounting adjustment	8,490
	16,140		16,140

Stock account (balance sheet)

	£		£
Per trial balance	7,650	Transfer to stock (profit and loss)	7,650
Accounting adjustment	8,490	Balance c/d	8,490
	16,140		16,140
Balance b/d (closing stock)	8,490		

(b) **Van disposal**

Van cost account

	£		£
Old van per trial balance	2,100	Disposal account	2,100
New van - cash paid (per trial balance)	2,200	Balance c/d	3,200
Part exchange value (disposal proceeds)	1,000		
	5,300		5,300
Balance b/d	3,200		

Van provision for depreciation account

	£		£
Disposal account	1,000	Old van per trial balance	1,000

Old van disposal account

	£		£
Van cost account	2,100	Accumulated depreciation	1,000
		Part exchange value	1,000
		Loss on disposal (bal fig) P&L a/c	100
	2,100		2,100

Note that the part exchange value is given in the question as £1,000.

(c) **Depreciation**

Calculation

| Motor van (3,200 × 20%) | £640 |
| Furniture and equipment (8,000 × 10%) | £800 |

Double entry

Van provision for depreciation account

	£		£
Disposal account	1,000	Old van per trial balance	1,000
Balance c/d	640	Depreciation expense a/c (P&L)	640
	1,640		1,640
		Balance b/d	640

Furniture and equipment provision for depreciation account

	£		£
Balance c/d	3,200	Per trial balance b/d	2,400
		Depreciation expense a/c (P&L)	800
	3,200		3,200
		Balance b/d	3,200

(d) Bad debt provision

Calculation of provision

Closing debtors per trial balance	=	£10,760
5% of debtors (5% × £10,760)	=	£538
Increase in provision required	=	(538 – 437) £101

Double entry

Provision for doubtful debts account

	£		£
Required bal c/d (see working above)	538	Per trial balance	437
		P&L a/c (bal fig)	101
	538		538
		Balance b/d	538

Bad debt expense account

	£		£
Per trial balance	1,791	P&L a/c	1,892
Provision for doubtful debts	101		
	1,892		1,892

CHAPTER 14 : PRODUCING THE ACCOUNTS

Step 2 Produce the adjusted trial balance from the original trial balance and your journals and workings. It is important to keep neat workings to support your figures.

Adjusted trial balance

	£	£
Capital		15,258
Drawings	5,970	
Purchases	73,010	
Returns inwards	1,076	
Returns outwards		3,720
Discounts	1,870	965
Credit sales		96,520
Cash sales		30,296
Customs duty	11,760	
Carriage inwards	2,930	
Carriage outwards	1,762	
Salesman's commission	711	
Salesman's salary	3,970	
Office salaries	7,207	
Bank charges	980	
Loan interest	450	
Light and heat	2,653	
Sundry expenses	2,100	
Rent and rates	7,315	
Printing and postage	2,103	
Advertising	1,044	
Bad debts (1,791 + 101)	1,892	
Provision for doubtful debts (437 + 101)		538
Stock (balance sheet)	8,490	
Debtors	10,760	
Creditors		7,411
Cash at bank	2,534	
Cash in hand	75	
Motor expenses	986	
Furniture and equipment:		
Cost	8,000	
Depreciation at 1 June 20X5		3,200
Delivery van:		
Cost	3,200	
Depreciation at 1 June 20X5		640
Loan account at 9% (repayable in five years)		5,000
Stock (P&L)	7,650	8,490
Depreciation expense:		
Van	640	
Equipment	800	
Loss on sale of van	100	
	172,038	172,038

Step 3 Prepare the profit and loss account and balance sheet.

(a)

Trading and profit and loss account for the year ended 31 May 20X6

	£	£	£
Sales:			
Credit			96,520
Cash			30,296
			126,816
Less: sales returns			(1,076)
			125,740
Opening stock		7,650	
Purchases	73,010		
Less: purchase returns	(3,720)		
	69,290		
Carriage inwards	2,930		
Customs duty	11,760		
	83,980		
	91,630		
Closing stock	(8,490)		
Cost of sales			83,140
Gross profit			42,600
Discount received			965
			43,565
Less: Expenses			
Depreciation:			
Van		640	
Equipment		800	
Loss on disposal		100	
Bad debts		1,892	
Light and heat		2,653	
Rent and rates		7,315	
Discount allowed		1,870	
Carriage outwards		1,762	
Salesman's commission		711	
Salesman's salary		3,970	
Office salaries		7,207	
Bank charges		980	
Loan interest		450	
Sundry expenses		2,100	
Printing and postage		2,103	
Advertising		1,044	
Motor expenses		986	
			(36,583)
Net profit			6,982

CHAPTER 14 : PRODUCING THE ACCOUNTS

(b)

Balance sheet at 31 May 20X6

	Cost £	Acc dep'n £	£
Fixed assets:			
Motor van	3,200	(640)	2,560
Furniture and equipment	8,000	(3,200)	4,800
	11,200	(3,840)	7,360
Current assets:			
Stock		8,490	
Debtors	10,760		
Less: Provision for doubtful debts	(538)		
		10,222	
Cash at bank		2,534	
Cash in hand		75	
		21,321	
Less current liabilities:			
Trade creditors		(7,411)	
			13,910
			21,270
Less: Long-term liability			(5,000)
			16,270
Capital account:			
Balance at 1 June 20X5			15,258
Net profit for the year			6,982
			22,240
			(5,970)
			16,270

Notes on presentation

(a) The trading account includes all expenditure incurred in bringing the goods to their present location and condition. This includes:

   (i)   purchase cost including import duty

   (ii) carriage inwards and freight costs.

In contrast carriage outwards is treated as an expense of selling and is included with all the other expenses. Note that both carriage inwards and carriage outwards are debits (i.e. expenses).

Definition   Carriage inwards is the cost of bringing in raw materials from suppliers. Carriage outwards is the delivery charge incurred in supplying goods to customers.

(b) 'Returns' often causes difficulties. Returns inwards are the same as sales returns. Since sales are credits, sales returns are debits. For presentation purposes, sales returns are deducted from sales. In the same way purchase returns are deducted from purchases.

(c) The discounts are shown as one line in the trial balance with both a debit and a credit balance. Remember that expenses are debit balances while items of income are credit balances. Therefore the discount allowed is the debit balance and the discount received the credit balance.

(d) In examinations the answers should precede the workings, which should clearly be labelled as such. The idea behind this is that the examiner only wishes to look at the workings if errors have been made - hopefully he will not need to.

If the workings are numbered then a reference to the working can be made in the final accounts.

5 PREPARING AN EXTENDED TRIAL BALANCE AND ACCOUNTS

This section follows the accounts production process from the extraction of the TB through to the preparation of the P&L and the Balance Sheet. Work through the Guidance and the Solution carefully and then attempt the Activity.

5.1 EXAMPLE - EXTENDED TRIAL BALANCE AND FINAL ACCOUNTS - JILL JAMBO

Jill Jambo is a sole trader running a business making and selling traditional jewellery both locally and overseas. She has just finished her second year of trade, and the trial balance for this year is noted below. Her year-end is 30 June 20X8.

Jill Jambo: Trial balance for the year ending 30 June 20X8

	Dr	Cr
Sales		685,000
Stock 1 July 20X7	43,250	
Purchases	327,500	
Fixed assets at cost		
Equipment	97,600	
Motor vehicles	43,400	
Fixed assets: Provision for depreciation: 1 July 20X7		
Equipment		14,280
Motor vehicles		13,500
Rent	71,898	
Salaries and wages	130,000	
Carriage inwards	3,456	
Carriage outwards	10,000	
Postage and stationery	11,892	
Trade debtors	65,200	
Trade creditors		28,478
Insurance	9,312	
Bad debts written off during the year	4,825	
Petty cash	1,190	
Sundry expenditure	28,017	
Capital account as at 1 July 20X7		100,000
Drawings	134,601	
10% Loan repayable in 20Y6		200,000
Loan interest paid	15,000	
Bank Balance	44,117	
	1,041,258	1,041,258

CHAPTER 14 : PRODUCING THE ACCOUNTS

Notes

(a) Stock was counted on 30 June 20X8 and valued at £32,900.

(b) Equipment is depreciated at 10% per annum on a straight line basis.

(c) Motor vehicles are depreciated at 25% pa on a reducing balance basis.

(d) Although only £15,000 interest has been paid (as shown on the Trial Balance), a full year's interest at 10% should be charged in the accounts.

(e) Insurance includes £3,504 paid on certain items covering the year to 30 November 20X8.

(f) The rent for the year was £15,000 per quarter. However, the landlord was accidentally over paid just before the year end.

(g) On 15 June 20X8 Jill paid a £900 electricity bill for the quarter to 30 April 20X8 and a £456 water bill for the quarter ending 31 May 20X8. These expenses are included in sundry expenditure. Jill has not paid or accounted for any electricity or water consumed since then.

Tasks

(a) Prepare an extended trial balance for Jill Jambo for the year-ending 30 June 20X8.

(b) Prepare a Profit and Loss Account, Balance Sheet and Capital Account for Jill Jambo for the year ending 30 June 20X8 in a format suitable for presentation to the proprietor, bank manager and other interested parties.

Use the formats provided for you.

Guidance

1 Copy the balances from the trial-balance given to you in the question onto the extended-trial-balance work-sheet supplied overleaf. Make sure that you have extracted the numbers correctly. This can be done by adding up the columns and making sure that they still balance.

2 Work through the information in the **Notes** methodically, noting any adjustments required in the appropriate column of the ETB work sheet.

(a) *Stock was counted on 30 June 20X8 and valued at £32,900.*

This adjustment will normally be shown in the adjustment columns of the ETB. Remember that the debit (asset) will be taken to the balance sheet and that the credit reduces cost of sales in the profit and loss account.

(b) *Equipment is depreciated at 10% per annum on a straight line basis.*

Calculate the charge and then enter it onto the ETB.

The charge will be a debit in the adjustments column and will be taken to the P&L. The work sheet has already allocated a line for this charge.

The credit will increase the provision in the balance sheet. The TB already shows the brought forward balance. This year's credit will be entered into the adjustments column of the TB on the same line as the brought forward balance.

(c) *Motor vehicles are depreciated at 25% pa on a reducing balance basis.*

As above. Because this is to be calculated on the reducing balance basis make sure that you work out the brought forward net book value before calculating the charge.

MAINTAINING FINANCIAL RECORDS AND PREPARING ACCOUNTS : UNIT 5

(d) *Although only £15,000 interest has been paid (as recorded in the N/L and on the TB), a full year's interest at 10% should be charged in the accounts.*

An accrual is probably needed here. Calculate the annual charge and compare this to what has been recorded in the trial balance. If the recorded amount is less than the full annual charge then the difference must be accrued for.

The ETB records accrued charges to the P&L on a line by line basis. In this case the accrual will be entered into the "accruals" column on the loan interest line, increasing the charge taken to the P&L.

The balance sheet entry will be dealt with later. See Guidance 4.

(e) *Insurance includes £3,504 paid on certain items covering the year to 30 November 20X8.*

Insurance is normally paid in advance, giving rise to prepayments at the year-end.

In this case work out how much of the £3,504 mentioned relates to the period after the year-end (i.e. July through to November).

The ETB records prepayments on a line by line basis against the relevant P&L charge. In this case the prepayment will be entered into the "prepayments" column on the insurance line, reducing the charge taken to the P&L.

The balance sheet entry will be dealt with later. See Guidance 5.

(f) *The rent for the year was £15,000 per quarter. However, the landlord was accidentally over paid just before the year end.*

This will also create a prepayment. Work out the correct annual charge and then put through a prepayment to counteract the overpayment.

(g) *On 15 June 20X8 Jill paid a £900 electricity bill for the quarter to 30 April 20X8 and a £456 water bill for the quarter ending 31 May 20X8. These expenses are included in sundry expenditure. Jill has not paid or accounted for any electricity or water consumed since then.*

These are both accruals which will be dealt with in the normal way. However, the amount accrued for will have to be estimated on the basis of past consumption.

The electricity bill is £900 per quarter, and there were two months between the date of the last bill and the year-end. Therefore the business has probably consumed about £600 since the last invoice and this will have to be accrued for.

The water bill is £456 per quarter. One month elapsed between the last bill and the year-end and so an accrual of £152 will be needed (£456 / 3 months).

The total accrual for these two items will be £752 which will be included in sundry expenditure.

3 Add up the adjustment columns. The debit and credit columns should be equal. If they aren't make sure that you have entered the adjustments on the correct sides and for the correct amounts.

4 Add up the accruals column. The total will be taken to the credit side of the balance sheet. (The charge will be taken to the P&L on a line by line basis.)

5 Add up the prepayments column. The total will be taken to the debit side of the balance sheet. (The credit entry will be taken to the P&L on a line by line basis.)

CHAPTER 14 : PRODUCING THE ACCOUNTS

6 Extend" the trial balance by adding the lines across and entering the totals into the correct columns in the "Profit and Loss" and "Balance Sheet" sections of the ETB.

   (a) Remember that capital and drawings belong in the balance sheet.

7 Balance off the "Profit and Loss" columns.

   (a) If the balancing figure is on the debit side than the business has made a profit. (Sales and other credits exceed expenses.) The other half of this entry will be a credit to capital in the balance sheet.

   (b) If the balancing figure is on the credit side than the business has made a loss. (Expenses are greater than the sales and other credits.) The other half of this entry will be a debit to capital in the balance sheet.

   If the P&L and balance sheet columns do not balance each other out then you have made a mistake when extending the trial balance. Go back and check stage six.

   You should have calculated a profit of £53,121.

8 Extract the figures from the profit and loss and balance sheet sections of the ETB and enter them into the financial statements using the formats provided.

Extended trial balance for Jill Jambo 30 June 20X8

	Trial balance		Adjustments		Accruals	Prepaid	Profit & loss		Balance sheet	
	Dr	Cr	Dr	Cr	Dr to P&L	Cr to P&L	Dr	Cr	Dr	Cr
	£	£	£	£	£	£	£	£	£	£
Sales										
Opening stock										
Purchases										
Equipment at cost										
Depreciation										
Vehicles at cost										
Depreciation										
Rent										
Salaries and wages										
Carriage inwards										
Carriage outwards										
Postage and stationery										
Trade debtors										
Trade creditors										
Insurance										
Bad debts written off										
Petty cash										
Sundry expenditure										
Opening Capital										
Drawings										
10% Loan (20Y6)										
Loan interest paid										
Bank Balance										
Closing Stock (B/S, P&L)										
Dep'n charge: Equipment										
Motors										
Total adjustments etc										
					Cr. B/S	Dr. B/S				
Profit transferred to B/S										

Jill Jambo: Profit and loss account for the year ending 30 June 2008

	£	£
	£	£

Sales

Cost of sales
- Opening stock
- Add: purchases
- Add: carriage inwards
- Less: closing stock

Gross profit

Expenses
- Rent and rates
- Wages and salaries
- Carriage outwards
- Postage and stationery
- Insurance
- Bad debts
- Sundry expenses
- Depreciation: Equipment
- Motors

Operating profit
Interest payable

PROFIT FOR THE YEAR

Jill Jambo: Balance sheet as at 30 June 2008

	Cost £	Depreciation £	NBV £

Fixed assets
- Equipment
- Motor vehicles

Current assets
- Stocks
- Trade debtors
- Prepayments
- Bank and cash

Current liabilities
- Trade creditors
- Accruals

Net current assets

CHAPTER 14 : PRODUCING THE ACCOUNTS

Total assets less current liabilities
10% Loan repayable 2026
NET ASSETS

CAPITAL
    Opening capital
    Add: profit for the year
    Less: drawings
    Closing capital

5.2 SOLUTIONS

Jill Jambo: Profit and loss account for the year ending 30 June 20X8

	£	£
Sales		**685,000**
Cost of sales		
Opening stock	43,250	
Add: purchases	327,500	
Add: carriage inwards	3,456	
Less: closing stock	(32,900)	
		(341,306)
Gross profit		**343,694**
Expenses		
Rent and rates	60,000	
Wages and salaries	130,000	
Carriage outwards	10,000	
Postage and stationery	11,892	
Insurance	7,852	
Bad debts	4,825	
Sundry expenses	28,769	
Depreciation: Equipment	9,760	
Motors	7,475	
		270,573
Operating profit		**73,121**
Interest payable		(20,000)
PROFIT FOR THE YEAR		**53,121**

Jill Jambo : Balance sheet as at 30 June 20X8

	Cost £	Depreciation £	NBV £
Fixed assets			
Equipment	97,600	24,040	73,560
Motor vehicles	(43,400)	(20,975)	(22,425)
	141,000	45,015	95,985
Current assets			
Stocks		32,900	
Trade debtors		65,200	

Prepayments	13,358	
Bank and cash (£44,117 + £1,190)	45,307	
	156,765	
Current liabilities		
Trade creditors	28,478	
Accruals	5,752	
	34,230	
Net current assets		**122,535**
Total assets less current liabilities		**218,520**
10% loan repayable 20Y6		(200,000)
NET ASSETS		**£18,520**
CAPITAL		
Opening capital		100,000
Add: profit for the year		53,121
Less: drawings		(134,601)
Closing capital		**£18,520**

CHAPTER 14 : PRODUCING THE ACCOUNTS

Jill Jambo trial balance for Jill Jambo 30 June 20X8

	Trial balance Dr £	Trial balance Cr £	Adjustments Dr £	Adjustments Cr £	Accruals Dr to P&L £	Prepaid Cr to P&L £	Profit and Loss Dr £	Profit and Loss Cr £	Balance sheet Dr £	Balance sheet Cr £
Sales		685,000						685,000		
Opening stock	43,250						43,250			
Purchases	327,500						327,500			
Equipment at cost	97,600								97,600	24040
Depreciation		14,280		b 9,760						
Vehicles at cost	43,400								43425	20915
Depreciation		13,500		c 7,475						
Rent	71,898					f 11,898	60,000			
Salaries and wages	130,000						130,000			
Carriage inwards	3,456						3,456			
Carriage outwards	10,000						10,000			
Postage and stationery	11,892						11,892			
Trade debtors	65,200								65,200	
Trade creditors		28,478								28,478
Insurance	9,312					e 1,460	7,852			
Bad debts written off	4,825						4,825			
Petty cash	1,190								1,190	
Sundry expenditure	28,017				g 752		28,769			
Opening capital		100,000								100,000
Drawings	134,601								134,601	
10% Loan (20Y6)		200,000								200,000
Loan interest paid	15,000				d 5,000		20,000			
Bank balance	44,117								44,117	
	1,041,258									
Closing stock (B/S, P&L)			a 32,900	a 32,900				32,900	32,900	
Dep'n charge:										
Equipment			b 9,760				9,760			
Motors			c 7,475				7,475			
Total adjustments etc			50,135	50,135	5,752	13,358	64,779		13,358	5,752
					Cr. B/S	Dr. B/S			432,366	379,245
							53,121			53,121
							717,900	717,900	432,366	432,366

FOULKS LYNCH PUBLICATIONS

193

ACTIVITY 1

The activity below practices all the financial accounting skills that you have leared so far.

Sally Sana owns and manages a panel beating business in Gabs West. She has traded successfully for a number of years and the Trial Balance for the Year Ending 30 November 20X9 is set out below:

Sally Sana
Trial balance for the year ending 30 November 20X9

	Dr £	Cr £
Sales		756,293
Opening stock	21,645	
Purchases	285,365	
Equipment at cost	157,954	
Depreciation		45,487
Motor vehicles at cost	45,999	
Depreciation		32,876
Rent	8,000	
Salaries and wages	163,996	
Motor expenses	35,947	
Certification costs	7,354	
Training	14,987	
Trade debtors	2,253	
Trade creditors		32,756
Insurance	14,298	
Bad debts written off	132	
Petty cash	5,750	
Sundry expenditure	49,310	
Opening capital account		250,000
Drawings	254,999	
15% loan repayable in 20Y9		100,000
Loan interest paid	3,500	
Bank balance	145,923	
	1,217,412	1,217,412

Notes

(a) Stock was counted on 30 November 20X9 and valued at £24,680.

(b) Equipment is depreciated at 15% per annum on a straight line basis.

(c) Motor vehicles are depreciated at 33% pa on a reducing balance basis.

(d) Although only £3,500 interest has been paid (as shown on the Trial Balance), a full year's interest should be charged in the accounts.

(e) Insurance includes £6,432 paid on certain items covering the year to 28 February 20Y0.

(f) The rent for the year was £18,000 per quarter. However, owing to a dispute the Landlord has not been paid for many months. Eventually the rent will have to be paid.

(g) On 15 November Sally paid out £28,000 on an advertising campaign which will commence on New Year's Day to cash in on any seasonal smashes mayhem on the roads. It has been included within sundry expenditure.

CHAPTER 14 : PRODUCING THE ACCOUNTS

Tasks

Prepare a Profit and Loss Account, Balance Sheet and Capital Account for Sally Sana for the year-ending 30 November 20X9 in a format suitable for presentation to the proprietor, bank manager and other interested parties.

This activity covers performance criterion A in element 5.3.

For a suggested answer, see the 'Answers', section at the end of the book.

CONCLUSION

This chapter on producing accounts is the final step in learning how an accounting system works. It is one step further on than basic bookkeeping.

From a given trial balance, a series of adjustments are required and, following those adjustments, the production of a profit and loss account and a balance sheet is then possible.

Questions set in this area use all the learning in the previous chapters and thus it is important that the principles covered in those chapters are fully understood.

SELF TEST QUESTIONS

		Paragraph
1	What is an error of omission?	2.3
2	How do you deal with closing stock in the trial balance?	3.1
3	Set out the trial balance entries for the bad debt adjustment.	3.3
4	Define carriage inwards.	4

KEY TERMS

Error of omission - a transaction has not been recorded at all and its correction necessitates the posting of the complete double entry.

Compensating errors - two entirely separate errors have been made but both are incorrect by the same amount.

Suspense account creating errors - these errors are known as original entry errors and result in the creation of a suspense account.

Chapter 15

PARTNERSHIP ACCOUNTS

This chapter covers the preparation of partnership accounts. The basic profit and loss account and balance sheet are the same as for a sole trader. The differences are in the ownership interests, where profits have to be shared and arrangements made for the retirement and admission of partners.

CONTENTS

1 Partnerships – basic principles

2 Profit appropriation

3 Partnership financial statements

4 Partnership changes

5 Retirement

6 Admission of partner

KNOWLEDGE AND UNDERSTANDING

		Reference
1	Legal requirements relating to the division of profits between partners	Item 4
2	The structure of the organisational accounts of sole traders and partnerships	Item 6
3	The form of final accounts of sole traders and partnerships	Item 8
4	How to draft year-end final accounts of sole traders and partnerships	Item 21
5	The function and form of a profit and loss account and balance sheet for sole traders and partnerships	Item 28

PERFORMANCE CRITERIA

		Reference
1	Prepare final accounts of partnership in proper form in compliance with the partnership agreement, from the trial balance.	Item B in element 5.3

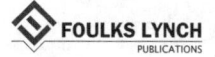

CHAPTER 15 : PARTNERSHIP ACCOUNTS

2   Observe the organisation's policies, regulations, procedures and timescales in relation to preparing final accounts of sole traders and partnerships   Item C in element 5.3

LEARNING OUTCOMES

At the end of this chapter you should know the following topics.

- Basic principles of partnership
- Capital accounts and current accounts
- Drafting partnership accounts
- Admission of a new partner
- Retirement of an existing partner

1   PARTNERSHIPS - BASIC PRINCIPLES

1.1   INTRODUCTION

Definition   A partnership is a natural progression from a sole trader, the sole proprietor taking in one or more partners (co-proprietors) in common with a view to profit. A partnership is not a corporate entity, but a collection of individuals jointly carrying on business.

Although partnerships are covered by statutory rules, mainly by the Partnership Act 1890, these are often varied by agreement between the partners. Since no limitation of the liability of the partners is (usually) involved, there is no need for the detailed statutory rules to protect creditors typical of the Companies Act. Therefore, those matters which the partners agree between them provide the legal structure within which the partners operate.

1.2   THE ADVANTAGES AND DISADVANTAGES OF A PARTNERSHIP

Comparing a partnership to sole trading, the advantages of operating as a partnership are as follows.

(a)   Business risks are spread among more than one person.

(b)   Individual partners can develop special skills upon which the other partners can rely rather than being a jack of all trades.

(c)   Certain partners may be able to draw upon larger capital resources to set up the partnership or expand the partnership.

The disadvantages are:

(a)   There may be disputes between partners on such matters as the direction the business is taking or how much money individual partners are taking out of the business. Some partners may feel they are contributing more time and effort to the partnership than others and not being sufficiently financially rewarded as a result.

(b)   A partner is 'jointly and severally liable' for his partners. This means that if one partner is being sued in relation to the business of the partnership, the other partners share in the responsibility.

1.3 PARTNERSHIP AGREEMENT

Definition A partnership agreement, which need not necessarily be in written form, will govern the relationships between the partners.

Important matters to be covered include:

(a) name of firm, the type of business, and duration

(b) capital to be introduced by partners

(c) distribution of profits between partners

(d) drawings by partners

(e) arrangements for dissolution, or on the death or retirement of partners

(f) settling of disputes

(g) preparation and audit of accounts.

The division of profit stated in the partnership agreement may be quite complex in order to reflect the expected differing efforts and contributions of the partners. For example, some or all of the partners may be entitled to a salary to reflect the differing management involvement in the business. Interest on capital may be provided to reflect the differing amounts of capital contributed. The profit shares may differ to reflect seniority or greater skills.

It is important to appreciate, however, that all of the above examples are means of dividing the profits of the partnership and are not expenses of the business. A partnership salary is merely a device for calculating the division of profit; it is not a salary in the normal meaning of the term.

Conclusion A partnership is made up of a number of sole traders trading together normally with some agreement drawn up between them.

1.4 ACCOUNTING FOR PARTNERSHIPS

The accounting techniques developed for sole traders are generally applicable to partnerships, but there are certain important differences. These can be summarised as:

Item	Sole trader's books	Partnership's books
Capital introduced	Capital account	Partners' fixed capital accounts
Drawings and share of the profit	Capital account	Partners' current accounts
Division of profits	Inapplicable - one proprietor only	Appropriation account

Definition The appropriation account is an account is used to split the profit of the partnership amongst the individual partners.

1.5 CAPITAL ACCOUNTS

At the commencement of the partnership an agreement will have to be reached as to the amount of capital to be introduced. This could be in the form of cash or other assets. Whatever the form of assets introduced and debited to asset accounts, it is normal to make the credit entry to fixed capital accounts. These are so called because they are not then used to record drawings or shares of profits but only major changes in the relations between partners. In particular, fixed capital accounts are used to deal with:

(a) capital introduced or withdrawn by new or retiring partners

(b) revaluation adjustments (see later in this study text).

The balances on fixed capital accounts do not necessarily bear any relation to the division of profits. However, to compensate partners who provide a larger share of the capital, it is common for notional interest on capital accounts to be paid to partners. This is dealt with through the appropriation account.

1.6 CURRENT ACCOUNTS

These are used to deal with the regular transactions between the partners and the firm i.e. matters other than those sufficiently fundamental to be dealt with through the capital accounts. Most commonly these are:

(a) share of profits, interest on capital and partners' salaries usually computed annually

(b) monthly drawings against the annual share of profit.

Example

Nab and Crag commenced business in partnership on 1 January 20X6, contributing as fixed capital £5,000 and £10,000 cash respectively. All profits and losses are shared equally. The profit for the year ended 31 December 20X6 amounted to £10,000. Drawings for Nab and Crag amounted to £3,000 and £4,000 respectively.

You are required to prepare the capital and current accounts, appropriation account and balance sheet extracts.

Solution

Partners' capital accounts

	Nab £	Crag £		Nab £	Crag £
			20X6		
			1 Jan Cash	5,000	10,000

Appropriation account

	£		£
20X6		20X6	
31 Dec Share of profit - current account		31 Dec Net profit b/d	10,000
Nab	5,000		
Crag	5,000		
	10,000		10,000

Partners' current accounts

		Nab £	Crag £			Nab £	Crag £
20X6				20X6			
1 Dec	Drawings	3,000	4,000	31 Dec Share of profits	5,000	5,000
	Balance c/d	2,000	1,000				
		5,000	5,000			5,000	5,000
				20X7			
				1 Jan	Balance b/d	2,000	1,000

Note: The above accounts are presented in a columnar format. This is quite common in a partnership set of books as each partner will have similar transactions during the year. A columnar format allows two (or more) separate accounts to be shown using the same narrative. It is important to remember though that each partner's account is separate from the other partner(s).

Balance sheet at 31 December 20X6 (extract)

	Capital accounts £	Current accounts £	Total £
Partners' accounts:			
Nab	5,000	2,000	7,000
Crag	10,000	1,000	11,000
	15,000	3,000	18,000

Note that the current account balances of £2,000 and £1,000 will be credited in the following year with profit shares and debited with drawings.

One of the main differences between the capital section of the balance sheet of a sole trader and a partnership is that the partnership balance sheet will often only give the closing balances whereas the sole trader's movements in capital are shown. The main reason for the difference is simply one of space. Movements in the capital and current accounts for a few partners cannot be easily accommodated on the face of the balance sheet.

Example

The information is the same as in the previous example, except that Nab's drawings are £5,300. Rewrite the partners' current accounts.

Solution

Partners' current accounts

		Nab £	Crag £			Nab £	Crag £
20X6				20X6			
	Drawings	5,300	4,000		Share of profits	5,000	5,000
31 Dec	Balance c/d		1,000	31 Dec	Balance c/d	300	
		5,300	5,000			5,300	5,000
20X7				20X7			
1 Jan	Balance b/d	300		1 Jan	Balance b/d		1,000

Note that Nab's current account is overdrawn. How do we present this in the balance sheet?

Balance sheet at 31 December 20X6 (extract)

	Capital accounts £	Current accounts £	Total £
Partners' accounts:			
Nab	5,000	(300)	4,700
Crag	10,000	1,000	11,000
	15,000	700	15,700

Conclusion Partners' drawings and share of the annual profit are recorded in their current accounts. Their capital accounts are used to record fixed capital introduced.

ACTIVITY 1

Tom, Dick and Harry trade in partnership. The balances on their current accounts at the start of the year were as follows:

Tom	Dick	Harry	Total
£17,000 Cr	£9,000 Cr	£7,300 Cr	£33,300 Cr

During the year their business made a profit of £99,000, which is to be shared equally.

Their drawings during the year were as follows:

Tom	Dick	Harry	Total
£45,000	£22,000	£18,000	£85,000

Task

Prepare the partnership current accounts for the year.

This activity covers performance criterion B in element 5.3.

For a suggested answer, see the 'Answers' section at the end of the book.

2 PROFIT APPROPRIATION

2.1 APPROPRIATION ACCOUNT

Definition The appropriation account is a ledger account dealing with the allocation of net profit between the partners.

In practice it is often included as the final part of the trading and profit and loss account.

An important point is that all allocations of profit to partners in their capacity as partners, and during the time they actually are partners, are made through the appropriation account. This applies even though such allocations may be described as partners' salaries, interest on capital or a share of profits.

Example

Pike and Scar are in partnership and have the following profit-sharing arrangements:

(a) interest on capital is to be provided at a rate of 8% pa

(b) Pike and Scar are to receive salaries of £6,000 and £8,000 pa respectively

(c) the balance of profit or loss is to be divided between Pike and Scar in the ratio 3 : 2.

Net profit for the year amounts to £20,000 and capital account balances are Pike £12,000 and Scar £9,000.

You are required to prepare:

(a) a statement showing the allocation of profit between the partners and

(b) relevant entries in the trading and profit and loss and appropriation account.

Solution

(a) **Allocation of net profit of £20,000**

	Pike £		Scar £		Total £
Interest on capital (8% × £12,000/9,000)	960		720		1,680
Salaries	6,000		8,000		14,000
					15,680
Balance of profits (£20,000 – £15,680) in ratio 3:2	2,592	(3/5)	1,728	(2/5)	4,320
Totals	9,552		10,448		20,000

Note that this is only a calculation of the allocation of profit and not part of the double-entry bookkeeping system, merely providing the figures for the appropriation account.

CHAPTER 15 : PARTNERSHIP ACCOUNTS

(b) **Extract from trading and profit and loss and appropriation account for the year ended**

	£	£
Sales		X
Cost of sales		X
Gross profit		X
Expenses		X
Net profit		20,000
Alloacted to:	9,552	
Pike	10,448	
Scar		20,000

The profit and loss appropriation account is closed by transferring the profit shares to the credit of the partners' current accounts. The double entry is therefore:

Debit	Credit	With
Profit and loss appropriation account	Pike's current account	£9,552
Profit and loss appropriation account	Scar's current account	£10,448

For the purposes of examinations (and in practice) parts (a) and (b) above can be amalgamated as follows:

Extract from trading and profit and loss and appropriation account for the year ended ...

	£
Sales	X
Cost of sales	X
Gross profit	X
Expenses	X
Net profit for year	20,000

Appropriation statement

	Pike £	Scar £	Total £
Interest on capital	960	720	1,680
Salaries	6,000	8,000	14,000
Balance of profits (£20,000 – £15,680) in ratio 3:2	2,592 (3/5)	1,728 (2/5)	4,320
Totals	9,552	10,448	20,000

The debits actually being made are as before (£9,552 and £10,448).

This treatment of the appropriation of profit in the appropriation statement is exactly the same as debiting an appropriation ledger account and crediting the partner's current accounts.

Conclusion The appropriation account is used to deal with the allocation of net profit between the partners.

MAINTAINING FINANCIAL RECORDS AND PREPARING ACCOUNTS : UNIT 5

ACTIVITY 2

Freddie and Roger have been trading in partnership for a number of years. This year their business made a net profit of £150,000.

The Trial Balance for their business was as follows:

	Dr £	Cr £
Net profit		150,000
Opening Capital		
Freddie		35,000
Roger		25,000
Opening Current Accounts balances		
Freddie		18,000
Roger		12,000
Drawings		
Freddie	67,500	
Roger	32,500	
Net assets	140,000	
	240,000	240,000

The partnership agreement was as follows:

Interest on Capital	9%	
Salaries	Freddie	£24,000 pa
	Roger	£36,000 pa
Profit sharing ratio	Freddie : Roger	3 : 2

Tasks

1   Share out the profits for the year according to the partnership agreement.
2   Write up the capital and current accounts for the year.
3   Draft a summary balance sheet as at the year-end.

This activity covers performance criterion B in element 5.3.

For a suggested answer, see the 'Answers' section at the end of the book.

2.2 PROFITS AND LOSSES

It is entirely possible for a partnership to make such a small profit that this will not cover all of the agreed appropriation such as interest on capital and salaries. Nevertheless these appropriations must be carried out first as they are part of the partnership agreement. Then the remaining loss is split amongst the partners in the profit-sharing ratio.

Example

The facts are the same as in Example 2.2 except that net profit is now only £3,680.

You are required to show the allocation of profit between the partners.

205

Solution

Allocation of net profit of £3,680

	Pike	Scar	Total
	£	£	£
Interest on capital	960	720	1,680
Salaries	6,000	8,000	14,000
Balance of loss (£3,680 – £15,680 = £12,000) to be shared in ratio 3:2	(7,200)	(4,800)	(12,000)
Totals	(240)	3,920	3,680

The profit share is always carried out last after all other appropriations e.g. interest, salaries, even if this means that it becomes a loss share.

The double entry in this case is

Debit	Credit	With
Profit and loss appropriation account	Scar's current account	£3,920
Pike's current account	Profit and loss appropriation account	£240

The relevant part of the profit and loss account would show:

	£	£
Net profit		3,680
Allocated to:		
Scar	3,920	
Pike	(240)	
Total		3,680

ACTIVITY 3

Brian and John have been trading in partnership for a number of years. Their Capital and Current Accounts are as follows:

	Capital	Current	Total
	£	£	£
Brian	100,000	12,000	112,000
John	140,000	32,000	172,000
	240,000	44,000	284,000

This year their business made a net profit of £97,000. The partnership agreement was as follows:

Interest on Capital   15%
Salaries   Brian   £44,000 pa
           John   £33,000 pa
Profit sharing ratio   Brian : John   5 : 3

Task

Share out the profits for the year according to the partnership agreement.

This activity covers performance criterion B in element 5.3.

For a suggested answer, see the 'Answers' section at the end of the book.

MAINTAINING FINANCIAL RECORDS AND PREPARING ACCOUNTS : UNIT 5

2.3 PARTNERS' SALARIES

One point which regularly causes difficulties is the partners' salaries. The key is to remember at the outset that a partner's salary is an appropriation of profit, whereas a salary paid to an employee is an expense.

Accordingly a salary to which a partner is entitled is included as part of the appropriation statement. Questions sometimes state that a partner has withdrawn his salary. In this case:

(a) include the salary in the appropriation statement as usual and

(b) quite separately treat the withdrawal of the salary as drawings.

Debit	Credit	With
Partners' current account	Bank	Amount withdrawn

2.4 GUARANTEED MINIMUM PROFIT SHARE

In certain partnership agreements a partner may be guaranteed a minimum share of profits. The appropriation of profit would proceed in the normal way. If the result is that the partner has less than this minimum, the deficit will be made good by the other partners (normally in profit-sharing ratio).

Example

Tessa, Laura and Jane are in partnership and have the following profit-sharing arrangements:

(a) Tessa and Laura are to receive salaries of £20,000 and £30,000 respectively

(b) the balance of profit or loss is to be divided Tessa 1, Laura 2, Jane 3

(c) Tessa is guaranteed a minimum profit share of £25,000.

The net profit for the year is £68,000.

You are required to show the appropriation account for the year.

Solution

Appropriation account

	Tessa £	Laura £	Jane £	Total
Net profit				68,000
Salaries	20,000	30,000	-	(50,000)
				18,000
Balance of profits in ratio 1 : 2 : 3	3,000	6,000	9,000	(18,000)
	23,000	36,000		
Adjustment		3,920	3,680	
Tessa 2000	(240)			
Laura 2/5 × 2,000 (800)		(800)		
Jane 3/5 × 2,000 (1200)				(1,200)
Totals	25,000	35,200	7,800	68,000

CHAPTER 15 : PARTNERSHIP ACCOUNTS

Conclusion The partner with the guaranteed minimum profit share must receive that amount. Any shortfall must be made up by the remaining partners.

2.5 THE PROVISIONS OF THE PARTNERSHIP ACT 1890

The essence of a partnership is the mutual agreement of the partners. The Partnership Act allows partners wide powers in determining their relationships with each other. Partnership agreements may be written or oral, although the former are preferable in order to prevent misunderstandings or disputes. However, in the absence of a specific agreement, Section 24 of the Act lays down the following rules:

1. Partners' capitals to be contributed equally.
2. No partner is entitled to interest on capital.
3. No partner is entitled to a salary.
4. Profits and losses, both of a capital and revenue nature are to be shared equally.
5. Any loan made to the business by a partner is to carry interest at the rate of 5% pa.

3 PARTNERSHIP FINANCIAL STATEMENTS

3.1 INTRODUCTION

The profit and loss account and balance sheet for a partnership are generally very similar to those for a sole trader. The differences are in the areas of appropriation and capital and current accounts dealt with earlier in this chapter.

Example

You are provided with the following information regarding the partnership of Dacre, Hutton and Tod.

(a) The trial balance at 31 December 20X6 is as follows:

	Dr £	Cr £
Sales		50,000
Stock at 1 January 20X6	6,000	
Purchases	29,250	
Carriage inwards	250	
Carriage outwards	400	
Creditors		4,000
Cash at bank	3,900	
Current accounts:		
Dacre		900
Hutton		750
Tod		1,350
Capital accounts:		
Dacre		4,000
Hutton		5,000
Tod		6,000

MAINTAINING FINANCIAL RECORDS AND PREPARING ACCOUNTS : UNIT 5

Drawings:		
Dacre	2,000	
Hutton	3,000	
Tod	5,000	
Sundry expenses		2,800
Debtors	13,000	
Shop fittings:		
Cost	8,000	
Accumulated depreciation		1,600
	73,600	73,600

(b) Closing stock is valued for accounts purposes at £5,500.

(c) Depreciation of £800 is to be provided on the shop fittings.

(d) The profit-sharing arrangements are as follows:

    (i) Interest on capital is to be provided at a rate of 10% per annum

    (ii) Dacre and Tod are to receive salaries of £3,000 and £4,000 per annum respectively

    (iii) the balance of profit or loss is to be divided between Dacre, Hutton and Tod in the ratio of 3 : 8 : 4.

You are required to prepare final accounts together with current accounts of the partners.

Solution

Step 1   Prepare the trading and profit and loss account as if it were for a sole trader.

Step 2   Calculate the total appropriation of profit to each partner using an appropriation statement

Dacre, Hutton and Tod
Trading and profit and loss account for the year ended 31 December 20X6

	£	£
Sales		50,000
Opening stock	6,000	
Purchases	29,250	
Carriage onwards	250	
	35,500	
Less: Closing stock	5,500	
		30,000
Gross profit		20,000
Sundry expenses	2,800	2,800
Carriage outwards	400	
Depreciation	800	
		4,000
Net profit		16,000
Allocated to:		
Dacre	4,900	
Hutton	4,500	
Tod	6,600	16,000

CHAPTER 15 : PARTNERSHIP ACCOUNTS

Profit appropriation

The new development is that, having calculated the profit for the period, it has to be appropriated between Dacre, Hutton and Tod. To calculate their respective shares an appropriation statement is used:

	Dacre £	Hutton £	Tod £	Total £
Interest on capital	400	500	600	1,500
Salaries	3,000	-	4,000	7,000
				18,000
Balance of profit (£16,000 – £8,500) in ratio 3 : 8 : 4	1,500	4,000	2,000	7,500
Total	4,900	4,500	6,600	16,000

This gives us the figures for the double entry:

    Dr   Profit and loss appropriation

    Cr   Partners' current accounts

Step 3   Prepare balance sheet as for a sole trader.

Balance sheet as at 31 December 20X6

	Cost £	Acc dep'n £	£
Fixed assets			
Shop fittings	8,000	2,400	5,600
Current assets			
Stock		5,500	
Debtors		13,000	
Cash		3,900	
		22,400	
Current liabilities			
Creditors		4,000	
Net current assets			18,400
			24,000

Step 4   Prepare partners' capital and current accounts and put balances onto the capital section of the balance sheet.

Partners' accounts

	Capital accounts £	Current accounts £	Total £
Dacre	4,000	3,800	7,800
Hutton	5,000	2,250	7,250
Tod	6,000	2,950	8,950
	15,000	9,000	24,000

Partners' current accounts

	Dacre £	Hutton £	Tod £			Dacre £	Hutton £	Tod £
20X6:				20X6:				
Drawings	2,000	3,000	5,000	1 Jan	Balance b/d	900	750	1,350
31 Dec Balance c/d	3,800	2,250	2,950		P&L app	4,900	4,500	6,600
	5,800	5,250	7,950			5,800	5,250	7,950
				20X7:				
				1 Jan	Balance b/d	3,800	2,250	2,950

A final point:

The majority of examination questions specify separate capital and current accounts. Occasionally you may be faced with a question specifying only one account for each partner. Such an account acts as a capital and current account combined.

To prepare a set of partnership accounts:

1 Draw up a proforma balance sheet and profit and loss account and enter figures as soon as you calculate them.

2 Work through any adjustments required.

3 Complete the profit and loss account and appropriate the profit as per the partnership agreement.

4 Open up partners' current accounts; enter the opening balances, appropriation of profit and drawings.

5 Find the new balances on the partners' current accounts.

6 Complete the balance sheet.

---

4 PARTNERSHIP CHANGES

4.1 INTRODUCTION

Changes in a partnership may occur for a variety of different reasons:

- a partner leaves, dies or retires from the partnership
- a new partner enters the partnership
- the existing partners change their profit-sharing arrangements
- the partnership is merged or sold
- the partnership is dissolved.

4.2 ACCOUNTING ASPECTS

From the accounting viewpoint there are two main aspects:

(a) dividing profits between old and new partners when the change occurs during the course of the financial period.

(b) the problem of valuing partnership assets, especially goodwill, at the time of the change.

4.3 DIVISION OF PROFITS

There will be many occasions when a partnership change does not take place at a convenient date (such as the accounting year end!).

For the purpose of dividing profits equitably between the partners concerned, it is necessary to apportion (or allocate) profits between those arising before the change, and those arising afterwards.

In most cases where the trade is not of a seasonal nature, sales occur at an even rate during the year. It will then be reasonable to apportion sales and profit on a time basis. Having apportioned the profit between the different parts of the year, it is then allocated between the partners according to their arrangements for sharing profits during those periods.

Example

Gavel and Kirk are in partnership, sharing profits in the ratio 3 : 2, after Gavel has received a salary of £2,000 per annum. The accounting year end of the partnership is 31 December. On 30 June 20X6 Blea is admitted to the partnership. The new profit-sharing arrangements provide for Gavel's salary of £2,000 per annum to be maintained, and for Blea to receive a salary of £3,000 per annum. The balance is to be shared between Gavel, Kirk and Blea in the ratio 2 : 2 : 1.

The net profit for the year to 31 December 20X6 is £22,000.

You are required to show the transfer to the partners' current accounts for the year ended 31 December 20X6.

Solution

Step 1 Apportion the profit to the pre and post change periods.

Assuming that the net profit of £22,000 accrues evenly over the year, it may be apportioned on a time basis as follows:

		£
1 January 20X6 to 30 June 20X6	$\frac{6}{12} \times £22,000$	11,000
1 July 20X6 to 31 December 20X6	$\frac{6}{12} \times £22,000$	11,000
		22,000

Step 2 Allocate each period's profit to the partners according to the profit share agreement in that period.

The net profit relating to each six month period is allocated according to the profit-sharing arrangements operating during that period.

MAINTAINING FINANCIAL RECORDS AND PREPARING ACCOUNTS : UNIT 5

Statement of allocation of profit

	Gavel £	Kirk £	Blea £	Total £
Six months to 30 June 20X6 ~~30 June~~ 30/6 20X6				
Salary:				
Gavel 6/12 × £2,000	1,000	-	-	1,000
Balance of profit (£11,000 – £1,000) in ratio 3 : 2	6,000	4,000	-	10,000
	7,000	4,000	-	11,000
Six months to ~~30 June 20X6~~ 31 Dec 20X6	Gavel £	Kirk £	Blea £	Total £
Salary:				
Gavel 6/12 × £2,000	1,000	-	-	1,000
Blea 6/12 × £3,000	-	-	1,500	1,500
Balance of profit (£11,000 – £2,500) in ration 2 :2 : 1	3,400	3,400	1,700 3,400	1,700 8500
	4,400	3,400	3,200	11,000
Totals – 12 months	11,400	7,400	3,200	22,000

Remember that the salaries are expressed at an annual rate! Interest on capital percentages are also expressed at an annual rate so a similar problem of time apportionment could apply elsewhere.

Partners' current accounts - Extract

Gavel £	Kirk £	Blea £		Gavel £	Kirk £	Blea £
			Profit and loss appropriation:			
			To 30 June	7,000	4,000	-
			To 31 Dec 20X6	4,400	3,400	3,200

4.4 APPORTIONMENT OF PROFIT

Unless otherwise instructed, it is acceptable to apportion profits (step 1) on a time basis. However, occasionally the question may specify some alternative basis.

Example

Assume that in the previous example the net profit of £22,000 was arrived at as follows

	£	£
Sales (£96,000 in six months to 30 June 20X6)		160,000
Cost of sales	118,000	
	~~42,000~~	
Gross profit		~~5,500~~ 42,000
Selling and distribution expenses	15,500	
Administrative expenses	~~2,000~~ 12500	
Financial expenses	22,000	
Net profit	Sub Total 20000	22,000

You are required to show the apportionment of profit between the two parts of the year. Assume that gross profit and selling expenses are to be apportioned on a turnover basis and all other items on a time basis. The allocation of profit between the partners is not required.

Solution

Step 1 Apportion profit to the pre and post change periods.

	£
Turnover:	
Six months to 30 June 20X6	96,000
Six months to 31 December 20X6	64,000
	160,000

The ratio of turnover is therefore 96 : 64 or 3 : 2.

	Six months to 30 June 20X6		Six months to 31 December 20X6		Total	
	£	£	£	£	£	£
Gross profit (3:2)	25,200		16,800		42,000	
Selling expenses (3:2)	3,300		2,200		5,500	
Administrative Expenses (1:1)	6,250		6,250		12,500	
Financial expenses (1:1)		1,000		1,000		2,000
		10,550		9,450		20,000
Net profit		14,650		7,350		22,000

The apportionment of net profit is therefore:

	£
Six months to 30 June 20X6	14,650
Six months to 31 December 20X6	7,350
	22,000

As can be seen, in a seasonal business, where sales fluctuate greatly from month to month, the apportionment of net profit on a time basis may give a misleading picture.

Conclusion Where there is a change of profit share arrangement part way through an accounting period then the profit must be apportioned to the pre and post change periods on an equitable basis.

5 RETIREMENT

5.1 RETIREMENT OF AN EXISTING PARTNER

Definition Retirement of a partner is where he leaves the partnership and therefore requires repayment of all amounts due to him from the partnership.

When a partner retires it is important first of all to ensure that his current account is credited with his share of profits and debited with his drawings up to the date of retirement. The balances on his current and capital accounts are then transferred to a loan account and becomes a liability of the business. The manner and timing of the payment of this liability are likely to be regulated by the partnership agreement. In practice the amount will probably be paid in instalments, with allowance for interest on the unpaid balance. Since the former partner is no longer a partner of the business, the interest cannot be regarded as an appropriation of profit and must be regarded as an expense of the partnership (in the same way as interest on a bank overdraft).

Example

Birk, How and Stile have been in partnership for many years. Birk retired from the partnership on 1 July. At 30 June the summarised balance sheet showed the following position:

		£
Sundry assets		27,296

Partners' accounts	Capital accounts	Current accounts	Total
	£	£	£
Birk	12,000	1,735	13,735
How	8,000	2,064	10,064
Stile	3,000	497	3,497
	23,000	4,296	27,296

Show the partnership balance sheet after Birk's retirement.

Solution

It is assumed that the current account balances reflect profit shares and drawings up to 30 June. At that date the balances on Birk's capital and current accounts should be transferred to a loan account and regarded as a liability of the partnership. The double entry for this is:

Dr   Birk's capital/current account
Cr   Loan account - Birk

A balance sheet at 1 July would then appear:

	£
Sundry assets	27,296
Less: Loan account – Bank	13,735
Net assets	13,561

Partners' accounts	Capital accounts	Current accounts	Total
	£	£	£
How	8,000	2,064	10,064
Stile	3,000	497	3,497
	11,000	2,561	13,561

The retiring partner is now a creditor of the partnership as he is no longer a partner. The loan account will eventually be paid off according to the partnership agreement.

ACTIVITY 4

Braine, Amis and Thomas are in partnership producing television plays. They share profits equally. On 30 June 20X8 Braine took early retirement, but as yet no entries have been made in the books to record this. The Balance Sheet, Capital Accounts and Current Accounts for the partnership as at 31 December 20X8 are noted below. These have been drawn up BEFORE accounting for the profit for the year to 31 December 20X8 for the retirement.

Balance sheet

	£
Fixed assets	476,000
Sundry current assets	123,000
Bank and cash	43,000
Sundry current liabilities	(87,000)
	555,000

	Capital £	Current £	Total £
Braine	225,000	33,000	258,000
Amis	100,000	7,000	107,000
Thomas	55,000	15,000	70,000
	380,000	55,000	435,000
Profit for the year			120,000
Total			555,000

The terms of the retirement are as follows:

(a) Braine will claim his share of profits up to his date of retirement. (This is standard procedure.)

(b) Braine will be paid £66,000 in cash. The Bank has agreed to any overdraft facility that might be required.

(c) The balance due to Braine will be transferred to a loan account.

Tasks

1 Prepare an appropriation statement for the year. Assume that all profits have accrued evenly over the year.

2 Prepare the Capital and Current Accounts for the year. They should reflect both the profit for the year and the retirement.

3 Prepare a Balance Sheet as at 31 December 20X8 immediately after the retirement.

This activity covers performance criterion B in element 5.3.

For a suggested answer, see the 'Answers' section at the end of the book.

6 ADMISSION OF A PARTNER

A new partner will bring in cash (or another asset) which will be credited to his capital account. His capital account will then be charged with the fair value of his share of the partnership assets (including goodwill). The procedure is similar as for retirements, and will be illustrated by the following example.

The new partner will get the benefit of the reputation of the existing partnership. This is known as goodwill. This goodwill is accounted for in one of two ways:

- Goodwill left in the balance sheet as an asset.
- Goodwill written off.

MAINTAINING FINANCIAL RECORDS AND PREPARING ACCOUNTS : UNIT 5

The double entry for these two situations is as follows:

Goodwill left in the balance sheet

Debit	B/S fixed assets	With the agreed value of the goodwill
Credit	**Old** partner's capital accounts in the **old** profit sharing ratio	With the agreed value of the goodwill

Goodwill written off

Credit	**Old** partner's capital accounts in the **old** profit sharing ratio	With the agreed value of the goodwill
Debit	**New** partner's capital accounts in the **new** profit sharing ratio	With the agreed value of the goodwill

Example - Big and large; introducing huge

Big and Large are trading in partnership. Details of the partnership as at 31 December 2000 are as follows:

		£	
Capital accounts	Big	50,000	Cr
	Large	40,000	Cr
Current accounts	Big	14,000	Dr
	Large	6,000	Cr
		82,000	
Balance sheet	Bank overdraft	17,000	Cr
	Sundry net assets	99,000	
		82,000	
Profit sharing ratio	Big:Large	6:5	

On 1 January 2001 Huge was invited to join the partnership.

He would introduce £30,000 cash as capital.

The new profit sharing ratio would be B:L:H, 4:4:2.

Goodwill will be valued at £44,000.

Tasks

1   Prepare the T accounts to reflect these changes.

2   Draft the balance sheet (including partners' interests) after the change.

This should be done:

(a) Assuming that goodwill will be maintained in the books of the new partnership, and

(b) Assuming that goodwill will be written off immediately.

Solution - Goodwill maintained in the books of the new partnership

Capital account

	BIG £	LARGE £	HUGE £	TOTAL £		BIG £	LARGE £	HUGE £	TOTAL £
					B/f	50,000	40,000	-	90,000
					Goodwill IN	24,000	20,000	-	44,000
C/d	74,000	60,000	30,000	164,000	Cash	-	-	30,000	30,000
	74,000	60,000	30,000	164,000		74,000	60,000	30,000	164,000

CHAPTER 15 : PARTNERSHIP ACCOUNTS

Balance sheet

	£
Goodwill	44,000
Cash (from memo a/c)	13,000
Sundry net assets	99,000
Net Assets	156,000

Financed by	Capital £	Current £	Total £
Big	74,000	(14,000)	60,000
Large	60,000	6,000	66,000
Huge	30,000	-	30,000
Total	164,000	(8,000)	156,000

In this question the current accounts are not affected by the changes.

Memorandum cash account

		B/f	17,000
Capital	30,000		
		C/d	13,000
	30,000		30,000

Solution - Goodwill NOT maintained in the books of the new partnership

Capital account

	BIG £	LARGE £	HUGE £	TOTAL £		BIG £	LARGE £	HUGE £	TOTAL £
					B/f	50,000	40,000	-	90,000
Goodwill OUT	17,600	17,600	8,800	44,000	Goodwill IN	24,000	20,000	-	44,000
					Cash	-	-	30,000	30,000
C/d	56,400	42,400	21,200	120,000					
	74,000	60,000	30,000	164,000		74,000	60,000	30,000	164,000

Current and Cash accounts are the same as before.

Balance Sheet

	£
Cash	13,000
Sundry net assets	99,000
Net assets	112,000

Financed by	Capital £	Current £	Total £
Big	56,400	(14,000)	42,400
Large	42,400	6,000	48,400
Huge	21,200	-	21,200
Total	120,000	(8,000)	112,000

MAINTAINING FINANCIAL RECORDS AND PREPARING ACCOUNTS : UNIT 5

ACTIVITY 5

Small and Little are trading in partnership. Details of the partnership as at 31 December 2000 are as follows:

		£	
Capital accounts	Small	25,000	Cr
	Little	15,000	Cr
Current accounts	Small	3,000	Cr
	Little	7,000	Cr
		50,000	
Balance sheet	Bank	12,000	
	Sundry net assets	38,000	
		50,000	

Profit sharing ratio   Small:Little   3:2

On 1 January 2001 Micro was invited to join the partnership.

- He would introduce £20,000 cash as capital.
- The new profit sharing ratio would be Small : Little : Micro, 4:3:2.
- Goodwill will be valued at £22,500.

Tasks

1   Prepare the T accounts to reflect these changes.

2   Draft the balance sheet (including partners' interests) after the change.

This should be done:

(a) Assuming that goodwill will be maintained in the books of the new partnership, and

(b) Assuming that goodwill will be written off immediately.

This activity covers performance criterion B in element 5.3.

For a suggested answer, see the 'Answers' section at the end of the book.

SELF TEST QUESTIONS

		Paragraph
1	What is a partnership?	1.1
2	What advantages does trading as a partnership have over sole trading?	1.2
3	What typical points might be covered in a partnership agreement?	1.3
4	What is recroded in partners' fixed capital accounts?	1.5
5	What is recorded in partners' current accounts?	1.6
6	What is the purpose of the appropriation account?	2.1
7	How is a partner's salary treated in partnership accounts?	2.3

KEY TERMS

Partnership - a natural progression from a sole trader, the sole proprietor taking in one or more partners (co-proprietors) in common with a view to profit. A partnership is not a corporate entity, but a collection of individuals jointly carrying on business.

Partnership agreement - which need not necessarily be in written form, will govern the relationships between the partners.

Appropriation account - a ledger account dealing with the allocation of net profit between the partners.

Capital accounts - record major changes in the relations between partners.

Partners' current accounts - record transactions between partners that do not go on the capital accounts. Most commonly these are share of profits, interest on capital, and partners' salaries, usually computed annually; and monthly drawings against the annual share of profit.

Retirement of a partner – the partner leaves the partnership and therefore requires repayment of all amounts due to him from the partnership.

Chapter 16

INCOMPLETE RECORDS: TECHNIQUES

This chapter explains how to calculate the profit or loss for the year when proper accounting records have not been kept, or when they have been destroyed.

CONTENTS

1. Introduction
2. Net asset approach
3. T account approach

KNOWLEDGE AND UNDERSTANDING

		Reference
1	The methods of restructuring accounts from incomplete evidence	Item 18

LEARNING OUTCOMES

At the end of this chapter you should be able to:

- recognise which incomplete record technique to use for a question
- prepare a schedule of movements in net assets to calculate profit
- use cost structures to work out gross profit percentages and mark-ups
- find missing information on:
  - bank accounts
  - cash accounts
  - debtors control accounts
  - creditors control accounts
- link the trading account with cost structures.

1 INTRODUCTION

There are two types of incomplete records situations that might be encountered.

The first is where there are absolutely no accounting records for the year. The approach to this type of situation is to use the business's net assets to work out the profit or loss via the accounting equation.

The second situation is where the business has not kept proper records and it is necessary to prepare the financial accounts from not much more than the bank statements.

These types of questions will test a candidate's accounting knowledge to the limit as they usually involve aspects of all the accounting learning to date.

2 NET ASSET APPROACH

2.1 REVISION OF THE NET ASSET PRINCIPLE

From the very first chapter the accounting equation was established:

Net assets = Capital + profit – drawings

After the profit and drawings are cleared to the owner's capital account, the equation becomes:

Net assets = Capital

After a further year of profitable trading the net assets will have increased as a profit has been made and further capital may have been introduced by the owner. Drawings, of course, will have reduced the net assets, if taken. This affects the accounting equation as follows:

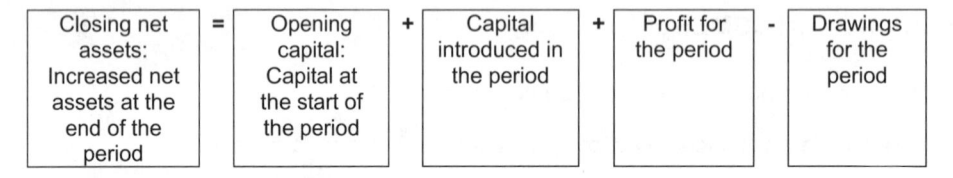

| Closing net assets: Increased net assets at the end of the period | = | Opening capital: Capital at the start of the period | + | Capital introduced in the period | + | Profit for the period | − | Drawings for the period |

This provides a method of finding profit in the absence of proper accounting records; if the amount of capital introduced, drawings and changes in net assets are known, then profit will be the balancing figure that completes the equation.

2.2 QUESTION TECHNIQUE

The way to approach this type of question is to produce the top half of two balance sheets, one for the end of the current year and one for the end of the previous year. This will show the net assets at the beginning and end of the year, from which the increase or decrease in net assets is found.

Find out if any capital has been introduced or drawings been taken out and insert all the figures into the following proforma:

CHAPTER 16 : INCOMPLETE RECORDS: TECHNIQUES

	£
Net assets at end of year	x
Less net assets at beginning of year	(x)
Increase/decrease in net assets	x
Less capital introduced in the year	(x)
Add drawings for the year	x
Profit/(loss) for the year	**x**

Problems that will be encountered may be:

- adjusting for a specific bad debt
- providing for a general doubtful debt provision
- calculating depreciation
- working out the net realisable value of some stock.

In each case the double entry would normally be to the balance sheet on one side and the profit and loss account on the other. With these type of 'net asset' incomplete records questions, only the balance sheet adjustment needs to be worried about.

Suppose the stock of £3,200 in the example below has a net realisable value of £2,900. Look at the effect on the profit calculation of this adjustment.

	Without stock write off £	With stock write off £
Fixed assets	800	800
Stock	3,200	2,900
Bank	14,000	14,000
Trade creditors	(3,200)	(3,200)
Net assets at end of 20X4	14,800	14,500
Net assets at beginning of 20X4	(12,000)	(12,000)
Increase in net assets	2,800	2,500
Less capital introduced	(1,000)	(1,000)
Add drawings	1,200	1,200
Profit	3,000	2,700

The profit figure has automatically been adjusted for the £300 stock write off. Any modification to net assets will automatically affect the profit or loss.

Example

The financial accounts of James Wine Merchants at 31 December 20X1 showed net assets of £41,500.

On the 29 December 20X2, a burst water pipe caused a flood destroying all the accounting records. However the following has been ascertained for 31 December 20X2:

The net book value of fixed assets at 31 December 20X1 was £15,000. During the year a new machine costing £3,000 was purchased. Depreciation of £4,000 for 20X2 is to be provided.

Unpaid debtors' invoices amounted to £12,300, including one debt of £200 which is to be written off.

Stocks of wine at cost were £25,000 but the net realisable value was £23,000.

The bank statements showed a balance of £15,000 with no outstanding cheques or lodgements.

Outstanding purchases invoices were £8,000.

There was a capital input of £5,000 and drawings of £14,000 during the year.

Find the profit for the year ending 31 December 20X2.

Step 1   Produce a balance sheet at the end of the year making all the adjustments.

	Year end balance sheet £
Fixed assets (15,000 + 3,000 – 4,000)	14,000
Debtors (12,300 – 200)	12,100
Stock (at net realisable value)	23,000
Bank	15,000
Trade creditors	(8,000)
Net assets at end of 20X2	56,100

Step 2   Produce a balance sheet at the end of the previous year.

In this case it is not necessary because the net assets at the end of 20X1 have already been calculated at £41,500.

Step 3   Find out if any capital has been introduced or money drawn out.

Capital introduced   £5,000

Drawings   £14,000

Step 4   Insert the figures into the profit calculation proforma.

	£
Net assets at end of year	56,100
Less net assets at beginning of year	(41,500)
Increase in net assets	14,600
Less capital introduced in the year	(5,000)
Add drawings for the year	14,000
Profit for the year	**23,600**

CHAPTER 16 : INCOMPLETE RECORDS: TECHNIQUES

ACTIVITY 1

On 1 January 20X5 Joan Updike started working as a freelance computer trainer and technician. She was not expecting her business to grow as rapidly as it did, and she kept on putting off installing any proper accounting systems.

You have been asked to calculate how much profit she has made in her first year of trade.

The following information is available and can be relied upon:

1. The business bank account shows transfers from Joan's private account, payments for capital items and for drawings. These can be summarised as follows:

Transfers from Joan's private account	£13,000
Purchase of computer hardware and software	£9,000
Drawings	£18,000

2. There has been no proper control over cash sales and purchases. However, you are confident that there are no cash purchases for capital items or cash drawings.

3. The computer hardware and software should have a three year-life.

4. At the year-end there was £37,247 in the business bank account. There were no unpresented cheques or outstanding lodgements.

5. Joan was owed £2,500 from one customer, and owed £157 to a supplier.

6. Sundry stock amounted to £54.

Tasks

(a) Prepare the closing balance sheet.

(b) Using the accounting equation, calculate Joan's net profit for the period. This can be done as part of the movement on capital.

This activity covers performance criterion A in element 5.3.

For a suggested answer, see the 'Answers' section at the end of the book.

3 T-ACCOUNT APPROACH

3.1 INTRODUCTION

Questions necessitating this approach are common in the examination because they test the understanding of all of the basic accounting principles and also the ability to work under pressure created by the time constraint of the question.

These questions are undoubtedly daunting because they appear to be a jumble of information, which the student must unravel and produce a profit and loss account and balance sheet.

Once the basic accounting skills required are mastered, the key to answering this type of question is to apply a set technique that will create a methodical approach to dealing with the information in the question, and thus will provide a satisfactory answer every time.

MAINTAINING FINANCIAL RECORDS AND PREPARING ACCOUNTS : UNIT 5

The following sections revise the most common basic accounting skills required in answering these questions and then show how they fit in to the technique needed to deal with this type of incomplete records problem.

3.2 COST STRUCTURES

(a) Gross profit percentage (margin)

In the trading account section of the profit and loss account the relationship between sales and gross profit is measured in terms of gross profit percentage.

Definition Gross profit percentage. Profit made per £100 of sales, expressed as a percentage.

For example, take the following trading account:

	£
Sales	100
Cost of sales	(80)
Gross profit	20

The business will make £20 of gross profit from sales of £100, therefore the gross profit percentage is 20%.

This figure can be worked out for any level of sales by dividing gross profit by sales and multiplying by 100. (The multiplication is to convert the figure to a percentage.)

So for the example above:

Gross profit percentage $= \dfrac{20}{100} \times 100 = 20\%$

(b) Mark up

When a business purchases stock for resale it will often add an amount on to the purchase price to get the selling price. For example, if goods are purchased for £100 and the selling price is £130, the mark up is £30.

Definition Mark-up. The amount of profit added to cost to get the selling price.

This figure is often expressed as a percentage of purchase price:

Mark-up on cost $= \dfrac{30}{100} \times 100 = 30\%$

(c) Establishing a cost structure

For any calculations involving gross profit margins or mark-ups it is imperative to work out a cost structure linking cost and selling price in % terms before any attempt is made at the calculation. The golden rule with cost structures is that whatever profit is based on is 100%.

For example, the cost structure for a gross margin of 20%:

	%
Cost	80
Add profit	20
Selling price	100

CHAPTER 16 : INCOMPLETE RECORDS: TECHNIQUES

A gross margin calculates profit as a percentage of sales, so profit is based on selling price. Therefore, selling price is 100%, profit is 20%, so cost must be the balancing figure of 80%.

In contrast, the cost structure for a mark-up of 30% on cost is:

	%
Cost	100
Add profit	30
Selling price	130

A mark-up is based on cost; it is the profit that is added on to cost and therefore cost is 100% this time.

The profit of 30% when added to cost gives a selling price of 130%.

Note: The cost structure is very important in calculating figures needed in incomplete records questions. To remember which figure is 100% in the cost structure learn these phrases:

- mark-up on cost
- gross margin on sales.

Example

(a) Jones applies a mark-up of 40% to his purchases. If his sales for the year are £150,000 what will be his expected gross profit?

Step 1 Establish the cost structure.

	%
Cost	100 (mark-up on cost)
Add profit	40
Sales	140

Step 2 Use the cost structure to find the profit from the sales figure given.

Sales = £150,000 (140%)

Profit = $\frac{40}{140} \times £150,000$

= £42,857

If you find the mathematics a little confusing, just look at the cost structure and you will see that we need to scale down the sales figure from 140% to 40%, so the appropriate fraction is $\frac{40}{140}$.

(b) Filbert has a consistent gross margin of 25%. What will his sales be to achieve a profit of £50,000?

Step 1   Establish the cost structure.

	%	
Cost	75	
Add profit	25	
Sales	100	(gross margin on sales)

Step 2   Use the cost structure to find sales from the profit figure.

Profit = 50,000 (25%)

Sales = $\dfrac{100}{25} \times £50{,}000$

= £200,000

This time we needed to scale up the profit figure from 25% to 100% to find the sales figure. The fraction required is $\dfrac{100}{25}$, giving us a larger figure than we started with.

ACTIVITY 2

A company sells two products, A and B. Last year, all product A's sales were at a gross margin of 30%. Purchases of product A totalled £200,000, and there were no opening or closing stocks.

All product B's sales were at a mark-up of 100%. Sales of product B totalled £300,000, and there were no opening or closing stocks.

You are required to prepare the company's trading account in total for last year.

For a suggested answer, see the 'Answers' section at the end of the book.

3.3 CASH AND BANK ACCOUNTS

The central part to an incomplete records type of question is a build up of the business's cash account (cash in hand) and bank account (cash at bank) from the information given in the question.

The use of these accounts is one of the techniques which enables the calculation of figures required in the balance sheet or profit and loss account. The technique involves the setting up of a cash account and a bank account and inserting all the entries given in the information in the question. Then, the accounts can be reviewed for missing figures, which may then be found as balancing figures on the accounts.

Recorded in the cash and bank accounts below are the typical entries that would be expected in a question. Revise the proformas and then read the associated notes.

Cash account

Balance b/d	X (note 4)	Cash expenses	X (note 2)
Cash receipts from customers	X (note 1)	Banking	X (note 3)
		Balance c/d	X (note 5)
	X		X

CHAPTER 16 : INCOMPLETE RECORDS: TECHNIQUES

Notes:

1   The main assumption that must be made in doing the bank and cash accounts is that all monies received by the business are recorded first in the cash account. This reflects the cash and cheques coming into the business being placed in a till or box before being banked. Therefore any cash from cash sales will be recorded under this heading along with any cheques received in respect of credit sales. The double entries to record these items are:

   Dr   Cash account
   Cr   Cash sales

   Dr   Cash account
   Cr   Debtors control account

2   The business will pay certain of its expenses in cash, for example wages or window cleaning. These expenses are entered on the credit side of the cash account, the other side of the double entry being a debit to the profit and loss account expenses section.

3   Having paid out cash expenses, the remaining money will be paid into the bank account, the double entry being:

   Dr   Bank account
   Cr   Cash account

4   The balance at the start of the year will be shown in the question unless the business began in the current year, in which case there will be no opening balance.

5   The closing balance may be given in the question in which case one of the other figures in the cash account will be a balancing figure which will have to be calculated, or it will have to be worked out from the other figures.

Bank account

Balance b/d	X (note 5)	Payment of expenses from bank	X (note 2)
Bankings from cash	X (note 1)	Payments to creditors	X (note 3)
		Drawings	X (note 4)
		Balance c/d	X (note 6)
	X		X

Notes:

1   This is the other side of the double entry in note 3 above in the cash account. You should always perform this complete double entry in the cash account and bank account.

2   Some expenses will be paid for specifically out of the bank account by cheque or standing order, for example salaries, rent or rates. These expenses are credited as normal to the bank account and debited to the relevant expense category in the profit and loss account.

3   Payments to creditors are usually made by cheque. The double entry is:

   Dr   Creditors control account
   Cr   Bank account

MAINTAINING FINANCIAL RECORDS AND PREPARING ACCOUNTS : UNIT 5

4   Drawings would be a typical figure where the examiner would require its calculation as a balancing figure on the bank account.

5   The balance at the start of the year will be shown in the question unless the business began in the current year, in which case there will be no opening entry.

6   The closing balance in the bank account may be given in the question, in which case one of the other figures in the bank account will be a balancing figure or it will have to be worked out from the other figures. The only potential complication with the closing balance in the bank is that the figure given in the question may be the balance per the bank statement. In this instance there will be some information in respect of unpresented cheques and outstanding lodgements enabling the calculation of the closing bank account balance by means of a bank reconciliation.

Example

The accounting books of Stevens and Sons have not been kept up to date. The bank and cash accounts need to be created from the following information.

The balances on the accounts from the previous year's financial accounts are:

Bank   £33,000
Cash   £2,000

During the year £40,000 was received from customers for sales. Cash expenses totalled £1,000 and £38,000 was paid into the bank.

Cheque payments for expenses were £20,000 for salaries and £5,000 for rent. Credit purchases paid for were £25,000.

The closing balance on the bank statement was £13,000 but there was a cheque not yet presented at the year end of £2,000.

Stevens regularly wrote cheques to himself for drawings, but could not remember how much a month.

Step 1   Set up a proforma cash account.

Cash account

	£		£
Balance b/d		Paid to bank	
Cash from customers		Cash expenses	
		Balance c/d	

Step 2   Set up a proforma bank account.

Bank account

	£		£
Balance b/d		Salaries	
Cash paid into bank		Rent	
		Purchases	
		Balance c/d	

CHAPTER 16 : INCOMPLETE RECORDS: TECHNIQUES

Step 3 Insert figures into the proformas from the question.

Note: At this point it is vital that all double entry is maintained. Apart from the opening and closing balances, every other figure has a double entry which should immediately be recorded in an appropriate place.

Cash account

	£		£
Balance b/d	2,000	Paid to bank	38,000
Cash from customers	40,000	Cash expenses	1,000
		Balance c/d	

Bank account

	£		£
Balance b/d	33,000	Salaries	20,000
Cash paid into bank	38,000		
		Rent	5,000
		Purchases	25,000
		Balance c/d (see note below)	11,000

Note: the bank statement showed a figure of £13,000 but there was still a cheque of £2,000 to pass through the account. Therefore the 'real' bank balance is only £11,000.

Step 4 Review the accounts for missing figures.

Note: At this point some assumptions have to be made. The note on drawings indicates that all drawings have been made via cheque and therefore come from the bank account. Any imbalance on the bank account must therefore be assumed to have come from drawings.

In the absence of any further information, it must be assumed that the balance remaining in the cash account is cash on hand at the year end.

Cash account

	£		£
Balance b/d	2,000	Paid to bank	38,000
Cash from customers	40,000	Cash expenses	1,000
		Balance c/d	3,000
	42,000		42,000

MAINTAINING FINANCIAL RECORDS AND PREPARING ACCOUNTS : UNIT 5

Bank account

	£		£
Balance b/d	33,000	Salaries	20,000
Cash paid into bank	38,000	Rent	5,000
		Purchases	25,000
		Drawings (balancing figure)	10,000
	71,000	Balance c/d	11,000
			71,000

3.4 DEBTORS CONTROL ACCOUNT

Having looked at the bank account and cash account, it is now necessary to piece together a debtors control account from the cash receipts information in the cash account and, also, other information in the question. The construction of the debtors control account enables the calculation of figures such as total sales or debtors for the profit and loss account and balance sheet respectively.

Proforma debtors control account:

Debtors control account

Balance b/d	X (note 1)	Cash received from customers	X (note 2)
Sales (bal fig)	X (note 4)	Balance c/d	X (note 3)
	XX		XX

Notes:

1   This figure will be given in the question unless the business started in the current year in which case there will be no opening debtors.

2   The cash received from customers is the credit entry resulting from the debit to the cash account.

3   The balance carried down on the debtors control account will usually be indicated in the question.

4   The missing figure on the control account is usually sales which can be worked out by completing the T-account.

Example

The balance on the debtors control account of Stevens and Sons at the end of last year was £12,000.

The total cash received from customers during the year was £40,000.

A review of outstanding sales invoices, unpaid at the year end showed a total of £16,000.

CHAPTER 16 : INCOMPLETE RECORDS: TECHNIQUES

Prepare the debtors control account.

Step 1   Set up a proforma debtors control account.

Debtors control account

	£		£
Balance b/d		Cash received from customers	
Sales (bal fig)		Balance c/d	

Step 2   Insert known figures into proforma.

Note: The entry for cash received from customers would already have been made to this account when completing the cash account because every entry (apart from year end balances) written in any proforma should always have a double entry.

Debtors control account

	£		£
Balance b/d	12,000	Cash received from customers	40,000
Sales (bal fig)	?	Balance c/d	16,000
	56,000		56,000

Step 3   Find the missing figure.

Debtors control account

	£		£
Balance b/d	12,000	Cash received from customers	40,000
Sales (bal fig)	**44,000**	Balance c/d	16,000
	56,000		56,000

3.5 CREDITORS CONTROL ACCOUNT

Finally, it is necessary to piece together a creditors control account from the credit purchase payments information and, also, other information in the question. This construction of the creditors control account is necessary to enable the credit purchases of the business to be calculated, or possibly the closing balance on creditors, depending upon the information given.

Proforma creditors control account

Creditors control account

Payments made to suppliers	X (note 2)	Balance b/d	X (note 1)
Balance c/d	X (note 3)	Purchases (bal fig)	X (note 4)
	XX		XX

Notes:

1. This figure will be given in the question unless the business started in the current year in which case there will be no opening creditors.
2. The payment to suppliers is the debit entry resulting from the credit for purchase payments in the bank account.
3. The balance carried down on the creditors control account will usually be indicated in the question.
4. The missing figure on the control account is usually credit purchases which can be worked out by completing the T-account.

Example

The payments made in respect of credit purchases per the bank account totalled £25,000 (see example above). Stevens says that the business currently owes about £5,000 for building materials. At the same time last year the business owed £7,000.

Work out the purchases for the year.

Step 1 Set up a proforma creditors control account.

Creditors control account

	£		£
Payments made to suppliers		Balance b/d	
Balance c/d		Purchases (bal fig)	

Step 2 Insert the known figures.

Note: In a full question the payments made to suppliers would already have been posted to this account as part of the double entry of the bank account.

Creditors control account

	£		£
Payments made to suppliers	25,000	Balance b/d	7,000
Balance c/d	5,000	Purchase (bal fig)	?
	30,000		30,000

Step 3 Work out the missing purchases figure.

Creditors control account

	£		£
Payments made to suppliers	25,000	Balance b/d	7,000
Balance c/d	5,000	Purchases (bal fig)	**23,000**
	30,000		30,000

CHAPTER 16 : INCOMPLETE RECORDS: TECHNIQUES

3.6 THE TRADING ACCOUNT AND COST STRUCTURES

In the last few sections it has been shown how the sales figures and purchases figures can be worked out by knowledge of the bank and cash account and the control accounts for debtors and creditors. This section ties up the cost structure section with those sections and shows how a missing figure in the trading account can be worked out by combining all these sections. The good news is that this final technique is as hard as any question will get!

The trading account section of the profit and loss account will contain the following figures:

	£	£
Sales		x
Opening stock	x	
Purchases	x	
	x	
Less: Closing stock	(x)	
Cost of sales		(x)
Gross profit		£xx

Work through the example below to see how they may be found.

Example

Stevens and Sons forgot to do a year-end stocktake so no closing stock figure is available. However they do know that a mark-up of 100% is applied to building materials to get the final selling price. Stock at the end of last year was £5,000.

Step 1   Set up a proforma trading account to see what figures are available.

Stevens and Sons trading account

	£	£	
Sales		44,000	(from the debtors control account)
Opening stock (given in the question)	5,000		
Purchases (from the creditors control account)	23,000		
	28,000		
Less: Closing stock	?		
Cost of sales		?	
Gross profit		??	

Using cost structures and the sales figure, the cost of sales and gross profit can be found.

Step 2 Establish the cost structure.

	%
Cost	100
Add profit	100
Sales	200

Step 3 Use the cost structure to find cost of sales and gross profit from sales.

Sales = £44,000

Cost of sales = $44,000 \times \dfrac{100}{200}$

= £22,000

Gross profit = $44,000 \times \dfrac{100}{200}$

= £22,000

or = 44,000 − 22,000

= £22,000

Step 4 Complete the trading account, with the closing stock as the balancing figure.

Stevens and Sons trading account

	£	£
Sales		44,000
Opening stock	5,000	
Purchases	23,000	
	28,000	
Less: Closing stock (bal fig see note 2)	(6,000)	
Cost of sales (bal fig see note 1)		22,000
Gross profit		22,000

Note 1: If sales are £44,000 and gross profit is £22,000 then cost of sales must be £22,000

Note 2: If the cost of sales is £22,000 and opening stock and purchases total £28,000, then it must mean that closing stock was £6,000.

Step 5 Insert the closing stock figure in the balance sheet.

The whole point of the last exercise was to find closing stock by completing the trading account and to find the stock figure for the balance sheet.

CHAPTER 16 : INCOMPLETE RECORDS: TECHNIQUES

3.7 A STRUCTURED APPROACH TO EXAM QUESTIONS

So far, the basic building blocks of the T-account approach have been demonstrated, namely cost structures, control accounts and cash and bank accounts. The next step is to use these within an overall approach to incomplete records questions in order to gain as many marks as possible within the relatively short timescale of an exam. The next chapter deals with this overall approach and will rely upon your understanding of the techniques covered in this chapter.

ACTIVITY 3

You have been asked to investigate the losses made by the bar at your local sports club. You have established the following facts.

(a) The stock was counted and valued on 1 January 20X8. It had a cost of £2,341.

(b) During 20X8 stock with a cost of £56,475 was delivered.

(c) On 31 December 20X8 the stock was counted and valued. It had a cost of £3,816.

(d) Bar takings during the year were £59,328.

(e) All drinks are sold at a 30% mark-up on cost.

(f) The physical security procedures at the Bar mean that it is highly unlikely that any stock has been stolen.

Tasks

1   Calculate the cost of goods sold during the year.

2   Calculate the theoretical sales revenues during the year.

3   Identify the shortfall in takings during the year.

This activity covers performance criterion A in element 5.3.

For a suggested answer, see the 'Answers' section at the end of the book.

ACTIVITY 4

At the month-end a computer virus wiped out your employer's sales ledger. Fortunately this happened after you had printed out a list of balances, but you do not know what the sales for the month were. The most important piece of information to find out is the value of output VAT during the month.

The information that you do have is as follows:

	£
Opening balance on the sales ledger control account. (Taken from the hard-copy)	243,957
Cash received during the month. (Taken from the cash book)	128,365
Discounts allowed during the month. (Taken from the cash book)	3,289
Closing balance on the sales ledger control account. (Taken from the hard-copy)	310,264

All values are gross of VAT at 17.5%.

MAINTAINING FINANCIAL RECORDS AND PREPARING ACCOUNTS : UNIT 5

Tasks

1. Recreate the sales ledger control account for the month, and calculate the sales made during the month.
2. Calculate the output VAT for the month.

This activity covers performance criterion A in element 5.3.

> For a suggested answer, see the 'Answers' section at the end of the book.

CONCLUSION

This chapter looked at two methods of construction of financial accounts from incomplete records.

The net asset approach uses the accounting equation to find a profit figure.

The T account approach can be used to find all the figures required to prepare a balance sheet and profit and loss account using three basic techniques:

- cost structures
- debtors and creditors control accounts
- cash and bank accounts.

SELF TEST QUESTIONS

		Paragraph
1	Write down the accounting equation used in the net assets approach.	2.1
2	What is the gross profit percentage?	3.2
3	What is mark-up?	3.2
4	Set out the proforma of the trading account and of the profit and loss account.	3.6

KEY TERMS

Limited accounting records - refers to the situation where a sole trader maintains records of his transactions, but not a full set of double entry books of account. Additional information is needed before final accounts can be prepared.

Incomplete accounting records - records which the trader has not fully completed or where no records at all have been kept of transactions.

Gross profit percentage - profit made per £100 of sales, expressed as a percentage.

Mark-up - the amount of profit added to cost to get the selling price.

Debtors ledger control account – records the total value of transactions with debit customers.

Creditors ledger control account - records the total value of transactions with credit customers.

Chapter 17

INCOMPLETE RECORDS: EXAMPLE

This chapter explains how to approach incomplete records questions in a structured and methodical manner.

CONTENTS

1 The overall T account approach

KNOWLEDGE AND UNDERSTANDING

		Reference
1	The methods of restructuring accounts from incomplete evidence	Item 18

LEARNING OUTCOMES

At the end of this chapter you should be able to:

- prepare a profit and loss account and balance sheet from incomplete records information using the basic techniques learnt in the previous chapter.

1 THE OVERALL T-ACCOUNT APPROACH

1.1 STEPS TO A GOOD ANSWER

Step 1 Read the requirements.

This is an important first step. If the examiner only asks for a profit and loss account then it will be a waste of time doing a balance sheet in the answer as well. No marks will be given, even if it does balance!

Step 2 Glance through the notes.

Before writing any part of the answer, very briefly read through the question to ascertain what type of question it is and what potential problems there are. At this stage of the answer, it is vital that nothing is read more than once and that no time is spent dwelling on difficult parts to the question. To do so at this point is very demoralising as the focus is immediately on the hard parts of the question, ignoring the many easy marks that are up for grabs.

Step 3   Set out proforma as required.

The next step is to write out the following proformas:

- profit and loss account
- balance sheet
- cash account
- bank account
- debtors control account
- creditors control account.

Do this very quickly, as the examiner will be expecting a candidate at this level to be able to produce such statements and therefore few marks will be available for just the words.

At this point you may wish to slot in some final figures if they are given in the question, such as opening and closing stock, debtors, creditors, bank and cash.

Step 4   Work through the cash/bank account.

Starting with the cash account, post all the information given in the question concerning the cash account to this account and also post the opposite side of each entry to the relevant place. Tick each figure on the face of the question paper as it is dealt with. The year-end cash balance will require insertion into the cash account and the balance sheet.

So for example, when posting cash received from customers, write the entry in the cash account, and straight away put the credit into the debtors control account.

For cash expenses, post the credit to cash account and post the debit to the profit and loss account by writing the figure in brackets next to the category heading in expenses. For example:

Suppose wages were £5,000 paid from the cash account. The credit is written in the cash account. The debit would be written like the following:

Profit and loss account extract - expenses

Rates

Wages and salaries (5,000)

Rent

etc

This figure will be added to later on.

Note: If there is a difficult figure to deal with that cannot be dealt with in about 10 seconds put a circle around the figure and go back to it later.

Having dealt with the cash account information, move on to the bank account and follow the same process with regard to posting the information in the question. So for example, suppose salary payments were £15,000. Write this figure into the bank account proforma and immediately write it against the salary category in the margin of the profit and loss account as follows:

Profit and loss account extract - expenses

Rates

Wages and salaries (5,000 + 15,000)

Rent

etc

Step 5 Complete debtors.

Find the opening and closing debtors from the question and insert the figures into the proforma. Find the balancing sales figure and put it into the profit and loss account proforma. The closing debtors figure may be put into the balance sheet at this point.

Step 6 Complete creditors.

Find the opening and closing creditors from the question and insert the figures into the proforma. Find the balancing purchases figure and put it into the profit and loss account proforma. The closing creditors figure may be put into the balance sheet at this point.

Step 7 Balance up the cash account and bank account.

Until this point it is possible that some figures might be needed to finish the cash and bank accounts from debtors and creditors. Once these accounts are balanced it is probably safe to finish the cash and bank accounts and to put their closing balances into the balance sheet.

Step 8 Finish the trading account.

Use the cost structure technique to find any missing figures in the trading account, for example, closing stock. Post the closing stock to the balance sheet.

Step 9 Other accounting adjustments.

Other likely adjustments will be:

- depreciation
- accruals
- prepayments.

Deal with these in the normal double entry fashion

Step 10 Finish the profit and loss account.

Add up all the figures in the margin and put the final total of each expense category in the expenses column of the profit and loss account.

Total up the expenses and deduct them from gross profit to arrive at net profit.

Step 11   Finish the balance sheet.

Find the opening capital balance by adding up the opening assets and taking away the opening liabilities in the same way as for a net assets approach question. The resulting figure will be the capital brought forward.

Ensure the balances given in the question are adjusted for the amounts noted in the margin.

Total up the balance sheet.

Example

The above structured approach can be demonstrated using Stevens and Sons. Most of the information has already been seen in the separate examples of the specific techniques.

This is how the Stevens and Sons example would appear in an exam question.

The accounting books of Stevens and Sons are incomplete, however it was possible to find out the following information.

Last year's accounts showed the following balances:

Fixed assets	£50,000
Stock	£5,000
Debtors	£12,000
Cash at bank	£33,000
Cash in hand	£2,000
Creditors	£7,000

During the year £40,000 was received from customers for sales.

Cash expenses totalled £1,000 made up as follows:

Wages	£800
Sundry expenses	£200

£38,000 was paid into the bank.

An analysis of the cheque book (including the unpresented cheque below) revealed the following payments:

Salaries	£20,000
Rent	£5,000
Purchases on credit	£25,000

The closing balance on the bank statement was £13,000 but there was a cheque not yet presented at the year end of £2,000.

Stevens regularly wrote monthly cheques to himself for drawings, but had not recorded their amounts.

A review of outstanding sales invoices, unpaid at the year end showed a total of £16,000.

Stevens says that the business currently owes about £5,000 for building materials.

CHAPTER 17 : INCOMPLETE RECORDS: EXAMPLE

Stevens forgot to do a year-end stocktake so no closing stock figure is available. However, a mark-up of 100% is applied to building materials to get the final selling price.

There is a sundry expense accrual of £50 and a rent prepayment of £300

Depreciation is to be provided at 20% on net book value

Required:

Prepare a profit and loss account for the year and a balance sheet as at the year end.

Note: If the technique sections above were followed and understood, then the information being presented in the question is identical apart from the final parts on accruals, prepayments and depreciation, which incidentally, are probably the easiest parts.

Faced with a block of information like the above, it is very easy to panic. Stay calm, follow the structured approach and a good pass mark will be obtained.

Solution

Step 1 & 2   Read the requirements and glance through the notes.

A profit and loss account and balance sheet is required, whilst a glance through the question reveals that it is an incomplete records type of question with a bank and cash account.

Potential problems appear to surround drawings and closing stock as there is some information but no figures (which is always a good indication that some calculations are needed).

Step 3   Set out proformas.

Draft out blank proformas for both financial statements and the necessary accounts. Note that only the profit and loss account and balance sheet is shown here to save repeating the proformas in the steps below:

Stevens and Sons - profit and loss account

	£	£
Sales		
Opening Stock		
Purchases	_____	
Less: Closing stock	_____	
Cost of sales		_____
Gross profit		
Wages and salaries		
Rent		
Sundry expenses	_____	
Net profit		_____

Stevens and Sons - balance sheet

	Cost £	Accumulated depreciation £	£
Fixed assets			
Current assets			
Stock			
Debtors			
Bank			
Cash			
Current liabilities			
Creditors			
Capital			
Profit for the year			
Drawings			

Step 4   Work through the cash/bank account.

Cash account

	£		£
Balance b/d	2,000	Bankings	38,000
		Wages	800
Cash from customers	40,000		
		Sundry expenses	200
		Balance c/d (balancing figure)	

Bank account

	£		£
Balance b/d	33,000	Salaries	20,000
		Rent	5,000
Bankings from cash	38,000		
		Credit purchases	25,000
		Balance c/d (13,000 – 2,000)	11,000

CHAPTER 17 : INCOMPLETE RECORDS: EXAMPLE

Step 5 Complete debtors control account.

Debtors control account

	£		£
Balance b/d	12,000	Cash received from customers	40,000
Sales (bal fig)	**44,000**	Balance c/d	16,000
	56,000		56,000

Step 6 Complete creditors control account.

Creditors control account

	£		£
Payments made to suppliers	25,000	Balance b/d	7,000
Balance c/d	5,000	Purchases (bal fig)	**23,000**
	30,000		30,000

After these accounts have been finished the profit and loss account would include further items, as follows:

	£	£
Sales		44,000
Opening Stock		
Purchases	23,000	
Less: Closing stock	————	
Cost of sales		————
Gross profit		
Wages and salaries (800 + 20,000)		
Rent (5,000)		
Sundry expenses (200)	————	
Net profit		————

245

MAINTAINING FINANCIAL RECORDS AND PREPARING ACCOUNTS : UNIT 5

Step 7   Balance the cash account and bank account.

Cash account

	£		£
Balance b/d	2,000	Bankings	38,000
		Wages	800
Cash from customers	40,000		
		Sundry expenses	200
		Balance c/d (balancing figure)	3,000
	42,000		42,000

Bank account

	£		£
Balance b/d	33,000	Salaries	20,000
		Rent	5,000
Bankings from cash	38,000		
		Credit purchases	25,000
		Drawings (bal fig)	10,000
		Balance c/d (13,000 – 2,000)	11,000
	71,000		71,000

The completion of the control accounts and the cash and bank account enable the following balances to be established in the balance sheet at this point:

	Cost	Accumulated depreciation	
	£	£	£
Fixed assets	———	———	
Current assets			
Stock			
Debtors		16,000	
Bank		11,000	
Cash		3,000	
		———	
Current liabilities			
Creditors	(5,000)	———	
	———		———
			———
Capital			
Profit for the year			
			———
Drawings			(10,000)

Step 8   Finish the trading account using the cost structures.

CHAPTER 17 : INCOMPLETE RECORDS: EXAMPLE

	Cost structure %
Cost	100
Add profit	100
Sales	200

Sales	=	£44,000
Cost of sales	=	$44,000 \times \dfrac{100}{200}$
	=	£22,000
Gross profit	=	$44,000 \times \dfrac{100}{200}$
	=	£22,000

	£	£
Sales		44,000
Opening Stock	5,000	
Purchases	23,000	
	28,000	
Less: Closing stock	(6,000)	
Cost of sales		(22,000)
Gross profit		22,000

The balance sheet would now include the closing stock found as the balancing figure in the trading account.

	Cost	Accumulated depreciation	
	£	£	£
Fixed assets			
Current assets			
Stock		6,000	
Debtors		16,000	
Bank		11,000	
Cash		3,000	
Current liabilities			
Creditors		5,000	
Capital			
Profit for the year			
Drawings			(10,000)

Step 9   Other accounting adjustments

Perform the double entry for depreciation, accruals and prepayments directly on the face of the financial accounts if you feel confident enough. Otherwise, use T accounts as workings.

Depreciation charge (50,000 × 20%) = £10,000

    Dr   Depreciation expense (P&L) a/c £10,000
    Cr   Provision for depreciation £10,000
                (accumulated depreciation in balance sheet)

Rent account

	£		£
Bank account	5,000	Balance c/d	300
		P&L a/c	4,700
	5,000		5,000
Balance b/d	300		

Sundry expenses

	£		£
Cash account	200	P&L a/c	250
Balance c/d	50		
	250		250
		Balance b/d	50

Stevens and Sons - profit and loss account

	£	£
Sales		44,000
Opening stock	5,000	
Purchases	23,000	
	28,000	
Less: Closing stock	(6,000)	
Cost of sales		(22,000)
Gross profit		22,000
Wages and salaries (800 + 20,000)		
Rent (5,000)		
Sundry expenses (200)	10,000	
Net profit		

CHAPTER 17 : INCOMPLETE RECORDS: EXAMPLE

Stevens and Sons - balance sheet

	Cost £	Accumulated depreciation £	£
Fixed assets		(10,000)	
Current assets			
Stock		6,000	
Debtors		16,000	
Prepayments		300	
Bank		11,000	
Cash		3,000	
		36,300	
Current liabilities			
Creditors	5,000		
Accruals	50		
		(5,050)	
			31,250
Capital			
Profit for the year			
Drawings			(10,000)

Step 10 Finish profit and loss account.

Stevens and Sons
Profit and loss account for the year

	£	£
Sales		44,000
Opening stock	5,000	
Purchases	23,000	
	28,000	
Less: Closing stock	(6,000)	
Cost of sales		(22,000)
Gross profit		22,000
Wages and salaries (800 + 20,000)	20,800	
Rent (5,000 – 300)	4,700	
Sundry expenses (200 + 50)	250	
Depreciation	10,000	
		(35,750)
Net profit		(13,750)

MAINTAINING FINANCIAL RECORDS AND PREPARING ACCOUNTS : UNIT 5

Step 11 Finish the balance sheet.

This will mean:

- working out the opening capital
- inserting balances where they haven't already been used in workings, for example, fixed asset cost
- inserting the year-end balances from the workings if not already done.

Stevens and Sons - Balance sheet as at the year end

	Cost	Accumulated depreciation	
	£	£	£
Fixed assets	50,000	(10,000)	40,000
Current assets			
Stock		6,000	
Debtors		16,000	
Prepayments		300	
Bank		11,000	
Cash		3,000	
		36,300	
Current liabilities			
Creditors	(5,000)		
Accruals	(50)		
		(5,050)	
			31,250
			71,250
Capital (see below)			95,000
Loss for the year			(13,750)
Drawings			(10,000)
			71,250

Note the opening capital figure is calculated by reference to last year-end's net assets:

	£
Fixed assets	50,000
Stock	5,000
Debtors	12,000
Bank account	33,000
Cash account	2,000
Creditors	(7,000)
Opening capital	95,000

CONCLUSION

This chapter builds up the T-account approach to provide a series of steps which can be applied in exam questions for this type.

There are no self-test questions in this chapter as it consists entirely of an example, rather than new material.

Chapter 18

THE ACCOUNTING AND BUSINESS FRAMEWORK

This chapter summarises the legal and professional framework within which sole traders and partnerships produce their financial statements.

CONTENTS

1. Why financial accounts are prepared
2. Accounting principles and concepts
3. Accounting standards

KNOWLEDGE AND UNDERSTANDING

		Reference
1	The relevant legislation and regulations	Item 2
2	The main requirements of relevant Statements of Standard Accounting Practice and Financial Reporting Standards	Item 3
3	The importance of maintaining the confidentiality of business transactions	Item 9
4	Basic accounting concepts that play a role in the selection of accounting policies – accruals and going concern	Item 22
5	The objectives and constraints in selecting accounting policies – relevance, reliability, comparability and ease of understanding, materiality	Item 23
6	The ways the accounting systems of an organisation are affected by its organisational structure, its administrative systems and procedures and the nature of its business transactions	Item 31

PERFORMANCE CRITERIA

		Reference
1	Conduct investigations into business transactions with tact and courtesy	Item G in element 5.2
2	Ensure that the organisation's policies, regulations, procedures and timescales relating to preparing final accounts are observed	Item H in element 5.2

MAINTAINING FINANCIAL RECORDS AND PREPARING ACCOUNTS : UNIT 5

LEARNING OUTCOMES

At the end of this chapter you should be able to:

- discuss why financial accounts are prepared
- be able to apply the correct principles and concepts when preparing financial accounts
- identify the limitations in using financial accounts
- identify the solutions offered by the accounting profession to those limitations.

1 WHY FINANCIAL ACCOUNTS ARE PREPARED

1.1 WHAT INFORMATION DO FINANCIAL ACCOUNTS GIVE?

In earlier chapters it was shown that the basic financial accounts of a business consist of a balance sheet and a profit and loss account. The balance sheet shows what a business owns - fixed assets, stock, debtors and cash, and what a business owes to people other than its owner - trade creditors and loans. The profit and loss account shows the financial performance of a business, including sales and all the costs incurred in making those sales.

There is a wealth of information about a business in a set of financial accounts, but it is only of relevance when it is put to a specific use. The use to which the information is put is dependent on who uses a set of financial accounts.

1.2 WHO USES THE INFORMATION AND FOR WHAT PURPOSE? – USER GROUPS

(a) The owner/management

The owner will use the profit figure to determine how much money can be drawn out of the business. In addition the owner will use the profit and loss account information to try to improve the sales performance and also to reduce costs if they are felt to be too high. The balance sheet items will be used to collect money owing to the business, pay debts due to suppliers and ascertain the amount of stock held by the business.

(b) The tax authorities/government agencies

The profit for the period is the basis on which the business will account for tax. A tax inspector, therefore, would like to see a set of financial accounts in order to work out the amount of tax a business will have to pay.

(c) Shareholders and potential shareholders

Anybody who wishes to invest in a business, either by buying shares if it is a company, putting capital into a partnership or by buying the whole business, will want to see a set of financial accounts to determine its profitability and financial position now as an indication of how it might perform in future.

(d) Employees and their trade union representatives

Employees of a business may want to see the financial statements of the business to use in wage negotiations or find out whether the company can offer them safe employment and promotion through growth over a period of years.

CHAPTER 18 : THE ACCOUNTING AND BUSINESS FRAMEWORK

(e) **Suppliers/customers/business contract group**

People who deal with a business will always be interested in the health of that business. A supplier will want reassurance that they will be paid, whereas a customer may want to make sure that the business they are dealing with will continue to supply them on a regular basis.

(f) **Lenders**

This group includes some who have financed the business over a long period by lending money which is to be repaid, as well as short-term creditors such as bank, and suppliers of raw materials, which permit a company to buy goods from them and pay in, say, four to twelve weeks' time.

(g) **The public**

From time to time the public may have an interest in the company, e.g. members of a local community where the company operates or environmental pressure groups.

2 ACCOUNTING PRINCIPLES AND CONCEPTS

2.1 INTRODUCTION

When preparing financial accounts, it is important to have a thorough knowledge of the recognised accounting principles, concepts and conventions. This section introduces some of these.

2.2 THE ENTITY CONCEPT

Definition Financial accounting information relates only to the activities of the business entity and not to the activities of its owners.

The business accounts are prepared as though the business is an entity that is separate from its owner. In the case of a company, this concept reflects the legal reality. A company is both legally and for accounting purposes a separate entity distinct from its owners, the shareholders. On the other hand, the business of a sole trader is **not** a legal entity distinct from its proprietor. Even so, for accounting purposes, the business is **regarded** as being a separate entity and accounts are drawn up for the business separately from the trader's own personal financial dealings.

2.3 THE ACCOUNTING EQUATION

Definition Assets – Liabilities = Capital

Understanding the accounting equation is the key to understanding the double entry accounting system. Profits add to net assets (assets minus liabilities) and capital. Drawings by the owner reduce assets and capital.

2.4 THE MATCHING (ACCRUALS) CONCEPT

Definition Income is recognised in financial accounts as it is earned, not when the cash is received. Expenditure is recognised as it is incurred, not when it is paid for. When income is incurred over time (e.g. rental income) or expenditures are time-related (e.g. rental payments), the income and expenditure recognised in the profit and loss account should relate to the time period, not to the receipts or payments of cash.

An accounting system must follow commercial reality. Sales revenue is recognised as the transaction occurs not as the cash is received. Similarly expenditure is recorded as the cost is actually incurred, not when the supplier is paid.

2.5 THE PRUDENCE CONCEPT

Definition   **Prudence**

Sales and profit should not be included in the profit and loss account until the cash has been received or there is reasonable certainty that the cash will be received.

In contrast, losses should be recognised in the profit and loss account as soon as they are foreseen and considered reasonably certain.

2.6 CONFLICT BETWEEN ACCRUALS AND PRUDENCE

There are many instances where the accruals concept and the prudence concept conflict. For example, the prudence concept says that a sale should only be recognised when the cash is received or its receipt is reasonably certain. Accruals, on the other hand, states that a sale is recognised as earned when the transaction takes place, which is before the cash is received.

The argument is resolved by the words, 'reasonably certain'. These allow the operation of the accruals concept within the boundaries of prudence because a sale on credit is legally enforceable and therefore the cash receipt is reasonably certain.

Preparers should aim for a 'neutral' view of events, that is neither too optimistic nor too pessimistic.

2.7 COMPARABILITY AND CONSISTENCY

Financial information prepared by an entity should be comparable between one period and the next. Comparability is achieved by consistency. A business should be consistent in its accounting treatment of similar items, both **within** a particular accounting period and **between** one accounting period and the next

Consistency prevents the problems that would be caused for example, by similar items of expenditure being treated as capital items and included as fixed assets one year, but as revenue items deducted from profit another year.

2.8 GOING CONCERN

Definition   Financial statements are usually prepared on the assumption that the business (or enterprise) will **continue in operational existence for the foreseeable future.**

This means that the financial statements are drawn up on the assumption that there is **no intention or necessity to close down the business.**

If the financial accounts are not prepared on the going concern basis then they must be prepared on what is known as the break-up basis.

The break-up basis reflects the following:

- Some fixed assets may be sold at less than their value in the balance sheet because, whilst a machine may have a use for a specific business, it may be scrap metal to anyone else.

- In contrast, property may be sold for a value in excess of that shown in the balance sheet based on original cost.
- If all the stock is sold at once then it will not be sold for as much money as if it were sold in the normal way.
- Some debtors may decide not to pay the business if it is known the business is about to go into liquidation.

2.9 HISTORICAL COST ACCOUNTING CONVENTION

Definition The figure shown in the financial accounts for an item is the value of the item when the transaction occurred, not a current market value.

For example, a property is shown in the financial accounts at its original cost, not at a value that the property could be currently sold for. Whilst there may be some questions about whether this is showing a true value of the business, it is at least objective, in that the property was purchased for a price (the historical cost) and this is the value it is shown at in the financial accounts. Any current market valuations would be based on opinions of the various valuers and thus would be subjective.

In practice, the historical cost accounting convention is used for most assets and liabilities, and income and expenditure, but might not be used for all of them. In particular, some businesses might regularly revalue some fixed assets, especially land and buildings, to a current value.

2.10 NO NETTING-OFF

Definition All related assets and liabilities should be shown separately and not netted off with one another to give a smaller net value.

Suppose the business had purchased goods from a supplier for £10,000 which it had in stock at the year end. It had paid £3,000 to the supplier and therefore still owed £7,000.

This principle says that:

- the stock should be shown at £10,000
- the trade creditor is shown at £7,000.

The *wrong* alternative is to show the stock at the net £3,000 (that is £10,000 stock less £7,000 trade creditor).

2.11 MATERIALITY

Definition Financial statements should separately disclose items which are significant enough to require their inclusion.

The significance of an item stems from its importance in the overall context of the financial statements.

3 ACCOUNTING STANDARDS

3.1 INTRODUCTION

The accounting profession and the government have produced, and continue to produce, regulations that set out how information is shown in financial accounts.

Regulations prepared by the accounting profession are known as accounting standards. Most accounting standards are called Financial Reporting Standards (FRS's), but some that have been in existence for longer are known as Statements of Standard Accounting Practice (SSAP's).

3.2 ACCOUNTING STANDARDS

The standards themselves are not law. The Companies Act 1985, however, does require large companies to state that their financial accounts have been prepared in accordance with applicable standards. If the board of directors of a company decides not to follow the standards then the accounts must explain why.

Non-corporate businesses such as sole traders and partnerships do not have the same constraints, but tend to follow the standards anyway as the owners of the business still require reliable information. The Inland Revenue also takes the view that accounts should be prepared in accordance with the reporting standards.

3.3 COMPANIES ACT 1985 STATUTORY FORMATS

The Companies Act 1985 specifies the layout or format for a profit and loss account and balance sheet, and what each item should contain. For businesses that are not companies there is no such legal requirement for the format of the P&L account and balance sheet. In practice, however, the same format is normally used for these types of businesses.

3.4 CONCLUSION

The potential limitations of financial accounts have been addressed by accounting standards and statutory formats for the presentation of financial information.

A detailed knowledge of accounting standards and the Companies Act is not required for the purpose of the examination at this level. However, some of the topics in the syllabus do have standards attached. The standards are only examinable to the extent that the accounting treatment specified in the standards relates to an item in the syllabus.

CONCLUSION

This chapter has looked at the need for basic accounting concepts and principles by putting them into the context of why and for whom financial accounts are prepared.

SELF TEST QUESTIONS

		Paragraph
1	Who uses financial information?	1.2
2	Define the entity concept.	2.2
3	Give the definition of the accounting equation.	2.3
4	What is the prudence concept?	2.5
5	Name three accounting conventions.	2

CHAPTER 18 : THE ACCOUNTING AND BUSINESS FRAMEWORK

KEY TERMS

Entity concept - financial accounting information relates only to the activities of the business entity and not to the activities of its owners.

Accounting equation - Assets – Liabilities = Capital

Matching (accruals) concept - income is recognised in financial accounts as it is earned, not when the cash is received. Expenditure is recognised as it is incurred, not when it is paid for. When income is incurred over time (e.g. rental income) or expenditures are time-related (e.g. rental payments), the income and expenditure recognised in the profit and loss account should relate to the time period, not to the receipts or payments of cash.

Prudence concept - Sales and profit should not be included in the profit and loss account until the cash has been received or there is reasonable certainty that the cash will be received. In contrast, losses should be recognised in the profit and loss account as soon as they are foreseen and considered reasonably certain.

Going concern - financial statements are usually prepared on the assumption that the business (or enterprise) will continue in operational existence for the foreseeable future.

Historical cost accounting convention - the figure shown in the financial accounts for an item is the value of the item when the transaction occurred, not a current market value.

No netting off - all related assets and liabilities should be shown separately and not netted off with one another to give a smaller net value.

Materiality - financial statements should separately disclose items which are significant enough to require their inclusion.

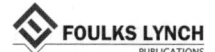

ANSWERS TO ACTIVITIES

CHAPTER 2

ACTIVITY 1

	Suppliers	VAT element
(a)	£117.50 gross	VAT = £17.50
(b)	£470.00 gross	VAT = £70.00
(c)	£200.00 net	VAT = £35.00
(d)	£1,245.50 gross	VAT = £185.50
(e)	£17,117.40 gross	VAT = £2,549.40

ACTIVITY 2

HM Customs & Excise (VAT)

		£			£
VAT on Purchases	(W2)	23,625	Balance b/f		24,837
			VAT on Sales	(W1)	38,500
		23,625			63,337
Balance c/d		39,712			
		63,337			63,337

Workings:

(W1)   £258,500 * 17.5/117.5   =   £38,500

(W1)   £158,625 * 17.5/117.5   =   £23,625

Flagon will have to pay over £39,712 to HM Customs and Excise.

ACTIVITY 3

Loan (Principal only)

		£			£
			1 – 1 – X6 Initial loan		15,000
1 - 4	Capital element of repayment	1,875			
1 - 7	Capital element of repayment	1,875			
1 - 10	Capital element of repayment	1,875			
	Closing balance	9,375			
		15,000			15,000

MAINTAINING FINANCIAL RECORDS AND PREPARING ACCOUNTS : UNIT 5

Interest expense

			£		£
1 - 4	Interest element of repayment		225		
1 - 7	Interest element of repayment		225		
1 - 10	Interest element of repayment		225		

Bank and cash

		£			£
1 – 1 – X6	Initial loan	15,000	1 – 4 – X6	First instalment	2,100
			1 – 7 – X6	Second instalment	2,100
			1 – 10 – X6	Third instalment	2,100

CHAPTER 3

ACTIVITY 1

Purchase day book

Date	Invoice number	Supplier	Ledger Ref	Total £	VAT £	Aviation Fuel £	Repairs £	Chemicals £
April								
6	67	Lightning Avgas	L23	8,225.00	1,225.00	7,000.00		
9	291	Wildcat Services	W36	2,115.00	315.00		1,800.00	
15	618	Avenger Agrochemicals	A17	5,875.00	875.00			5,000.00
19	CN99	Wildcat Services	W36	(470.00)	(70.00)		(400.00)	
				15,745.00	2,345.00	7,000.00	1,400.00	5,000.00

ACTIVITY 2

Petty cash book - July

Date	Details	Voucher reference	Total £	Cleaning £	Repairs £	Coffee/Tea £	Parking £	Sundry £
01 Jul	J Smith	7-1	10.00				10.00	
04 Jul	Cleaning materials	7-2	15.00	15.00				
16 Jul	Tea/Milk	7-3	3.00			3.00		
20 Jul	Keys	7-4	2.00		2.00			
25 Jul	Flowers	7-5	25.00					25.00
			55.00	15.00	2.00	3.00	10.00	25.00

Imprest Voucher

	£
Balance brought down	70.00
Less total expenses	(55.00)
Add cash replenishment	65.00
Balance carried down	80.00

UNIT 5 : ANSWERS TO ACTIVITIES

Petty cash account

	£		£
Balance b/d	70.00	Petty cash book (expenses paid)	55.00
Cash at bank account	65.00	Balance c/d	80.00
	135.00		135.00

Cash at bank account

	£		£
Balance b/d	x	Petty cash account	65.00

Cleaning account

	£		£
Balance b/d	x		
Petty cash book	15.00		

Repairs account

	£		£
Balance b/d	x		
Petty cash book	2.00		

Staff catering account

	£		£
Balance b/d	x		
Petty cash book	3.00		

Parking account

	£		£
Balance b/d	x		
Petty cash book	10.00		

Sundry expenses account

	£		£
Balance b/d	x		
Petty cash book	25.00		

CHAPTER 4

ACTIVITY 1

(a)	New cars held by a motor dealership.	These will be classified as the current asset of stock. They are held with the intention of resale. They should be sold within twelve months.
(b)	A car owned by a driving school.	This will probably be a fixed asset. The car is being held form use within the business, not for resale.
(c)	Finished aeroplanes held by an aircraft manufacturer.	These are held for sale and they will be stock items.
(d)	Aeroplanes held by an airline.	These are held for use and they will be fixed assets.
(e)	The costs incurred by an aircraft manufacturer when developing an improved version of an existing plane.	These are development costs. they may be classified as *intangible fixed assets*.

CHAPTER 5

ACTIVITY 1

Fixed asset register

Asset number	Description	Location	Supplier	Date	Useful life	Dep method	Cost £	Scrap value £	Acc dep b/d £	Dep for year £	NBV £
10907	Cement pump	Site	PP	23/06/X4	6 years	SL	3,600	400	-	800	2,800
10908	Digger	Site	JD	17/09/X4	10 years	SL	23,000	3,000	-	2,000	21,000

CHAPTER 7

ACTIVITY 1

		20X7		20X8	
(a)	Straight line depreciation with a full year's charge in the year of acquisition.	**£700**	(£1,900 - £500) / 2 years. The life is based upon how long Billy intends to use it.	**£700**	
(b)	Straight line depreciation on a time apportioned basis.	**£175**	£700 * 3 months / 12	**£700**	
(c)	Depreciated on a 60% reducing balance basis.	**£840**	(£1,900 - £500) * 60%	**£336**	(£1,900 - £500 - £840) * 60%

CHAPTER 8

ACTIVITY 1

Task (a) Prepare the T accounts to record the disposal of this asset.

Fixed Asset at Cost account (B/S)

		£				£
Balance b/d		39,000	Disposal a/c	a		39,000
		39,000				39,000

Fixed Asset : Provision for Depreciation (B/S)

			£				£
Disposal a/c	b		21,000	Balance b/d	W1		21,000
			21,000				21,000

Cash at bank account (BS)

			£		£
Proceeds of disposal	c		12,300		

Disposal of fixed assets account

			£				£
Asset at cost	a		39,000	Provision for deprecation	b		21,000
				Proceeds	c		12,300
			39,000				33,300
				Loss on disposal			5,700
			39,000				39,000

W1 *Opening depreciation*

The annual charge was (£39,000 cost - £4,000 residual value) / five years = £7,000 per annum.

Depreciation will have been charged in 20X1, X2 and X3. This totals £21,000.

Task (b) Draft the Journal to record this transaction.

Account	Dr	Cr
Fixed asset disposal	39,000	
Machine at cost		39,000
Fixed asset disposal		21,000
Machine: provision for depreciation	21,000	
Cash at bank	12,300	
Fixed asset disposal		12,300
Fixed asset disposal		5,700
P&L: Loss on Disposal	5,700	

MAINTAINING FINANCIAL RECORDS AND PREPARING ACCOUNTS : UNIT 5

ACTIVITY 2

Fixed Assets at Cost: Elevators

	£			£
Balance b/d 20X9	45,000	Disposal a/c	a	45,000
Cost of fixed asset: Part-exchange	c 20,000			
Cost of Fixed Asset: Cash	79,000	Balance c/d		99,000
	144,000			144,000
Balance b/f 20Y0	99,000			

Provision for Depreciation on Fixed Assets: Elevators

		£			£
Disposal a/c	b	12,000	Balance b/d 20X9	W1	12,000
			Charge for the year	W2	3,000
Balance c/d		3,000			
		15,000			15,000
			Balance b/f 20Y0		3,000

Disposal of fixed assets account (P&L)

		£			£
Elevator at cost	a	45,000	Provision for deprecation	b	12,000
			Proceeds: Part-exchange	c	20,000
		45,000			32,000
Profit on disposal			Loss on disposal		13,000
		45,000			45,000

W1 Opening depreciation

The annual charge was (£45,000 cost - £5,000 residual value) / twenty years = £2,000 per annum.

Depreciation will have been charged in 20X3, X4, X5, X6, X7, X8. This totals £12,000.

W2 Depreciation charge for 20X9

The annual charge is (£99,000 cost - £9,000 residual value) / thirty years = £3,000 per annum.

CHAPTER 9

ACTIVITY 1

1 & 2 Ledger Accounts

Profit and Loss Account Ledger Accounts

Sales

			Smart	475
		6	Trendy	500
		6	Cool	1,240
P&L	6,603	15	Smart	470
		15	Cool	956
			Cash	2,962
	6,603			6,603

Purchases

2	Pewter	533		
2	Tin	687		
2	Ring	354		
3	Cash	867	P&L	4,441
3	Bank	2,000		
		4,441		4,441

264

UNIT 5 : ANSWERS TO ACTIVITIES

		Sales returns						Purchase returns			
13	Trendy	80	P&L	80		P&L	345	10	Tin	345
		80		80			345			345

		Motor Depreciation						Motor			
	Charge	80	P&L	80		21	Cash	65	P&L	65

		Rent & Rates						Office			
4	Cash	100				5	Bank	109	P&L	109
11	Cash	100								
19	Bank	200	P&L	400						
		400		400						

		Wages						Maintenance			
7	Cash	230				18	Cash	265	P&L	265
23	Cash	290	P&L	520						
		520		520						

		Advertising		
18	Bank	1,276	P&L	1,276

Balance Sheet Ledger Accounts

		Bank							Cash				
1	Capital	4,500	3	Goods	2,000		1	Capital	2,000	3	Purch.	867
24	Cool	750	5	Office	109			Cash sales	2,962	4	Rent	100
24	Smart	945	18	Adverts	1,276					7	Wages	230
			19	Rent	200					11	Rent	100
			27	Pewter	533					16	Maint.	265
			27	Bakkie	2,250					21	Motor	65
		6,195								23	Wages	290
											Drawings	1,200
												3,117
c/d		173								c/d		1,845
		6,368			6,368				4,962			4,962

		Capital							Drawings			
			1	Bank	4,500			Cash	1,200	To TB	1,200
			1	Cash	2,000						
	c/d	6,500									
		6,500			6,500				1,200		1,200

		Suppliers: Pewter							Suppliers: Tin			
27	Bank	533	2	Purch.	533		10	Returns	345	2	Purch.	687
								c/d	342			
									687			687

		Suppliers: Ring							Suppliers: Bakkie			
	c/d	354	2	Purch.	354		27	Bank	2,250	20	FA	2,250
		354			354							

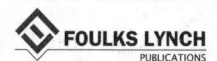

Customers: Smart						Customers: Trendy				
6	Sales	475	24	Bank	945	6	Sales	500	13 Returns	80
15	Sales	470				15	Sales	956	c/d	1,376
		945			945			1,456		1,456

Customers: Cool					
6	Sales	1,240	24	Bank	750
				c/d	490
		1,240			1,240

Fixed Assets : Motor Van						Fixed Assets : Motor Van : Depreciation			
20	C Bakkie	2,250						Charge	80
				c/d	2,250	c/d	80		
		2,250			2,250		80		80

3 Preparing the Trial Balance

Trial Balance for
Carlo Argenti 28 February 2005

	Dr £	Cr £
Profit and Loss		
Sales		6,603
Sales returns	80	
Purchases	4,441	
Purchase returns		345
Motor depreciation	80	
Motor Expenses	65	
Rent and rates	400	
Office Expenses	109	
Wages	520	
Maintenance	265	
Advertising	1,276	
Balance Sheet		
Bank		173
Cash	1,845	
Capital		6,500
Drawings	1,200	
Supplier Accounts		
Pewter		-
Tin		342
Ring		354
Bakkie		-
Customer Accounts:		
Smart	-	
Trendy	1,376	
Cool	490	
Pick-up truck	2,250	
Depreciation		80
Closing stock		
Dr: Balance sheet	1,630	
Cr: P&L		1,630
TB Total	**16,027**	**16,027**

UNIT 5 : ANSWERS TO ACTIVITIES

ACTIVITY 2

The only error that leads to an imbalance in the trial balance is the original entry error (2.6) when different amounts are debited and credited. All the other entries maintain the double entry correctly, even though the entries themselves are incorrect.

ACTIVITY 3

	Classification and Effect on the Suspense Account	**How the error might be identified**
A sales invoice for £500 was entered as a Credit Note onto the Purchase Day Book. On the same day a Credit Note for £500 from a supplier was entered into the Sales Day Book.	These are both errors of principle. Sales have been recorded as purchases and vice versa. Together, they form a compensating error. They will not affect the Suspense Account.	These might be discovered when supplier statement reconciliations are performed.
An invoice for £950 in respect of repairs made to the office interior has been posted to cleaning by mistake.	This is an error of commission. Although this has been posted to the wrong account, it is at least to the correct type of account (an expense account). It will not affect the Suspense Account.	It may be brought to light if the cleaning charge for the year appears to be far to high.
An invoice has been entered into the Sales Day Book twice.	This is an error of original entry. The Day Book will still add up and cross casts, but the totals will be incorrect. Because the Day Book still cross-casts, it will not affect the Suspense Account.	It may be identified when the Control Account is reconciled to the list of customer balances.
A cash sale for £75 was made without raising an invoice. The cash was locked in the petty cash tin but it has not been entered into the Petty Cash Book.	This is an error of omission. Because no entries have been made this will not affect the Trial Balance.	This will only be discovered when a Petty Cash count takes place.
A £15,000 business loan received from a friend of the proprietor has been credited to Capital.	This is an error of principle. A loan is a liability that must be repaid, whereas Capital belongs to the owner and need never be repaid. This will not affect the Suspense Account because Capital and Loans are both credit balances in the balance sheet.	This will be noted if the owner or lender reviews the accounts, or if the Tax authorities query where the £15,000 came from.

MAINTAINING FINANCIAL RECORDS AND PREPARING ACCOUNTS : UNIT 5

The Purchase Day Book has been correctly added-up and cross-cast. However, when the Total of £56,789 was posted to the Purchase Ledger control Account the clerk accidentally entered £57,689 in the PLCA.

This is an error of original entry. It is also a transposition error. Because the sum of the debit entries (the analysis) will still add up to £56,789, there will be a difference on the Trial Balance creating a Suspense Account Balance.

The Suspense Account will warn the accountants that an error has been made. The reconciliation of the PLCA to the list of supplier balances should identify where the error has been made.

ACTIVITY 4

Account	Debit £	Credit £
Motor vehicles	15,000	
Office equipment	10,000	
Opening stock	30,000	
Debtors	20,000	
Bank	12,000	
Creditors		45,000
Loan		20,000
Capital		5,000
Sales		100,000
Purchases	45,000	
Expenses	23,000	
Drawings	10,000	
	165,000	170,000
Suspense account	5,000	
	170,000	170,000

Suspense account

	£		£
Balance b/d	5,000		

ACTIVITY 5

Suspense account

	£		£
Journal 1	46,912	From trial balance	49,628
Journal 2	18,000	Journal 4	15,284
	69,912		64,912

Journals

1   Debit: Suspense   A/C   46,912
    Credit: Sales returns   A/C   23,456
    Credit: Sales   A/C   23,456
    With sales recorded as sales returns.

UNIT 5 : ANSWERS TO ACTIVITIES

2	Debit: Suspense	A/C	18,000	
	Credit: Sundry expenses	A/C		18,000
	To correct transposition error.			
3	Debit: Sales ledger control	A/C	10,000	
	Credit: Sales			10,000
	With missing invoices.			
4	Debit: Rent	A/C	15,284	
	Credit: Suspense	A/C		15,284
	To complete one-sided entry.			

CHAPTER 10

ACTIVITY 1

Date of purchase		Number of boxes	Cost per Box	£
31 December		65	£34	2,210
17 December		99	£40	3,960
3 December	Balance	72	£38	2,736
		236		8,906

The cost of the stock is £8,906.

ACTIVITY 2

Range	Number of boxes	Cost	Expected Selling Price	Lower of Cost & NRV	Valuation £
Venus	35	£5.30	£4	£4	140.00
Earth	54	£5.70	£6	£5.70	307.80
Saturn	85	£7.80	£8	£7.80	663.00
Pluto	47	£9.90	£8	£8	376.00
Jupiter	72	£6.50 8.50	£8	£8	576.00
					2,062.8

The balance sheet value of these stock items is £2,062.80.

CHAPTER 11

ACTIVITY 1

(a) This bill covers June to August 20X8, and so June's electricity needs to be accrued for. £900 × 1/3 = **£300**.

(b) This bill covers May to July 20X8 and so two months (May and June) need to be accrued for. £780 × 2/3 = **£520**.

(c) The sewerage bill for June needs to be estimated on the basis of past usage. If the quarterly bill is for £642, then the bill for one month will be about **£214**.

(d) 453 units of gas have bee used but not yet invoiced. At 10 pence per unit the accrual is **£45.30**.

ACTIVITY 2

Electricity

	£		£
PDB Invoices	697	Opening accrual	172
Closing accrual	238	**P&L charge**	**763**
	935		935

Rates

	£		£
PDB Invoices	756	Opening accrual	365
Closing accrual	28	**P&L charge**	**419**
	784		784

ACTIVITY 3

(a) This insurance is prepaid for the eight months from July 20X8 through to February 20X9. The prepayment is £2,136 × 8/12 = **£1,424**.

(b) This rent is prepaid for the month of July. £7,800 × 1/3 = **£2,600**.

ACTIVITY 4

Insurance

	£		£
Opening prepayment	3,672	Closing prepayment	4,107
PDB Invoices	7,295	**P&L charge**	**6,860**
	10,967		10,967

Rent

	£		£
Opening prepayment	3,908	Closing prepayment	2,798
PDB Invoices	19,540	**P&L charge**	**20,650**
	23,448		23,448

ACTIVITY 5

P&L Franchise Income

	£		£
Opening income receivable	14,726	Income received in 20X6	56,364
P&L Franchise Income	**70,283**	Closing income receivable	28,645
	85,009		85,009

P&L Rent

	£		£
Closing rents invoiced in advance	23,985	Opening rents invoiced in advance	17,625
P&L Rental Income	**68,576**	Rental invoices issued in 20X6	74,936
	92,561		92,561

CHAPTER 12

ACTIVITY 1

B/S Sales Ledger Control Account

	£			£
Balance June 20X9	78,635	Debts written off June 20X9	a	2,385
		Balance carried down		76,250
	78,635			78,635
Balance brought forward July 20X9	76,250			

B/S Provision for Doubtful Debts

		£		£
			Brought forward July 20X8	4,300
Closing provision June 20X9	W1	5,440		
			Increase in provision (balancing figure) b	1,140
		5,440		5,440
			Brought forward July 20X9	5,440

P&L Bad and Doubtful Debt Expense Account

		£		£
Debts written off during the year		1,234	P&L Charge for 20X9	4,759
Debts written off June 20X9	a	2,385		
Increase in provision	b	1,140		
		4,759		4,759

271

Presentation in the Balance Sheet 30 June 20X9

	£	£
Current Assets		
Trade Debtors	76,250	
Less: Provision for Doubtful Debts	(5,440)	
		70,810

W1 Provision for doubtful Debts

	Debtors £	Provision £
Revised balance (after write-offs)	76,250	
Less: Specific provision	(3,250)	3,250
Balance	73,000	
General Provision at 3%.		2,190
Total provision		**5,440**

CHAPTER 13

ACTIVITY 2

PG Trading Extended trial balance at 31 December 20X6

Account	Trial balance Dr £	Trial balance Cr £	Ref	Adjustments Dr £	Adjustments Cr £	Profit and loss Dr £	Profit and loss Cr £	Balance sheet Dr £	Balance sheet Cr £
Capital account		63,000							
Stock	**22,500**								
Sales		150,000							
Purchases	105,000								
Rent and rates	15,000								
Drawings	**18,000**								
Electricity	3,000								
Motor van cost	12,000								
Motor van provision for depreciation		6,000							
Bank balance	6,750								
Trade debtors	30,000								
Trade creditors		31,500							
Sundry expenses	750								
Wages and salaries	37,500								
	250,500	250,250							

The highlighted items were the suspense account corrections.

UNIT 5 : ANSWERS TO ACTIVITIES

ACTIVITY 3

PG Trading Extended trial balance at 31 December 20X6

Account	Trial balance Dr £	Trial balance Cr £	Ref	Adjustments Dr £	Adjustments Cr £	Profit and loss Dr £	Profit and loss Cr £	Balance sheet Dr £	Balance sheet Cr £
Capital account		63,000							
Stock	22,500								
Sales		150,000							
Purchases	105,000								
Rent and rates	15,000		3		300				
Drawings	18,000								
Electricity	3,000								
Motor van cost	12,000								
Motor van provision for depreciation		6,000	2		750				
Bank balance	6,750								
Trade debtors	30,000		1		1,500				
Trade creditors		31,500							
Sundry expenses	750								
Wages and salaries	37,500		3	300					
Depreciation expenses			2	750					
Bad debt expense			1	1,500					
	250,500	250,500		2,550	2,550				

ACTIVITY 4

PG Trading Extended trial balance at 31 December 20X6

Account	Trial balance Dr £	Trial balance Cr £	Ref	Adjustments Dr £	Adjustments Cr £	Profit and loss Dr £	Profit and loss Cr £	Balance sheet Dr £	Balance sheet Cr £
Capital account		63,000							
Stock	22,500								
Sales		150,000							
Purchases	105,000								
Rent and rates	15,000		5		300 + 1,200				
Drawings	18,000								
Electricity	3,000								
Motor van cost	12,000								
Motor van provision for depreciation		6,000			750				
Bank balance	6,750								
Trade debtors	30,000				1,500				
Trade creditors		31,500							
Sundry expenses	750		4	75					
Wages and salaries	37,500		4	300 + 225					
Depreciation expenses				750					
Bad debt expense				1,500					
Accruals			4		300				

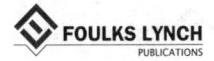

MAINTAINING FINANCIAL RECORDS AND PREPARING ACCOUNTS : UNIT 5

Account			Ref				
Prepayments			5	1,200			
	250,500	250,500		4,050	4,050		

(Note that the reference column only shows the reference of the new entries.)

ACTIVITY 5

PG Trading Extended trial balance at 31 December 20X6

Account	Trial balance		Ref	Adjustments		Profit and loss		Balance sheet	
	Dr £	Cr £		Dr £	Cr £	Dr £	Cr £	Dr £	Cr £
Capital account		63,000							
Stock	22,500		6	25,500	22,500				
Sales		150,000							
Purchases	105,000								
Rent and rates	15,000				300+ 1,200				
Drawings	18,000								
Electricity	3,000								
Motor van cost	12,000								
Motor van provision for depreciation		6,000			750				
Bank balance	6,750								
Trade debtors	30,000				1,500				
Trade creditors		31,500							
Sundry expenses	750			75					
Wages and salaries	37,500			300 + 225					
Depreciation expenses				750					
Bad debt expense				1,500					
Accruals					300				
Prepayments				1,200					
Stock (profit and loss)			6	22,500	25,500				
	250,500	250,500		52,050	52,050				

ACTIVITY 6

PG Trading Extended trial balance at 31 December 20X6

Account	Trial balance		Ref	Adjustments		Profit and loss		Balance sheet	
	Dr £	Cr £		Dr £	Cr £	Dr £	Cr £	Dr £	Cr £
Capital account		63,000							63,000
Stock	22,500			25,500	22,500			25,500	
Sales		150,000					150,000		
Purchases	105,000					105,000			
Rent and rates	15,000			300 + 1,200		13,500			
Drawings	18,000							18,000	
Electricity	3,000					3,000			
Motor van cost	12,000							12,000	

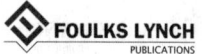

UNIT 5 : ANSWERS TO ACTIVITIES

Account	Trial balance Dr £	Trial balance Cr £	Adjustments Dr £	Adjustments Cr £	Profit and loss Dr £	Profit and loss Cr £	Balance sheet Dr £	Balance sheet Cr £
Motor van provision for depreciation		6,000		750				6,750
Bank balance	6,750						6,750	
Trade debtors	30,000			1,500			28,500	
Trade creditors		31,500						31,500
Sundry expenses	750			75	825			
Wages and salaries	37,500		300 + 225		38,025			
Depreciation expenses			750		750			
Bad debt expense			1,500		1,500			
Accruals				300				300
Prepayments			1,200				1,200	
Stock (profit and loss)			22,500	25,500	22,500	25,500		
	250,500	250,500	52,050	52,050	185,100	175,500	91,950	101,550

ACTIVITY 7

PG Trading Extended trial balance at 31 December 20X6

Account	Trial balance Dr £	Trial balance Cr £	Ref	Adjustments Dr £	Adjustments Cr £	Profit and loss Dr £	Profit and loss Cr £	Balance sheet Dr £	Balance sheet Cr £
Capital account		63,000							63,000
Stock	22,500			25,500	22,500			25,500	
Sales		150,000					150,000		
Purchases	105,000					105,000			
Rent and rates	15,000			300 +	1,200	13,500			
Drawings	18,000							18,000	
Electricity	3,000					3,000			
Motor van cost	12,000							12,000	
Motor van provision for depreciation		6,000			750				6,750
Bank balance	6,750							6,750	
Trade debtors	30,000				1,500			28,500	
Trade creditors		31,500							31,500
Sundry expenses	750			75		825			
Wages and salaries	37,500			300 + 225		38,025			
Depreciation expenses				750		750			
Bad debt expense				1,500		1,500			
Accruals					300				300
Prepayment				1,200				1,200	
Stock (profit and loss)				22,500	25,500	22,500	25,500		
Loss	250,500	250,500		52,050	52,050	185,100	175,500	91,950	101,550
							9,600	9,600	
						185,100	185,100	101,550	101,550

CHAPTER 14

ACTIVITY 1

Sally Sana
Profit and Loss Account for the Year Ending 30 November 2009

	£	£
Sales		756,293
Cost of sales		
Opening stock	21,645	
Add: purchases	285,365	
Less: closing stock	-24,680	
		-282,330
Gross profit		473,963
Expenses		
Wages and salaries	163,996	
Rent and rates	72,000	
Motor expenses	35,947	
Certification costs	7,354	
Training	14,987	
Insurance	12,690	
Heat, light, water, power		
Sundry expenses	21,310	
Depreciation: Equipment	23,693	
Motors	4,374	
Bad debt expense	132	
		-356,483
Operating profit		117,480
Interest payable		-15,000
PROFIT FOR THE YEAR		**102,480**

Sally Sana
Balance Sheet as at 30 November 2009

	Cost £	Depreciation £	Net Book Value £
Fixed Assets			
Equipment	157,954	69,180	88,774
Motor Vehicles	45,999	37,250	8,749
	203,953	106,430	97,523
Current Assets			
Stocks		24,680	
Trade debtors		2,253	
Prepayments		29,608	
Bank and cash (145,923 + 5,750)		151,673	
		208,214	
Current Liabilities			
Trade creditors		32,756	
Accruals		75,500	
		108,256	
Net Current Assets			99,958
Total Assets less Current Liabilities			197,481
15% Loan repayable 2019			-100,000
NET ASSETS			**£97,481**
Capital			
Opening capital			250,000
Add: profit for the year			102,480
Less: drawings			-254,999
Closing capital			**£97,481**

UNIT 5 : ANSWERS TO ACTIVITIES

Trial balance for Sally Sana 30 November 2009

	Trial balance Dr £	Trial balance Cr £	Adjustments Dr £	Adjustments Cr £	Accruals Dr to P&L £	Prepaid Cr to P&L £	Profit and Loss Dr £	Profit and Loss Cr £	Balance sheet Dr £	Balance sheet Cr £
Sales		756,293						756,293		
Stock 1 Dec 2008	21,645						21,645			
Purchases	285,365						285,365			
FA: Cost										
Equipment	157,954								157,954	
Motor vehicle	45,999								45,999	
FA: Dep'n 1-12-08										
Equipment		45,487		23,693						69,180
Motor vehicles		32,876		4,374						37,250
Rent	8,000				64,000		72,000			
Salaries and wages	163,996						163,996			
Motor expenses	35,947						35,947			
Certification costs	7,354						7,354			
Training	14,987						14,987			
Trade debtors	2,253								2,253	
Trade creditors		32,756								32,756
Insurance	14,298					1,608	12,690			
Bad debts written off	132						132			
Petty cash	5,750								5,750	
Sundry expenditure	49,310					28,000	21,310			
Capital account 1-12-08		250,000								250,000
Drawings	254,999								254,999	
15% Loan repayable (2019)		100,000								100,000
Loan interest paid and payable	3,500				11,500		15,000			
Bank balance	145,923								145,923	
	1,217,412	1,217,412								
Closing stock (B/S, P&L)			24,680	24,680				24,680	24,680	
Dep'n charge:										
Equipment			23,693				23,693			
Motors			4,374				4,374			
Total accruals & prepayments to B/S					75,500	29,608			29,608	75,500
Sub-total			52,747	52,747			678,493	780,973	667,166	564,686
Profit/loss transferred to B/S							102,480			102,480
							780,973	780,973	667,166	667,166

277

CHAPTER 15

ACTIVITY 1

Current Accounts

	Tom £	Dick £	Harry £	Total £		Tom £	Dick £	Harry £	Total £
					B/f	17,000	9,000	7,300	33,300
					Profits	33,000	33,000	33,000	99,000
Drawings	45,000	22,000	18,000	85,000					
C/d	5,000	20,000	22,300	47,300					
	50,000	42,000	40,300	132,300		50,000	42,000	40,300	132,300

ACTIVITY 2

Appropriation Statement

	Freddie £	Roger £	Total £
Net profit for the year			150,000
Interest on capital @ 9%	3,150	2,250	-5,400
Salaries	24,000	36,000	-60,000
Residual profit			84,600
Shared 3 : 2	50,760	33,840	-84,600
Total profit shares	77,910	72,090	150,000

Capital Accounts

	Freddie £	Roger £	Total £		Freddie £	Roger £	Total £
				B/f	35,000	25,000	60,000
C/d	35,000	25,000	60,000				
	35,000	25,000	60,000		35,000	25,000	60,000

Current Accounts

	Freddie £	Roger £	Total £		Freddie £	Roger £	Total £
				B/f	18,000	12,000	30,000
				Profits	77,910	72,090	150,000
Drawings	67,500	32,500	100,000				
C/d	28,410	51,590	80,000				
	95,910	84,090	180,000		95,910	84,090	180,000

Balance Sheet

			£
Net Assets			140,000

		£	£
Financed by			
Capital Accounts	Freddie	35,000	
	Roger	25,000	
			60,000
Current Accounts	Freddie	28,410	
	Roger	51,590	
			80,000
			140,000

UNIT 5 : ANSWERS TO ACTIVITIES

ACTIVITY 3

Appropriation Statement

	Brian £	John £	Total £
Net profit for the year			97,000
Interest on capital @ 15%	15,000	21,000	(36,000)
Salaries	44,000	33,000	(77,000)
Residual loss			(16,000)
Shared 5 : 3	(10,000)	(6,000)	16,000
Total profit shares	49,000	48,000	97,000

ACTIVITY 4

Appropriation Statement

	Braine £	Amis £	Thomas £	Total £
Profit for the first six months shared equally between three partners	20,000	20,000	20,000	60,000
Profit for the second six months shared equally between two partners	-	30,000	30,000	60,000
	20,000	50,000	50,000	120,00

Capital Accounts

	Braine £	Amis £	Thomas £	Total £		Braine £	Amis £	Thomas £	Total £
					B/F	225,000	100,000	55,000	380,000
					Transfer	53,000	-	-	53,000
Cash	66,000	-	-	66,000					
Loan	212,000			212,000					
C/D		100,000	55,000	155,000					
	278,000	100,000	55,000	433,000		278,000	100,000	55,000	433,000

Current Accounts

	Braine £	Amis £	Thomas £	Total £		Braine £	Amis £	Thomas £	Total £
					B/F	33,000	7,000	15,000	55,000
					Profits	20,000	50,000	50,000	120,000
Transfer	53,000	-	-	53,000					
C/D	-	57,000	65,000	122,000					
	53,000	57,000	65,000	175,000			57,000	65,000	175,000

Balance Sheet

		£
Fixed Assets		476,000
Sundry current assets		123,000
Bank and Cash	43,000 – 66,000	(23,000)
Sundry current liabilities		(87,000)
		489,000
Loan from Braine		(212,000)
		277,000

MAINTAINING FINANCIAL RECORDS AND PREPARING ACCOUNTS : UNIT 5

	Capital £	Current £	Total £
Amis	100,000	57,000	157,000
Thomas	55,000	65,000	120,000
	155,000	122,000	277,000

ACTIVITY 5

A Goodwill maintained in the books of the new partnership:

Capital Account

	Small £	Little £	Micro £	Total £		Small £	Little £	Micro £	Total £
					B/f	25,000	15,000	-	40,000
					Goodwill IN	13,500	9,000	-	22,500
					Cash	-	-	20,000	20,000
C/d	38,500	24,000	20,000	82,500					
	38,500	24,000	20,000	82,500		38,500	24,000	20,000	82,500

In this question the current account is not affected by the changes.

Memorandum Cash Account

B/f	12,000		
Capital	20,000		
		C/d	32,000
	32,000		32,000

Balance Sheet

		£
Goodwill	From Q	22,500
Cash (from memo a/c)		32,000
Sundry net assets	From Q	38,000
Net Assets		92,500

Financed by	Capital £	Current £	Total £
Small	38,500	3,000	41,500
Little	24,000	7,000	31,000
Micro	20,000	-	20,000
Total	82,500	10,000	92,500

B Goodwill NOT maintained in the books of the new partnership:

Capital Account

	Small £	Little £	Micro £	Total £		Small £	Little £	Micro £	Total £
					B/f	25,000	15,000	-	40,000
Goodwill OUT	10,000	7,500	5,000	22,500	Goodwill IN	13,500	9,000	-	22,500
					Cash	-	-	20,000	20,000
C/d	28,500	16,500	15,000	60,000					
	38,500	24,000	20,000	82,500		38,500	24,000	20,000	82,500

Current and Cash accounts are the same as before.

Balance Sheet : NO Goodwill

		£
Cash (from memo a/c)		32,000
Sundry net assets	From Q	38,000
Net Assets		70,000

Financed by	Capital £	Current £	Total £
Small	28,500	3,000	31,500
Little	16,500	7,000	23,500
Micro	15,000	-	15,000
Total	60,000	10,000	70,000

CHAPTER 16

ACTIVITY 1

Joan Updike
Balance Sheet as at 31 December 20X5

		£	£
Fixed Assets			
Computer software and hardware	Cost		9,000
	Depreciation (1/3)		3,000
			6,000
Current Assets			
Stock		54	
Trade Debtors		2,500	
Bank and Cash		37,247	
		39,801	
Current Liabilities			
Trade Creditors		157	
Net Current Assets			39,644
Net Assets			**45,644**
Capital			
Opening capital			-
Add: Capital introduced			13,000
Less: Drawings			(18,000)
			(5,000)
Profit for the year (balancing figure)			**50,644**
Closing Capital (Net Assets)			45,644

ACTIVITY 2

Product A

Step 1 Establish the cost structure.

	%
Cost	70
Add profit	30
Sales	100

Step 2 Use the cost structure to find the sales and profit from cost of sales (purchases).

Purchases = £200,000 (70%)

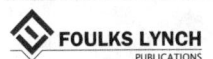

Sales $= 200{,}000 \times \dfrac{100}{70}$

$= £285{,}714$

Profit $= 200{,}000 \times \dfrac{30}{70}$

$= 85{,}714$

or

Profit $=$ Sales – cost of sales

$= 285{,}714 - 200{,}000 = £85{,}714$

Product B

Step 1   Establish the cost structure.

	%
Cost	100
Add profit	100
Sales	200

Step 2   Use the cost structure to find the cost and profit from sales.

Sales $=$ £300,000

Cost of sales $= 300{,}000 \times \dfrac{100}{200}$

$=$ £150,000

Profit $= 300{,}000 \times \dfrac{100}{200}$

$=$ £150,000

or

Profit $=$ Sales – cost of sales

$= 300{,}000 - 150{,}000 = £150{,}000$

Trading account

	Product A £	Product B £	Total £
Sales	285,714	300,000	585,714
Cost of sales	200,000	150,000	350,000
Gross profit	85,714	150,000	235,714

ACTIVITY 3

1	Cost of goods sold	£
	Opening stock	2,341
	Purchases	56,475
	Closing stock	3,816
	Cost of goods sold	**55,000**

2	Theoretical takings	
	Cost of goods sold	55,000
	Mark-up (30%)	16,500
	Theoretical takings	**71,500**

3	Shortfall in takings	
	Theoretical takings	71,500
	Actual	59,328
	Shortfall in takings	**12,172**

ACTIVITY 4

Sales Ledger Control Account

	£		£
Opening balance	243,957	Cash received	128,365
		Discounts allowed	3,289
		Closing balance	310,264
Sales for the month (balancing figure)	197,961		
	441,918		441,918

Gross Sales for the month was £197,961, therefore the Output VAT must have been **£29,483.55**. (£197,961 × 17.5 / 117.5)

INDEX

A
Accounting equation, 222, 253
Accounting for depreciation, 86
Accounting for part exchange, 97
Accounting for partnerships, 199
Accounting for stock, 126
Accounting principles and concepts, 253
Accounting standards, 256
Accruals, 82, 148, 165
Accruals concept, 56, 134
Accruals or matching concept, 148
Accrued expenses, 135
Admission of a partner, 216
Analysed cash payments book, 35
Analysed cash receipts book, 37
Appropriation account, 203
Asset, 10

B
Bad debt, 148
Bad debt recovered, 155
Bad debts expense, 149
Books of prime entry, 24

C
Capital, 10
Capital accounts, 199
Capital expenditure, 57, 74
Capital expenditure authorisation, 74
Cash book, 24
Change in the method of depreciation, 90
Classifying expenditure, 57
Companies Act 1985, 256
Comparability, 254
Compensating error, 109, 118
Conflict between accruals and prudence, 254
Consistency, 254
Control account, 45
Control account reconciliations, 46
Cost of conversion, 121
Cost structures, 226
Credit purchases, 14
Credit purchases and VAT, 18
Credit sales, 15
Credit sales and VAT, 17

Credit sales invoices, 30
Current accounts, 200
Current asset, 57

D
Day book, 24
Depletion, 82
Depreciation, 82, 91
Discounts allowed, 34
Discounts received, 33
Disposal of fixed assets, 78, 93, 94, 95
Disposal and part-exchange, 97
Doubtful debts, 150
Drawings, 11

E
Elements of VAT, 15
Entity concept, 253
Error, 176
Error of commission, 108, 118
Error of entry, 118
Error of omission, 109, 118
Error of principle, 109, 118
Extended trial balance, 159, 174

F
Finance leases, 76
Finished goods, 120
First in first out (FIFO), 122
Fixed asset, 57
Fixed asset count, 69
Fixed asset register, 65, 88
Funding capital expenditure, 75

G
General ledger, 104
General provision, 150
General provision for doubtful debts, 151
Going concern, 254
Gross profit percentage, 226

H
Hire purchase, 76
Hire purchase agreements, 76
Historical cost accounting, 255

I
Imprest system, 49
Intangible fixed assets, 58, 59
Invoice, 25

J
Journals, 27

L
Last in last out (LIFO), 123
Leasing, 76
Liability, 10
Limited accounting records, 238
Loan, 21
Loan repayment, 21

M
Mark-up, 226
Matching (accruals) concept, 56, 253
Materiality, 255
Memorandum accounts, 43
Methods of depreciation, 83
Miscellaneous income, 143

N
Net asset principle, 222
Net book value (NBV), 84, 91
Net realisable value, 125
No netting-off, 255

O
Obsolescence, 82
Original entry errors, 109
Owner's capital, 10

P
Part exchange, 97
Partners' salaries, 207
Partnership Act 1890, 208
Partnership agreement, 199
Partnership changes, 211
Partnership financial statements, 208
Partnerships, 198
Period end adjustments, 163, 174
Personal accounts, 28, 43, 45
Personal ledgers, 43
Petty cash, 49
Petty cash book, 24, 49
Prepaid expenses, 138
Prepayments, 165
Profit, 11

Profit appropriation, 203
Profits and losses, 205
Provision accounting, 86
Prudence, 148
Prudence concept, 254, 257
Purchase day book, 24, 25
Purchase ledger control account, 28

R
Raw materials, 120
Reducing balance, 84
Repairs, 63
Residual value, 83
Retirement, 214

S
Sale or return, 131
Sales day book, 24, 30
Settlement discount, 32
Specific provision, 150
Specific provision for doubtful debts, 154
Standard rated supplies, 17
Stock, 11, 120, 167
Stock cost valuation, 122
Straight-line depreciation, 83
Suspense account, 110, 118
Suspense account adjustments, 176

T
Tangible fixed assets, 57, 59, 62
Trade discount, 32
Transfer journal, 24, 29
Trial balance, 104, 161
Types of doubtful debt, 150
Types or error in double entry, 108

U
Useful economic life, 83
User groups, 252

V
VAT, 15
VAT exempt suppliers, 17

W
Weighted average, 123
Work in progress, 120
Written down value (WDV), 84, 91

Z
Zero VAT rated supplies, 17

FOULKS LYNCH PUBLICATIONS

TEXTBOOK REVIEW FORM

Thank you for choosing a Foulks Lynch Textbook for the AAT NVQ/SVQ in Accounting. As we are constantly striving to improve our products, we would be grateful if you could provide us with feedback about how useful you found this textbook.

Name: ....

Address: ....

....

Email: ....

Why did you decide to purchase this textbook?

Have used them in the past ☐
Recommended by lecturer ☐
Recommended by friend ☐
Saw advertising ☐
Other (please specify) ☐

Have you used the Foulks Lynch workbooks?

Yes ☐
No ☐

How do you study?

At a college ☐
On a distance learning course ☐
Home study ☐
Other ☐

Please specify...

Overall opinion of this textbook

	Excellent	Adequate	Poor
Introductory pages	☐	☐	☐
Coverage of standards	☐	☐	☐
Clarity of explanations	☐	☐	☐
Diagrams	☐	☐	☐
Activities	☐	☐	☐
Self-test questions	☐	☐	☐
Layout	☐	☐	☐
Index	☐	☐	☐

If you have further comments/suggestions or have spotted any errors, please write them on the next page.

Please return this form to: Veronica Wastell, Publisher, Foulks Lynch, FREEPOST 2254, Feltham TW14 0BR

Other comments/suggestions and errors

AAT Order Form

4 The Griffin Centre, Staines Road, Feltham, Middlesex, TW14 0HS, UK.
Tel: +44 (0) 20 8831 9990 Fax: +44 (0) 20 8831 9991
Order online: www.foulkslynch.com Email: sales@ewfl-global.com

For assessments in 2003/2004		Textbooks	Workbooks	Combined Textbooks/ Workbooks
Foundation stage – NVQ/SVQ 2				
1 & 2	Receipts and Payments	£10.95 ☐	£10.95 ☐	
3	Preparing Ledger Balances and an Initial Trial Balance	£10.95 ☐	£10.95 ☐	
4	Supplying Information for Management Control			£10.95 ☐
21*	Working with Computers			£10.95 ☐
22 & 23#	Achieving Personal Effectiveness and Health & Safety			£10.95 ☐
Intermediate stage – NVQ/SVQ 3				
5	Maintaining Financial Records and Preparing Accounts	£10.95 ☐	£10.95 ☐	
6	Recording and Evaluating Cost and Revenue	£10.95 ☐	£10.95 ☐	
7	Preparing Reports and Returns	£10.95 ☐	£10.95 ☐	
8 & 9	Performance Management, Value Enhancement and Resource Planning and Control	£10.95 ☐	£10.95 ☐	
Technician stage – NVQ/SVQ 4				
10	Managing Systems and People in the Accounting Environment	£10.95 ☐	£10.95 ☐	
11	Preparing Financial Statements	£10.95 ☐	£10.95 ☐	
15	Cash Management and Credit Control	£10.95 ☐	£10.95 ☐	
17	Implementing Auditing Procedures	£10.95 ☐	£10.95 ☐	
18	Business Taxation FA 2003	£10.95 ☐	£10.95 ☐	
19	Personal Taxation FA 2003	£10.95 ☐	£10.95 ☐	

* Unit 21 can be taken at Foundation Level or Intermediate Level
\# Unit 23 can be taken at any level

Postage, Packaging and Delivery (Per Item):

	First	Each Extra
UK	£5.00	£2.00
Europe (incl ROI and CI)	£7.00	£4.00
Rest of World	£22.00	£8.00

Product Sub Total £................... Post & Packaging £................... Order Total £................... (Payments in UK £ Sterling)

Customer Details
☐ Mr ☐ Mrs ☐ Ms ☐ Miss Other ....
Initials:................................... Surname: ....
Address: ....
....
....
Postcode: ....
Telephone: ....
Email: ....
Fax: ....

Delivery Address – if different from above
Address: ....
....
Postcode: ....
Telephone: ....

Payment
1 I enclose Cheque/PO/Bankers Draft for £...............................
   Please make cheques payable to '**Foulks Lynch**'.
2 Charge MasterCard/Visa/Switch a/c no:

Valid from: ☐☐☐☐   Expiry date: ☐☐☐☐

Issue No: (Switch only) ☐☐

Signature: .... Date: ....

Declaration
I agree to pay as indicated on this form and understand that Foulks Lynch Terms and Conditions apply (available on request).
Signature: .... Date: ....

Delivery – United Kingdom – 5 working days
please Eire & EU Countries – 10 working days
allow: Rest of World – 10 working days

Notes: All orders over 1kg will be fully tracked & insured. Signature required on receipt of order. Delivery times subject to stock availability.

Notes: Prices are correct at time of going to print but are subject to change

FOULKS LYNCH PUBLICATIONS